MW00789995

"The contributors to *Evangelical Postcolonial Conversations* remind us that there is no view from nowhere. More importantly, they help Western evangelicals realize how often we have confused our finite and fallible human responses to God's self-disclosure with the Word of God itself—how often we have confined God's Word to our words. What I enjoyed most about this book is the way it invited me, the reader, into an ongoing conversation that itself models how self-identifying evangelicals can better listen to the voices of those in the Majority World and on the margins in a manner that engenders humility, repentance and even our ongoing conversion to something that more closely resembles God's reign on earth as it is in heaven."

Dennis Okholm, Azusa Pacific University

"The various 'isms' usually start outside evangelicalism. They arrive in nonevangelical packaging and may provoke questioning and anxiety, but then they may get thought through within an evangelical framework and become fruitful within evangelical thinking and commitments in a way that can be instructive for the whole church. It can take time to navigate the sequence, even though evangelicalism is related to Protestantism, and postcolonialism (as one of the contributors notes) is a protest movement. This collection is the marvelous fruit of the work of those who have reflected deeply on postcolonialism. It's neat that so many of the chapters are cowritten. And whereas terms like *empire* can sound as if they apply chiefly to the empire against which the American colonies rebelled, it's encouraging for a Brit to be able to note how much attention is paid to the colonial nature of thinking and action within the Americas."

John Goldingay, Fuller Theological Seminary

"This volume presents a groundbreaking endeavor toward evangelical postcolonial theology, articulating the intersection between evangelical and postcolonial discourse. It challenges the theological roundtable under the dominion of the Western metanarrative of Enlightenment that keeps the colonial project and its civilizing mission intact, undertaking a constructive task for evangelical-postcolonial relevance and praxis in the face of the empire driven by globalization. This is an important contribution toward postcolonial imagination, which deepens and reinterprets evangelical theological discourse and praxis."

Paul S. Chung, Luther Seminary

EVANGELICAL
POSTCOLONIAL
CONVERSATIONS

Global Awakenings in Theology and Praxis

Edited by

Kay Higuera Smith, Jayachitra Lalitha
and L. Daniel Hawk

IVP Academic

An imprint of InterVarsity Press
Downers Grove, Illinois

InterVarsity Press
P.O. Box 1400, Downers Grove, IL 60515-1426
World Wide Web: www.ivpress.com
Email: email@ivpress.com

©2014 by Kay Higuera Smith, Jayachitra Lalitha and L. Daniel Hawk

All rights reserved. No part of this book may be reproduced in any form without written permission from InterVarsity Press.

InterVarsity Press® is the book-publishing division of InterVarsity Christian Fellowship/USA®, a movement of students and faculty active on campus at hundreds of universities, colleges and schools of nursing in the United States of America, and a member movement of the International Fellowship of Evangelical Students. For information about local and regional activities, write Public Relations Dept., InterVarsity Christian Fellowship/USA, 6400 Schroeder Rd., P.O. Box 7895, Madison, WI 53707-7895, or visit the IVCF website at www.intervarsity.org.

Scripture quotations, unless otherwise noted, are from the New Revised Standard Version of the Bible, copyright 1989 by the Division of Christian Education of the National Council of the Churches of Christ in the USA. Used by permission. All rights reserved.

While all stories in this book are true, some names and identifying information in this book have been changed to protect the privacy of the individuals involved.

Cover design: Cindy Kiple
Interior design: Beth Hagenberg
Images: Quaker Peace Testimony by Ron Waddams. Private Collection/The Bridgeman Art Library

ISBN 978-0-8308-4053-3 (print)
ISBN 978-0-8308-9631-8 (digital)

Printed in the United States of America ∞

 InterVarsity Press is committed to protecting the environment and to the responsible use of natural resources. As a member of Green Press Initiative we use recycled paper whenever possible. To learn more about the Green Press Initiative, visit www.greenpressinitiative.org.

Library of Congress Cataloging-in-Publication Data
*Evangelical postcolonial conversations : global awakenings in theology and
praxis / edited by Kay Higuera Smith, Jayachitra Lalitha, and L. Daniel Hawk.*
    pages cm
  Includes bibliographical references and index.
  ISBN 978-0-8308-4053-3 (pbk. : alk. paper)
  *1. Evangelicalism—Congresses. 2. Postcolonial Networks—Congresses. 3.
  Postcolonial theology—Congresses. I. Smith, Kay Higuera, 1954- editor
of compilation.*
  BR1640.A2E93 2014
  270.8'3--dc23

                                                                        2014011879

P	22	21	20	19	18	17	16	15	14	13	12	11	10	9	8	7	6	5	4	3	2	1
Y	33	32	31	30	29	28	27	26	25	24	23	22	21	20	19	18	17	16	15	14		

In honor of Richard L. Twiss

June 11, 1954–February 9, 2013

A follower of the Jesus Way
and a real human being

··· ···

CONTENTS

Acknowledgments

Joseph Duggan

Founder and Strategic Relationships Leader for Postcolonial Networks

Postcolonial Networks joins with the editors and all of the contributors to express our appreciation and gratitude to the editorial staff at InterVarsity Press for their recognition of the timely importance of this project for readers around the world. *Evangelical Postcolonial Conversations* has been in the making for four years and has become a reality because of the passionate vision and tireless energy of a few key people and institutions.

Our thanks to Judith Oleson and Dan Russ of Gordon College, who rolled out the red carpet for the first Postcolonial Roundtable meeting in October 2010, with the generous provision of travel stipends for visiting scholars from South Africa and India, comfortable meeting rooms, delicious meals for scholars and competent administrative support. Debbie Drost, Dan Russ's secretary, managed meeting communications through the school website, room scheduling, hotel reservations and other meeting details.

Each of the members of the Postcolonial Roundtable made significant investments of time and money to be part of this project. Their scholarly innovation and passion gave flesh and blood to it.

Steve Hu, the roundtable's scholar-secretary, captured the flow of conversation in a way that facilitated all of the threads coming together in immediately productive ways. Brian McLaren and Mabiala Kenzo were central parts of the meeting. Brian and Mabiala's scholarship and leadership, alongside those of the 2009 Amahoro Conference, as well as their own postcolonial friendship, served as a model for the Postcolonial Roundtable conversations.

The second Postcolonial Roundtable meeting, at the 2011 American Academy of Religion Conference in San Francisco, was made possible by Azusa Pacific University through the support of Scott Daniels, dean of the School of Theology.

The editors, Kay Higuera Smith, Jayachitra Lalitha and L. Daniel Hawk, were selected at the Gordon College meeting by their peers. These editors began their work at the meeting and have been tirelessly committed, spending an extraordinary amount of time knitting the manuscript, from drafting an initial table of contents to reading chapters. They skillfully interwove multiple editors into a coherent text and worked with individual authors to prepare publishable chapters.

Finally, we are grateful to you, the readers of this book, and invite you to embody the pages of this book and take your part in the work of global justice through decolonized actions in your local churches and communities.

THE EDITORS, KAY HIGUERA SMITH, JAYACHITRA LALITHA AND L. DANIEL HAWK

The editors express our gratitude to Joseph Duggan of Postcolonial Networks, whose vision, initiative and collaborative spirit have played a vital role in bringing this project to fruition. We are also grateful to David Congdon at InterVarsity Press for his advocacy of the project and valuable assistance. We acknowledge the contributors who kept us inspired and engaged throughout the process, and we offer special thanks to Jason Craige Harris, who provided valuable support in the editing phase, and to Bryan Muirhead, who created the index. We are also grateful to one member of the Postcolonial Roundtable, Mabiala Kenzo, who was not ultimately able to contribute to this volume but whose vision, patience and encouragement were crucial to its development. Our thanks also go to Gordon College and to Azusa Pacific University for their financial support and encouragement. Finally, we are grateful to our beloved family members who sacrificed and endured while we devoted our time to this project.

INTRODUCTION

Why Postcolonial Conversations Matter

························· ✗ ·························

Reflection on
Postcolonial Friendship

Brian D. McLaren

FELT I WAS TAKING A BIG RISK BACK IN 2001 when I chose the title for my new book, *A New Kind of Christian*. The *new* I was talking about back then wasn't easily located on old polarities of Protestant or Catholic, conservative or liberal, traditional or contemporary, medieval or modern. The best word I had for it at the time was postmodern, and I knew that finding value in that term might cost me. To some the term was so mushy as to be worthless, while to others it was a red flag signaling the destruction of everything orthodox, civilized and rational.

Six years later I wrote *Everything Must Change*. It was in the writing of that book that I realized the paradigm shift I was grappling with was even bigger and deeper than I had previously realized. I wrote,

> I experienced a breakthrough one day when I was talking with an African theologian, Dr. Mabiala Kenzo, a delightful and brilliant Congolese scholar of Twa descent, now working in Canada. "You may have noticed my small stature as a

Twa [the tribe also known as Pygmies]," I once heard Kenzo say with a smile, and then he added, "I try to watch my height." He said that *postmodern* and *postcolonial* were simply two sides of one coin, two parts of one emerging global conversation. He helped me realize that *postmodernity* was a key term in a conversation among the excessively confident, trying to understand and undermine their own colonial culture's confidence-mania and uncertainty-phobia. To attack or undermine what they saw as the twin sources of that overconfidence—foundationalism and metanarratives—they focused on the field of epistemology (which explores how we have rational confidence that what we call knowledge or truth is really, truly true).[1]

Kenzo also helped me see that *postcolonial* was a key term in a parallel conversation among those who had been dominated and colonized by the excessively confident. They were also trying to rebuild a new kind of confidence among people whose confidence had been shattered and ground into the dirt through colonialism. They needed a restored confidence to face the ugly aftermath of centuries of domination and exploitation. They didn't start with philosophical questions of truth and epistemology, but rather with social questions of justice, morality and power (justice and injustice being about the moral or immoral uses of power).

Since then Kenzo has been spending more of his time in his homeland, and we've only crossed paths too briefly, once or twice in the United States and once or twice in Africa. But I can't overstate Kenzo's influence on my work—along with the work of other Africans like Kwame Bediako and Lamin Sanneh, Native Americans like Randy Woodley and Richard Twiss, feminist theologians like Rita Nakashima Brock and Sallie McFague, Latino and Asian theologians like Leonardo Boff and Peter Phan, gay theologians like Yvette Flunder and Dale Martin, and African Americans like James Cone and, of course, Dr. King. As a white, American, male Christian, I was unconscious of the various forms of privilege and power I had inherited until these voices, coming from what Kenzo would call "the subaltern position," helped awaken me.

For its first two thousand years, Christian theology has been a largely white male enterprise, the province of people born like me. It's a cliché to say so but still largely unacknowledged. I remember hearing Kenzo once ask whether our

---

[1]Brian McLaren, *Everything Must Change: Jesus, Global Crises, and a Revolution of Hope* (Nashville: Thomas Nelson, 2007), p. 44.

first two thousand years mean that Christian identity and thought is forever set in stone, that voices and perspectives like his will always be judged as marginal and "subaltern." I don't know. If our faith maintains longstanding patterns of racial, cultural, economic or sexual hegemony, I imagine that more and more smart and ethical people will avoid it, and with good reason. But if we break down those old patterns of hegemony, I think a new day can dawn, and we will all be better Christians for it.

That's why I hope and pray that more privileged white males will defect from their inherited privilege and use whatever vestiges of it they have to help their sisters and brothers classified as "other" to be heard. Doing so will require of us what Kenzo calls "the courage to differ graciously," one virtue among many that he has exemplified for me. One can only hope that more and more people like me will benefit from friends like Kenzo.

When Kenzo decided to shift his primary focus to the Congo, he was leaving a pleasant and safe (albeit cold) place for a more dangerous and unstable one. He realizes, I think, that the Christian faith of the future must be a joint enterprise in which the descendants of the colonized and the descendants of the colonizers come together, reflect on the past and imagine a different and better future together. That work will involve risks and dangers for both groups, and the contributions of both are essential. One lesson the gospel surely teaches us is this: we are all connected.

· · · ✖ · · ·

The Importance of Postcolonial
Evangelical Conversations

Steve Hu

M Y ENCOUNTER WITH POSTCOLONIAL discourse first arose from the
needs of ministry in a multicultural context. After graduating from an
evangelical seminary in 2007, I began full-time ministry at a Chinese American
megachurch in the New York metropolitan area. This congregation was an
amalgamation of various distinct but related Chinese cultures—Taiwanese,
mainland Chinese, Cantonese, and second-generation Chinese Americans—
that coalesced around a central commitment to evangelical Christianity. While
my seminary education did well in training me in Western theological thought,
I was unprepared to tackle the cultural and leadership issues in this context.
Many of the congregants I worked with in this ministry context struggled with
their identity as they tried to make sense of what it means to be both American
and Chinese while striving to live faithfully as people of God. Increasingly, I
found myself unable to address my congregants' identity crises since they
wished to jettison various elements of their Chinese heritage in a desire to be
more "devout" to God. Many of them believed culture to be antagonistic to a
life of faith. While my seminary training taught that knowing leads to being, it
misses the fact that as people we are foremost shaped by our experiences and
culture rather than a set of theological propositions. Issues of culture and
identity rarely addressed during my seminary days surfaced in my ministry,
and I fumbled in figuring out how to resolve them.

For me, the need to engage postcolonial thought also stems from the one issue the American evangelical church has failed to adequately address since its inception: race. Growing up as a second-generation Chinese American in a white suburban neighborhood in the Northeast, I faced a fair share of racist taunts and slurs. No matter how well I spoke and pronounced English words or how hard I tried to assimilate into majority culture, I still was seen as foreign, exotic—the Other. One illustration of my experience of marginalization is an incident that happened to me while I backpacked across the country. I was approached by a middle-aged, Anglo-European woman in the observation deck of an Amtrak train somewhere between New Orleans and San Antonio. She asked me the curious question, "What country are you from?" My experience is not unique, and many others like myself still experience stereotyping and, worse, discrimination and marginalization. My encounters with racism pushed me to seek out resources to help me understand race and identity, but I found few resources written by evangelicals on this subject. When it came to the question of race, I was at a loss.

The necessity to engage intelligently with identity and race in the context of my ministry first nudged me slowly toward postcolonial discourse. This nudging was gentle at first, but the push became stronger as I found the insight provided by postcolonial thought to be fruitful and instructive in interpreting and understanding a rapidly globalizing world in which the West is no longer the center of the globe. I've discovered that postcolonial discourse grants me voice and allows me to speak so that I can be heard by those sitting at the theological roundtable, a table that long has been the domain of Westerners and privy only to those who can speak its predetermined discourse. This table has been so embedded in Western forms and categories that when I attempt to converse, my words, as Tite Tiénou notes, "are perceived as threats to orthodoxy."[1] Yet no one will disagree that theological enterprise is conversational in nature, that it is an ongoing, multilateral exchange between the biblical text, tradition, reason and context among various dialogue partners. It is time that those sitting at the theological roundtable cease to exclude marginal voices from this conversation. The inclusion of marginal dialogue partners not

---

[1]Tite Tiénou, "Christian Theology in an Era of World Christianity," in *Globalizing Theology: Belief and Practice in an Era of World Christianity*, ed. Craig Ott and Harold A. Netland (Grand Rapids: Baker Academic, 2006), p. 50.

only will give voice to the voiceless but will also produce rich fruit for our theological conversation.

As an Asian American evangelical residing in North America and as one who represents those voices in the margins, I ask my fellow evangelicals to consider seriously taking up the charge of engaging postcolonial discourse. This is akin to learning a new literacy, and such new literacy is needed in light of the shifts in the center of Christianity. In this globalizing world, where we have also witnessed the dramatic growth of the Two–Thirds World church, we cannot afford not to consider the multiple contexts in which theology begins. If our discourse continues to remain in the domain of the West, the resultant theology will be powerless to address the issues of the global church. If evangelical theology seeks to redress this issue, what will this new theologizing look like? Our theology must incorporate a new vocabulary in order for us to engage postcolonial discourse and speak to the needs of the global church. To be conversant with the world, evangelical theology must find new dialogue partners. Toward this goal, this book offers a way to think and imagine the world through a postcolonial lens. This book provides a framework for rethinking and reimagining the issues of identity, power, interpretation and historiography. My hope is that in this rethinking and reimagining, readers will find new ways of understanding and bettering the world.

· · · ✗ · · ·

A Response to the Postcolonial Roundtable
Promises, Problems and Prospects

Gene L. Green

I WALKED OUT THE BACK DOOR, stood on the lawn and wept.
Deb, my wife, had been writing a book that began as a story told to our
children and their friends while driving them to school up the mountains in
Costa Rica. Upon their urging, she began to put the stories to paper but in the
process realized that she needed to do some research so the aboriginal characters in her tale would have substance and realism. She read broadly about
indigenous peoples in the Americas but then focused on the Native American
experience. As she read down into the stories of genocide, ethnic cleansing and
ethnocide that accompanied Euro-American expansion on this continent, she
began to relate what had been submerged throughout our education. "Gene,
did you know that . . . ?" was her constant query, and all I could do was register
surprise at the level of violence that characterized colonial expansion.

During this period, I was also teaching a course at Wheaton College titled
World Christian Perspectives. The course was a sprint through emerging African, Asian and Latin American theologies, both evangelical and otherwise.
Since we had lived in Latin America, the course attended closely to liberation
theologies, the emergence of the Latin American Theological Fellowship and
Pentecostalism. But among the readings for the class were texts by authors who
had embraced postcolonial biblical interpretation and theology. Through this

reading I became increasingly aware of how the biblical text had been used to justify the colonial enterprise and how that mission influenced biblical interpretation. The categories of postcolonialism, such as domination and hybridity, occupied my reflection.

And then it happened. The stories my wife told and the colonial stories from Africa and Asia intertwined in an agonizing encounter. *I* was the colonist; I *am* the colonist. The land where I live was taken under an ill-signed treaty in 1829, and the people who lived here, the Potawatomi, were gathered and forcibly removed from this area under the Indian Removal Act of 1830. When Black Hawk resisted this ethnic cleansing, President Andrew Jackson sent General Winfield Scott through this area to suppress the rebellion. Afterward immigration to the west of Chicago spiked and new communities were founded such as the one where I now live and teach. We are established on this land because of colonialism. We are the colonists.

Facing the colonial story has not been easy given the level of violence perpetrated by our predecessors on Native peoples. Their loss of land and life, as well as the suppression of their culture through agencies such as boarding schools, is an evil that my nation has yet to face fully. The disturbing story of American expansion west becomes more pain filled when we examine the part the church played, with Bible in hand, in the process of conquest, removal and "civilization" of Native peoples. The gospel got mixed with the grand agenda of Manifest Destiny as this land was viewed as a new Canaan and its inhabitants were likened to the ancient Canaanites.[1] The conquest narrative about Joshua was the other side of the exodus story we had learned so well in Latin America. How did we understand and use that story? Postcolonial theory and theology beckon us to look at the historical reality of colonialism and the dance that occurred between the colonial enterprise and the interpretation of Scripture.[2]

Postcolonial biblical interpretation and theology are helpful instruments for analyzing our approach to Scripture, our understanding of the American experiment and the nature of Christian mission. Yet subsequently when my graduate students read texts on postcolonialism, the resistance was unlike any-

---

[1] L. Daniel Hawk, *Joshua in 3-D: A Commentary on Biblical Conquest and Manifest Destiny* (Eugene, OR: Cascade, 2010).

[2] Compare the way the Bible was used during the Civil War era as the nation struggled with the question of slavery. See Mark Noll, *The Civil War as a Theological Crisis* (Chapel Hill: University of North Carolina Press, 2006).

thing I had seen in decades of teaching. The readings were intended to make them self-aware of the influences on their interpretive practices and theology. But they objected vigorously to the way postcolonial authors bifurcated Scripture into resistant and colonizing voices. They expressed concern at the way the biblical text was placed on the same level as other sacred texts. They reacted against the critique of Christian mission, a centerpiece of evangelical life and theology. While affirming many of their concerns, my plea was to listen well with a hermeneutic of charity, understanding the forces that had been unleashed through the merger of Christian theology and colonial aspirations.

Colleagues and administrators have sometimes echoed the concerns voiced in my classroom. As evangelicals they regard the possibility of lowering biblical authority as reason enough to remove postcolonial interpretive perspectives from the table. In the midst of the myriad critiques, I longed to hear evangelical scholars grapple with the agonizing realities of postcolonial theory and theology. Then news arrived about the Postcolonial Roundtable and the publication of this volume. "At last!"[3] While not a member of the roundtable, I have found it gratifying to listen in on the discussion. This volume fills a gap for the evangelical church and academy. Postcolonial approaches to the Bible can indeed yield fruitful insights that will contribute to the health of the interpretive enterprise within evangelicalism while, at the same time, not destroying the way the evangelical church has embraced the authority of Scripture. A high Christology and postcolonial insights are not necessarily antithetical to each other. Indeed, evangelically oriented postcolonial biblical interpretation yields deep insights into the New Testament as a resistant discourse against oppressive and totalizing Roman imperial power. Postcolonial perspectives offer us newly cleaned lenses to examine the biblical text and our theological heritage.

For many this volume will serve as a challenging yet friendly introduction to postcolonial biblical interpretation and theology. No doubt they and the Postcolonial Roundtable members understand that these are first steps and that considerable work remains. Since the examples here are few, much more reflection is still required to explore how postcolonial perspectives inform the reading of biblical texts. How might postcolonial perspectives deepen our understanding as we engage Scripture? Moreover, how can postcolonial perspec-

---

[3] Apologies to Etta James.

tives move beyond suspicion of the texts we receive and provide fruitful understanding that will assist us as followers of Christ? Postcolonial theory in general has been very adept at "writing back" to the centers of power, but will it be able to provide sufficiently constructive perspectives? And, as Lozano and Roth ask,[4] will it provide the necessary impetus to wed Christian theology with *praxis*?

Another task that remains on the table is an analysis of the pitfalls of postcolonial interpretation. In this new domain of evangelical postcolonial theory, may we anticipate critiques as well as appropriations? How can postcolonial criticism remain evangelical with its commitments to Scripture and Christ? Will it be able to speak about the canon of Scripture in a multitextual world? Can it affirm the uniqueness of Christ without allowing the confession of his lordship to lead to renewed dominance and control?

Furthermore, an evangelical postcolonial agenda needs to embrace the examination of the texts, classes and curricula of our theological institutions. Many schools remain devoid of engagement with emerging Majority World and minority biblical interpretation and theology of any kind. Students from the Majority World who come to study in the North Atlantic region receive Western theological traditions and methodologies. They return to their countries with a Western orientation that is then reduplicated in their schools. Rather than embracing the fact that all theology is contextual, they learn implicitly or explicitly the position that Western perspectives are universal and that somehow biblical studies and theology in the West are neutral or objective enterprises. Will our theological institutions recognize that biblical interpretation and theology are the task of the whole church and that all interpretation involves a fusion of horizons?[5] What we deem as "contextual" theologies from Africa, Asia, Latin America, Oceana and minority communities are none other than Christian theology. As a catholic church, all members have a place at the interpretive and theological table and are responsible before God to contribute to our common theological conversation. We all speak, and we all listen and receive. But if academic programs in biblical studies and theology continue to ignore perspectives that are non-Western,

---

[4]See the chapter in this volume by Gilberto Lozano and Federico A. Roth, "The Problem and Promise of Praxis in Postcolonial Criticism."
[5]Hans-Georg Gadamer, *Truth and Method* (New York: Continuum, 2000).

we demonstrate that not only are we unaware of the fact that the Majority World and minority church is self-theologizing but we also endorse the continuation of the colonial enterprise. Colonialism is not merely a chapter in the history book. Our present-day hallways, classrooms and conferences need decolonization.

Evangelical postcolonial perspectives need to address the church and its "mission." The language of "mission," which emerged from the realms of politics and military conflict, needs examination in the light of postcolonial perspectives. Should we continue to talk about "Christian mission," or can we find new ways of understanding our role as a church in the world that are more consonant with how Jesus engaged people? As we witness Jesus' interactions in the Gospels, we find him engaging in conversation, touching, inviting and welcoming. He hangs out with people on the margins, and he knows how to have a good time among them. The embrace of Jesus won the masses in his day. Although we have become accustomed to speaking of Paul's "missionary" journeys, the language of "mission" is distinctly absent from his lips and the New Testament, while imagery of invitation and banqueting is prominent. Love, touch, invitation, forgiveness and hope are not the stuff of colonialism but constitute a true evangelical postcolonial approach to our fellow human beings. Domination is placed to the side, while care for all our fellows in creation occupies the center of Christian concern. "Mission" agencies and "missional" churches will want to find and employ new language to describe their calling from Christ.

Postcolonial interpretation and theology can indeed contribute to our understanding of the nature of the gospel, the church and Christian calling in the world. But that goal will not be realized unless those who embrace evangelical postcolonial interpretation and theology press beyond the discovery of new perspectives to the utilization of this lens both to critique and to construct. Since the critique of our theologies and methodologies is a painful process that goes to the core of our cultural and theological identities, those who encounter these perspectives need discerning wisdom from God along with love and patience as members of the body of Christ.

Those who listen and read will want to take the difficult posture of disciples who learn from another, not from the center of power but rather from the margins. Jesus, our Teacher, was the Galilean and not the Jerusalemite, so we should know how to learn from the margins. Surprisingly, however, those once considered to be on the margins are now the majority in the church. The center of Christianity has shifted to the South and East. Evangelical postcolonial perspectives can help us understand this new Reformation and allow us to keep pace with what God is doing in our era.

· · · ♃ · · ·

The Postcolonial Challenge to Evangelicals

Editors

CAN EVANGELICALS BE POSTCOLONIAL SCHOLARS? Can postcolonial scholars be evangelical? These two pertinent inquiries have been the motivating questions behind the idea for a volume on intersections between evangelical and postcolonial thought. In our global scenario, marked by a shift in the center of gravity from the West to the Global South, evangelicalism's struggle to maintain its theological credibility calls for new thinking and a vigorous and forthright engagement with the undesired consequences of colonial history.

The Bible was used in the colonial past not only to save but also to "civilize" native peoples and thus to legitimate the claims made by the colonizers that their dominance over the colonized was justified. The consequent injustices committed against native populations through cultural demonization, religious intolerance, claims of the superiority of Western civilization and sanctioning of colonial partnerships pose an urgent challenge to the continuing legacy of evangelical convictions and scholarship today. Evangelicals both helped to mobilize those repressive efforts and vehemently opposed them. But in either case they participated in the processes and practices of colonialism.

Postcolonial theories and theologies attempt to decolonize the established colonial remnants of Western hegemony. Their interrogations of evangelicalism are important for two reasons. On the one hand, Western evangelicals are implicated in many of the ways that the colonial powers authorized and rationalized the dehumanization (at best) and genocide (at worst) of native populations. On the other hand, colonial norms, assumptions and values have created residues that have deeply influenced native elites. Many of those same native elites are now indigenous tradents of evangelicalism, often resulting in their mimicking colonial models in their own mission strategies.

The emergence of liberation theologies in the twentieth century exposed how evangelical theologies have failed to address various social justice issues that challenged scriptural and ecclesiastical prerogatives. In India, for instance, Dalit theology emerged in the 1970s in a sociocultural hegemonic context in which casteism was widely practiced by evangelical Christians. When evangelicals did not perceive casteism as a socially evil system contradictory to biblical truths, the Bible as projected by evangelical Christians gradually lost credibility as a source for social justice and projects for the social emancipation of Dalits.

It was at this crucial juncture that the Dalits, who form the majority of the Christian population in India, began to sense a need to develop a theology that would relate their pathos to that of Jesus in the Gospels. Tribal theologies have also identified the failure of evangelical theologies to address the existential life realities of tribals/Adivasis in the Indian subcontinent and of indigenous and *mestizo/métis* in the Americas. Similarly women have also struggled to liberate themselves from the spiritual control of males through developing feminist or womanist theologies. A postcolonial critical tool instantly identifies native elites who act as colonial agents in contemporary hierarchical societies. Those native elites are caste-ridden and represent nontribal and sexist-dominant voices, sweeping away indigenous agency ruthlessly.

In these critical times, in which evangelicals are being blamed for failing to address social justice issues, postcolonialism may function as a redemptive hermeneutical tool, especially as it presses evangelical adherents to re/read the Scriptures and rectify theologies. Jesus of Nazareth, after all, was an indigenous peasant whose message critiqued a European imperial power and the local elites who colluded with it. Professed commitment to Jesus of Nazareth through a renewed affirmation of his humanness therefore compels evangelicals to critique the imperial structures of both the ancient and contemporary worlds.

Developing a stronger theological bond between evangelical and post-colonial thought requires new, strong theologies that articulate authentic indigenous Christianities. In this volume, we revisit Christologies and pneumatologies in order to deconstruct the traditional norms that keep colonial projects intact. Postcolonial theology, then, is germane not only for missions and praxis but for all theological endeavors.

Commensurate with theological revisioning, evangelical postcolonial critical engagement should also strive to connect theory with praxis. Given evangelicalism's historic activism, praxis will be central to evangelical engagement with postcolonialism. For what is it to critique power if we do not create communities that intentionally interrogate the ways that we construct power and create alternative modes of social interaction—modes that concern themselves with giving voice to the silenced and exercising power on behalf of one another rather than over one another?

In the essays that follow, evangelicals and those teaching and working in evangelical contexts consider the intersections between evangelicalism and postcoloniality. Although the volume as a whole challenges the way that the academic world has spoken in a uniform voice, the essays in particular manifest the unique, culturally rooted voices of the various contributors. Some speak in the idiom of the academy, while others consciously reject the narrow confines of such discourse and opt for language that is more consistent with their own cultural-social space. The chapters, with a few exceptions, have been cowritten, a practice we have undertaken as a step toward the collaborative path we believe our conversations must take. It is our hope that in our discursive expansiveness we model, in a small way, the respect and understanding that might identify evangelical postcolonial conversations.

The conversation begins, in part one, with an interrogation of evangelical missions and the grand narratives that articulate/d and legitimate/d the missionary enterprise. Part two then exposes the racial and national ideologies that configured the grand narratives. As steps toward rectifying these and other colonial/missional metanarratives, the authors in part three revision evangelical theology in a postcolonial key, and those in part four revision evangelical practices and praxis. The conversation in part five circles back to an account and self-critique of the Postcolonial Roundtable, which generated this conversation, and ends with words of hope. We are grateful to Joe Duggan and the Postcolonial Networks for initiating the Roundtable, supporting our conversation and inviting evangelical scholars into the vibrant global discourse they are generating. The attentive reader will soon realize that, although the organization of the volume assumes a linear form, the conversation itself more resembles a talking circle, or as one member characterizes it, a spiral—with threads appearing and reappearing in new combinations and new meanings as the conversation proceeds. We do not tie the threads together at the end but leave them for our Creator to join with us and with others in weaving them together in ongoing collaboration.

Prospects and Problems
for Evangelical Postcolonialisms

Robert S. Heaney

T HE PURPOSE OF THE PRESENT CHAPTER is to begin to answer a simple
question. What should a postcolonial evangelicalism look like? This
question will be addressed in four main steps. First, evangelicalism, especially
as it emerged from the discussions of the Postcolonial Roundtable, will be
briefly defined.[1] Second, postcolonialism will be outlined. Third, evangelicalism and postcolonialism will be brought into dialogue in a bid to identify
the prospects for an evangelical postcolonialism. Fourth, potential problems
arising from such a dialogue will be identified.

EVANGELICALISM(S)

At least six evangelical attributes emerged from discussions and submissions at
the roundtable. Not all of the characteristics are affirmed explicitly by each
participant. Undoubtedly, certain respondents would be uncomfortable with
some of these evangelical attributes. Indeed, a degree of hesitancy to self-
identify as evangelical was present not least because of attendant thought and
practice sometimes associated with evangelicalism, including patriarchy, nationalism, social conservatism, racial discord, conservative Republicanism, the

---

[1] On the Postcolonial Roundtable, see in this volume Joseph F. Duggan, "The Evolution of the Postcolonial Roundtable."

privatization of faith, Reformed theology, imperialism and the desire to make evangelicalism a uniquely American civil religion. Despite such hesitancies, which should not be gainsaid but may indeed be the very loci for evangelical postcolonialisms, the following six evangelical attributes emerged from the group as a whole: christocentrism, conversionism, charism, textualism, activism and communitarianism. These articulated characteristics will be discussed and developed presently.

First, evangelicals declare a *christocentrism*, which means understanding God's mission and God's intent toward creatures and creation as inextricably grounded (incarnated) in the person and work of Jesus Christ. The gospel (*euangelion*) is the declaration that God's transformative action toward humanity's alienation (sin) comes through the sacrificial and redemptive agency of Christ and the cross of Christ. Second, this Christ is risen, and in this resurrection a re-created humanity emerges and a renewed kind of *communitarianism* is instantiated. Church, at its most basic, is an assembly of those who have met the risen Christ. Indeed, church is created by an encounter with the risen Christ. Third, in *conversionism* an evangelical community of Christ testifies to the conviction that the ministry, resurrection and ascension of Christ, as well as the crucifixion, are the means through which God reconciles the world to God's self. Because of this life-giving mission of God, humans are called to align themselves intentionally or be converted to God's ongoing mission toward the re-creation of all things. However, this realignment or conversion is not possible simply through human resolve. The fourth element, *charism*, signifies the effective work of the Holy Spirit in the life and gospel of Christ that evangelicals affirm. The Spirit who raised Christ from the dead is the same Spirit who re-creates and reorients human lives (Rom 8:11) and guides the church into God's future. Fifth, the guidance of the Spirit is mediated and tested through the practice of *textualism*. That is to say, the Bible is considered by evangelicals to be God's living and authoritative Word. In interpreting it they see themselves contextualizing God's will in their activism and thought. Sixth, evangelicals are well known for *activism*, and in part this comes from their desire to see God's will done in human societies. Thus, for example, evangelicals organize themselves into movements and missions for evangelism, social action, education, ecological practice, the arts, church growth and leadership development.

POSTCOLONIALISM

R. S. Sugirtharajah observes that postcolonialism is not so much a theory as it is criticism. It is the adoption of a critical stance in favor of those suppressed in colonial and postcolonial circumstances.[2] The purpose of the criticism is to generate "counterdiscursive practices" that correct and undo so-called Western hegemony.[3] I will argue that such counterdiscursive practice can be summarized as responses to five priorities: coloniality, agency for the marginalized, hybridity, critique of power relations and decolonization.

First, postcolonialism as *a response to coloniality* emerges out of the suffering of historic colonialisms and ongoing neocolonialisms. Coloniality can be understood as a state or process of subjugating culture and/or agency by incursive cultural and, in this case, theological discourses.[4] This is the locus of postcolonialism, and the most important voices in the movement are those who have "asserted themselves by foregrounding the tension with the imperial power, and by emphasizing their differences from the assumptions of the imperial centre."[5] Second, in coloniality, postcolonialism is concerned about *agency for those who are marginalized.* Postcolonialism seeks to disrupt relationships of domination by developing new forms of internationalist understanding and communication.[6] The "post" is concerned with going beyond coloniality as an "ethical intention and direction."[7] Third, postcolonialism is a "dialectical product" (hybrid) of interaction between so-called Western and non-Western thought.[8] *Hybridity*, a term not without difficulties, further describes what postcolonialism is and what postcolonialism does. As a practice, hybridity simply means the mixing of, for example, cultures, languages or patterns of thought. It can result in linguistic fusions and mixing with the

[2]See R. S. Sugirtharajah, *Postcolonial Reconfigurations: An Alternative Way of Reading the Bible and Doing Theology* (St. Louis: Chalice, 2003), pp. 13-14.
[3]Georg M. Gugelberger and Diana Brydon, "Postcolonial Cultural Studies," in *The Johns Hopkins Guide to Literary Theory and Criticism*, 2nd ed., ed. Michael Groden, Martin Kreiswirth and Imre Szeman (Baltimore: Johns Hopkins University Press, 2005), p. 757.
[4]See Robert S. Heaney, "Coloniality and Theological Method in Africa," *Journal of Anglican Studies* 7, no. 1 (2009): 56-61.
[5]Bill Ashcroft, Gareth Griffiths and Helen Tiffin, *The Empire Writes Back: Theory and Practice in Postcolonial Literatures*, 2nd ed. (London: Routledge, 2002), p. 2.
[6]Robert J. C. Young, "What Is the Postcolonial? Anglican Identities and the Postcolonial" (paper presented at Lambeth Conference, Canterbury, England, July 21, 2008), p. 3.
[7]Catherine Keller, Michael Nausner and Mayra Rivera, eds., introduction to *Postcolonial Theologies: Divinity and Empire* (St. Louis: Chalice, 2004), p. 6.
[8]Robert J. C. Young, *Postcolonialism: An Historical Introduction* (Oxford: Blackwell, 2001), p. 68.

result, sometimes, of new dialects, languages or worldviews.[9] Such hybridizing does not simply emerge from historical contingencies but is intentionally developed as resistance to imperialist hegemony and homogeneity. Fourth, postcolonialism is an exercise in *critiquing power*. In *Orientalism* (1978) Edward Said draws attention to the exercise of power not only in colonialist land grabbing but also in the production of "knowledge" about, in his case, the so-called Orient. Colonization can perpetuate both physical and epistemic violence. Colonization is both physical and epistemic violence.[10] Therefore, critiquing such power is found not only in revolutionary action but also in counterdiscourses. Fifth, the aim of postcolonialism is always some kind of *decolonization*. The processes of thought and practice in postcolonialism interrupt dominant and domineering thought and practice with alternative kinds of, for example, testimonies, knowledges and epistemologies. For Robert Young, postcolonialism means turning the world upside down.[11]

PROSPECTS FOR AN EVANGELICAL POSTCOLONIALISM

Young may well unwittingly reference Acts 17:6 in his summation of postcolonialism. There the apostles are accused of turning the world upside down because it is alleged they are "acting contrary to the decrees of the emperor" by declaring "another king named Jesus" (Acts 17:7). An evangelical christocentrism, at least in this scene, is understood to equate with resistance to empire. To what extent other evangelical attributes can also contribute to such resistance is the issue at hand in the present section. I will argue that an evangelical christocentric communitarianism results in protest against the center, that charismatic conversionism results in protest against the status quo, that textualism results in protest against liberal theology and that activism results in protest against globalization.

First, evangelical postcolonial communities of Christ will *protest against the center*. In principle, christocentric community is founded on a graced equali-

---

[9]M. M. Bakhtin, *The Dialogic Imagination: Four Essays* (Austin: University of Texas Press, 1981), pp. 355-62.
[10]Edward W. Said, *Orientalism* (1978; repr., London: Penguin, 2003), p. 95.
[11]Young, "Postcolonial," pp. 3-4. Young sums up the nature of postcolonialism well here. There is, nonetheless, a danger in the assumption that a scholar from the North Atlantic can simply take on the perspective of people "from below." See Robert S. Heaney, "Conversion to Coloniality: Avoiding the Colonization of Method," *International Review of Mission* 97, nos. 384/385 (2008): 65-77.

tarianism. Consequently the stories and testimonies of those who have experienced coloniality and marginality form a rich vein in evangelicalisms. Despite the apparent power evangelicals hold in some contexts, they live on the margins in many other contexts. Evangelicals suffer and minister on the underside of empire. They suffer in contexts where the dominant denomination or religion is hostile, where conversion puts their lives and livelihoods at risk and where Christian missionary or military incursion associates them with foreignness. Compounding such suffering is the suspicion they face from other evangelicals who doubt their orthodoxy because of, for example, race or because of perceived liberalist, syncretist or leftist tendencies. Consequently it is worth considering how such already existing geo-missional and politico-economic decentering might provoke or exhibit theological decentering.

Caesar pushes Christ beyond the margins of empire and life only to find that, in resurrection, Christ subverts and converts the margins of empire and death so that they become thresholds into God's mission. Jesus is the boundary-crossing Christ; he makes porous the very boundary that separates death from life. God's future seeps into the human present. God's re-creation springs up both amid the lands people call home and lands people are no longer able to call home (Lk 17:20).[12] Thus every boundary and border is problematized. The cross stands in opposition to all who proclaim themselves Lord by domination, whether in petty or grand fiefdoms. Consequently the community of Christ is called by the Spirit to unveil centers where domination and domineering practices emerge. Indeed, the Spirit may be calling evangelicals toward a renewed *conscientização* and pedagogy.[13] For example, evangelicals who are conscious of coloniality and marginality will teach a more expansive gospel. A gospel in solidarity with the marginalized lobbies against the center, whether understood in terms of national self-centeredness, economic self-centeredness, cultural self-centeredness, gendered self-centeredness or denominational self-centeredness. For evangelical fellowship is a worldwide hybrid community of pluralist nationalisms, economic models and denominations.

Second, evangelical conversionism brought about by the power of the Holy Spirit means *protest against the status quo*. Conversion cannot be reduced to a

---

[12]George E. Tinker, *Spirit and Resistance: Political Theology and American Indian Liberation* (Minneapolis: Fortress, 2004), Kindle ebook location 97.

[13]See Paulo Freire, *Pedagogy of the Oppressed* (1970; repr., Harmondsworth, UK: Penguin, 1972).

single event. Continued conversion, reformation, sanctification or hybrid-ization through the power of the Spirit is needed. Arguably an evangelical settlement does not exist. Rather, the Spirit of Christ leads believers forward as they hybridize and contextualize in the contexts the providence of God has led them to. Therefore, like other postcolonialists, evangelicals are called to radi-cally threaten the status quo. Cruciform power does not serve the status quo. It subverts it. Christ is Lord by his sacrificial death. Christ therefore subverts the very nature of "lordship" in his self-emptying, and this is a process of con-version that the Spirit beckons believers into. To be converted is to enter deci-sively into a Spirit-inspired process of re-creation. It is a transformation of the state in which rebellious humans exist against the Spirit's re-creative activity. Conversion is following the Christ who reveals his power in being margin-alized by empire. To take up the cross is to be drawn by the Spirit into a movement against the status quo. For the status quo is supported by cultural, patriarchal, racist, consumerist, economic, political and imperial systems and practices.[14] Maintaining the status quo depends on coercion.[15] Many theologies, including evangelical theologies, seldom challenge this collective or systemic sin. Revival is needed, and revival will include reparative relationships between those close to empire's centers and those on empire's margins. Furthermore, it remains urgent that evangelicals reassess how they relate to the powers that be in the nation states in which they find themselves. Theology is counter-discursive (hearing God's judgment from the Other) as well as discursive (for example, explicating postcolonial practice from the resources of one's own community and experience). For it is through the practice of discourses and counterdiscourses that critical practice and thought against the status quo are provoked and enhanced. However, being open to God's call and judgment from other perspectives and traditions does not necessarily equate to making evan-gelicalisms "liberal," as I will now demonstrate.

Third, evangelical textualism results in a critique and *protest against liberal theology.* Imperialism often includes the idea of expanding the rationalism of a superior culture to lesser cultures. Immanuel Kant, argues Tsenay Sereque-berhan, considered "reason and rationality . . . not indigenous . . . in . . . black

---

[14]See Tinker, *Spirit and Resistance,* loc. 102-28.
[15]Stanley Hauerwas, *After Christendom: How the Church Is to Behave If Freedom, Justice, and a Chris-tian Nation Are Bad Ideas* (Nashville: Abingdon, 1991), pp. 69-92.

African peoples."[16] It is unsurprising, therefore, that modern liberal theology emerges as the empowered voice of the middle classes within a context of "German colonial fantasies."[17] The presumed rationalism of humans, it appears, is not always as universal as claimed. Consequently, without engaging the critique of other wisdoms and rationalities, the whole modern intellectual project becomes suspect at its very point of acclaim.

When a society is fixated with addressing the rational skeptic, moral skeptics are often overlooked. A moral skeptic points to the widespread passivity of northern Christian theology in the face of modernity's brutality. Additionally a moral skeptic points to the part played by theology itself in motivating and justifying such violence. Neither coherency, demythologization, correlation nor contextualization is the only theological issue at stake. What is at stake, at a much more practical level, is the very denial of humanity (and human life) to vast swathes of the world. Evangelical postcolonialists will nurture moral skepticism more intentionally. For such skepticism unmasks the power of death and opens the way to the salvation of God. In doing so, evangelical theology begins to recapture its radical and prophetic vocation in standing against the hegemonic impulses and forces of continued imperialist practice, including top-down globalization. Unfortunately, despite an apparent commitment to taking the biblical text seriously, evangelicals too often miss biblical critiques of domineering exercises of power.[18] Yet it is God who brings down the mighty and lifts up the lowly (Ps 75:1-10; Lk 1:46-55). Jesus unmasks imperialist collusion (Mk 11:11–12:12). The demonic Legion is driven into the sea (Mk 5:1-9). The empire's power is relativized in light of allegiance to Jesus, and Caesar is to get what he deserves (Mk 12:17). The "patronal ethic" of the empire is critiqued.[19]

---

[16]Tsenay Serequeberhan, "The Critique of Eurocentrism and the Practice of African Philosophy," quoted in *Postcolonial African Philosophy: A Critical Reader*, ed. Emmanuel Chukwudi Eze (Oxford: Blackwell, 1997), p. 149. See Immanuel Kant, "Idea for a Universal History from a Cosmopolitan Point of View," *German History in Documents and Images*, http://germanhistorydocs.ghi-dc.org /pdf/eng/12_EnlightPhilos_Doc.3_English.pdf, accessed August 23, 2013.

[17]Joerg Rieger, *Christ and Empire: From Paul to Postcolonial Times* (Minneapolis: Fortress, 2007), p. 200.

[18]See Gayatri Chakravorty Spivak, *A Critique of Postcolonial Reason: Toward a History of the Vanishing Present* (Cambridge, MA: Harvard University Press, 1999), p. 191.

[19]Joel B. Green, "'Salvation to the End of the Earth' (Acts 13:47): God as Savior in the Acts of the Apostles," in *Witness to the Gospel: The Theology of Acts*, ed. I. Howard Marshall and David Peterson (Grand Rapids: Eerdmans, 1998), p. 94.

Eschatologically all "Babylons" are finally destroyed in the judgment of God.[20]
Here is biblical protest against the center, which in a postcolonial evangelicalism becomes part of evangelical activism.

Fourth, evangelical activism will include *protest against globalization*. Evangelical activism, especially cross-cultural activism, has created a source of
critical (and uncritical) thinking on mission and colonialism. For J. N. K Mugambi, "globalization" is the latest in a long line of Euro-American projects
predicated on the insight of both foreign anthropologists and missiologists to
"develop" and "civilize" the so-called Third (and Fourth) Worlds.[21] Yet impulses
and practices of top-down globalization do not necessarily come from outside
theology. Before the modern missionary movement and before evangelicalisms
existed, Christian theology, emerging within the world of the Roman Empire,
had an "unfolding history of globalization."[22] In contrast, a key component of
any postcolonial movement is to work against such top-down globalization
(hegemony). For evangelicals, the particularity of the practice of Jesus, the particularity of faith communities emerging from meeting the risen Christ, the
particularity of conversion by the power of the Spirit and the particularity of
reading the biblical text in context create identities and opportunities for
"bottom-up" mission. Ulrich Duchrow further explicates what that might mean
when he calls believers to

> listen to the Bible, to the cries of the poor, to take roots in God's saving activity
> and to continue stubbornly analysing present mechanisms and opposing the
> falsity and propaganda of the systems . . . to try out alternatives in one's own small
> sphere . . . to do one's utmost so that the marginalised of the earth can gather and
> unite and try out a new quality of stewardship against the political and economic
> systems of Pharaoh to the glory of the God of justice, mercy and truth (Mt.
> 23.23).[23]

Such processes toward decolonization, I argue, can become part of Sunday

---

[20]See Christopher Rowland, *Revelation* (London: Epworth, 1993), pp. 142-46.

[21]J. N. K. Mugambi, "Religions in East Africa in the Context of Globalization," in *Religions in Eastern
Africa Under Globalization*, ed. J. N. K. Mugambi and Mary N. Getui (Nairobi: Acton, 2004), pp.
9-10.

[22]Joerg Rieger, *Globalization and Theology* (Nashville: Abingdon, 2010), p. 1. See Thomas McCarthy,
Race, Empire, and the Idea of Human Development (Cambridge: Cambridge University Press, 2009),
p. 132.

[23]Ulrich Duchrow, "Political and Economic Wellbeing and Justice: A Global View," *Studies in Christian
Ethics* 3, no. 61 (1990): 92.

schools, missionary classes, seminary curricula, unions, picket lines and the activism of local churches and evangelical agencies. While such an approach may be contested, it is the conviction of the present author that such thought and practice will begin to define what evangelical postcolonialism will be and do.

PROBLEMS FOR AN EVANGELICAL POSTCOLONIALISM

Evangelicalism will not be embraced by all postcolonialists, and postcolonialism will not be embraced by all evangelicals. For evangelicals may be tempted to adopt a cheap postcolonialism, and evangelical attributes may stand in tension with postcolonial practice.

Cheap postcolonialisms. To engage in false moves, or cheap postcolonialisms, may be a temptation for evangelicals. These moves, I submit, could include emphasizing the postcoloniality of Reformation, democracy or geography. First, a particular reading of the emergence of evangelicalisms, especially during the European Reformations, can evoke an anti-imperialist pedigree. In this reading Reformation is seen as a strike against top-down power structures and empire. However, such readings are challenged by evangelical imposition of reform, nationalistically defined reform and the relationships of Protestant mission with empire, especially as they emerge in historic European centers.

Evangelicals might respond to such critique by claiming that they have learned their lesson from history. This gives rise to the second point, which is that evangelicals sometimes claim that their commitment to the gospel of Christ and the freedom it brings promotes democracy.[24] At the center of such a claim is often an affirmation of the United States of America and its supposed influence on other movements for democracy. However, the influence of evangelicalisms in the emergence and ongoing development of the United States is contested, as is the consistency of America's understanding and practice of democracy overseas.[25]

The center of Christianity and evangelicalism is apparently shifting to the South. This may be considered a postcolonial shift in itself, with power moving

---

[24]See Jim Wallis, "Dangerous Religion: George W. Bush's Theology of Empire," in *Evangelicals and Empire: Christian Alternatives to the Political Status Quo*, ed. Bruce Ellis Benson and Peter Goodwin Heltzel (Grand Rapids: Brazos Press, 2008), pp. 25-32.

[25]C. René Padilla, "United States Foreign Policy and Terrorism," in *Terrorism and the War in Iraq: A Christian Word from Latin America*, ed. C. René Padilla and Lindy Scott (Buenos Aires: Kairos Ediciones, 2004), pp. 63-106.

away from the dominance of old colonial centers. However, so-called southern voices critiquing the so-called liberal North are not enough to engender theological postcolonialism. This leads to the third form of cheap postcolonialism, which is using postcolonial rhetoric in a way that does not equate to critically postcolonial practice.[26] Thus neither Reformation, nor democracy, nor the southern shift in Christianity are successful loci for evangelical postcolonialisms. It appears that evangelical postcolonialism will need to emerge more straightforwardly from evangelical theology, beginning with its central claim that Jesus is "Lord."

Evangelical christocentrism and postcolonialism. If the lordship of Christ is domination then christocentrism may attest to an evangelical imperialism. Max Warren illustrates just this when he argues, in his defense of imperialism, that submission of one group to another is theologically justifiable.[27] In more recent times, the "Bush theology" provides similar justification for imperialism when the nation becomes the "hope of all mankind" and the Johannine light that shines in the darkness.[28] In contrast, marginalized theologizing will not confuse Christ with nation nor see Christ as some kind of über-Caesar.[29] Salvation is not the domination of Christ over all. Salvation is the ending of all dominations. The lordship of Christ is not Caesarian but subverts all Caesars.[30] The incarnated lord comes not as humanity in general but comes as one marginalized from the center and from communities of power.

Evangelical communitarianism and postcolonialism. Evangelical communitarianism may well be a corrective to evangelical individualism. However, such ecclesiological redress may veil an equally colonialist preoccupation—the drawing and policing of boundaries or borders. Ecclesiological practice then can move from a focus on the "orthodoxy" of the individual believer to the "orthodoxy" of the individual community. Well-defined community boundaries between "world" and "church" and between "believers" and "unbelievers" are, as has already been seen, problematic from a critically postcolonial perspective. A

[26]See Mercy Amba Oduyoye, *Introducing African Women's Theology* (Sheffield: Sheffield Academic Press, 2001), pp. 12-13.
[27]M. A. C. Warren, *Caesar the Beloved Enemy* (London: SCM Press, 1955), p. 24.
[28]Wallis, "Dangerous Religion," pp. 28-29.
[29]See N. T. Wright, *Jesus and the Victory of God* (London: SPCK, 1996), pp. 360-65; Rowland, *Revelation,* p. 145.
[30]Homi K. Bhabha, *The Location of Culture* (New York: Routledge, 1994), pp. 130-31.

postcolonial ecclesiologist may, because of the boundary-crossing Christ, seek a theological decolonization by promoting a practical porosity. That is to say, the christological center is given priority over ecclesiological/ecclesiastical boundaries. In simple terms, church cannot be reduced to a gathering of "believers."

Rather, centering on Christ means a turning away from border-policing while simultaneously being confronted by the margins of human experience/ coloniality in the broken body and poured-out life of Christ. Word and sacrament are like centrifugal forces, sending believers toward the margins. The task of Christians, as has been seen, is then to convert such margins into thresholds toward participating in the mission of God through networks of particularisms and localisms. Such bottom-up and "intimately organized" networking can be as straightforward as standing together when human dignity and human potential are being suppressed.[31] Networking can be more widespread, thus connecting, for example, local groups for workers' rights, alternative banks, reparations, ecological campaigns, evangelistic strategizing or spiritual renewal.

Evangelical charism and postcolonialism. An emphasis on the work of the Spirit can veil abuses of power. Evangelicals, with other Christians, can pneumatologically legitimize oppression and subjugation. Such a pneumatology might conclude that the Spirit of God at work in human histories seems to have determined or allowed imperialism, colonialism, slavery and patriarchy. A key part of evangelical motivation for postcolonial practice will come with clarification on the nature and work of the Holy Spirit.

For evangelicals the Spirit is not some sort of insubstantial phantom haunting the world. The Holy Spirit is the Spirit of Jesus Christ. The Spirit is gifted by the one from the margins, who died on the margins. Marginality embedded in evangelical pneumatology means that readings of histories will not simply see the hand of God in the rise of empires or superpowers. Rather, the providence or provision of God also comes to the world from the margins. Therefore, any reading of any history will not readily assume that top-down power or center-out expansion is evidence of the hand of God in history. God calls creation to align itself with the resisting lord of the margins. This means a rejection of a Caesarian Christ who blesses the tropes and troops of the

---

[31]Tinker, *Spirit and Resistance*, loc. 353.

powers that be. A postcolonial spirituality, hybridized by perspectives and practices from the margins, seeks the Spirit's empowerment for ongoing conversion to the one standing opposed to the status quo.

Evangelical conversionism and postcolonialism. While evangelical conversion seems to be built on dualisms unacceptable in postcolonial criticism, the conversional process is one where syntheses are always being made.[32] For example, the *theos*, god, or *Mungu*, introduced by evangelical missionaries, even during colonialism, was and is inevitably amalgamated with pre-evangelized concepts of tradition and creator.[33] Despite this, hybridity does not have automatic theological or postcolonial value. For it can disempower attempts at transformative (decolonizing) practices if oppositional stances are seen as comprising people and circumstances that are admixtures of good and bad. That is to say, hybridity is not transformative (decolonizing) if invoked to apportion blame to the colonized as well as the colonizers. Equally, hybridity may not result from the agency of believers. It may signal a loss of agency in a context where hybridity becomes a process of gradual assimilation into a dominant culture.[34] Conversional hybridity cannot be the playful bricolage of postmodernism. Rather, hybridization is decolonizing when it is set within the struggles that exist because of differentials of power.[35] Conversion is not, for many Christians in many cultures, a rejection of "heathenism" in favor of "Christianity." On the contrary, conversion to Christ clears a path for ongoing dialogue and discovery of the God who is already present before the biblical text is preached. Thus conversionism is a process of continuity as well as discontinuity.

Evangelical textualism and postcolonialism. For evangelicals God spans the distance between Creator and creature in the act of speaking. This spanning is both linguistic (Bible) and ontological (incarnation). The linguistic spanning cannot hold the whole weight of God. It carries what is necessary for creation and re-creation. But the texts include not only the voice of God but also the

---

[32]J. N. K. Mugambi, *African Christian Theology: An Introduction* (Nairobi: East African Educational Publishers, 1989), p. 44; Martin Brokenleg, "Themes in Contemporary Native Theological Education," *Anglican Theological Review* 90, no. 2 (2008): 278.

[33]See Kwame Anthony Appiah, *In My Father's House: Africa in the Philosophy of Culture* (Oxford: Oxford University Press, 1992), pp. 107-36.

[34]Tinker, *Spirit and Resistance*, loc. 753, 693.

[35]Rieger, *Globalization and Theology*, p. 31.

voices of angels, humans, demons and Satan. The Bible cannot simply be considered the "direct utterance" of God. Therefore, John Goldingay argues that inspiration applied to prophetic writing (direct utterance) cannot be applied in the same way to other biblical genres. God speaks God's own words, and God makes effective and relevant the words of others for the mission of God.[36] Given this, how do postcolonial evangelicals read the Bible when postcolonial criticism sees much of it as objectionable?

Just as postcolonial evangelicals will read history christologically (casting an eye not only to the center but also to the margins), so too the biblical text may be approached in the same manner. That is to say, the Bible will be read with power analysis in the hermeneutical foreground. Indeed, Jesus himself provides a rereading of the messianic expectations of his day from the perspective not of empowerment but of disempowerment (Lk 24:13-35). Today, reading the Bible in fellowship will include reading with those who experience disempowerment and reading ever watchful for the marginalized characters or plots within the text. Such reading, it is hoped, will lead to renewed action and activism.

Evangelical activism and postcolonialism. Euro-American missionary proselytizing is deeply problematic for postcolonialism because it is often based on and perpetuates divisive dualistic thinking and global inequalities. Evangelistic zeal may, to some degree, fuel missionary expansionism. But it is also fueled by the resources of those who possess a larger portion of disposable income and citizenships, which often guarantee visas and work permits. The power—and missionaries—often continue to flow from the center to the margins. Sugirtharajah argues that such mission is intrinsically imperialist.[37]

An evangelical *postcolonial* missiology, emerging from protests against globalization, will work against perpetuating models of expansionist, center-out or top-down practices of mission. Equally, an *evangelical* postcolonial missiology will not be reductionist. It will not abandon the ambiguous and dangerous task of mission by reducing it to relief work or advocacy. Nor will it simply correlate all mission with imperialism. It will be not only *misión integral* but also *misión participativa.* Mission is, then, not so much the spread of one truth to many locations as it is the redemptive, disciplining and hybridizing participation in many localisms, particularisms, reparations, perspectives and

---

[36]See John Goldingay, *Models for Scripture* (Carlisle, UK: Paternoster Press, 1987), pp. 252-60.
[37]Sugirtharajah, *Postcolonial Reconfigurations*, pp. 17-36.

practices. In practice this means a continued development of grassroots networks and an openness to participate in the mission of God found in organizations, community groups, lobbying groups, spiritual movements and indeed
churches, including those that do not identify themselves with evangelical faith.

CONCLUSION

If postcolonial evangelicalisms are practicable, they will be, I argue, a re-
discovery of "Protestantisms" in the context of neoimperialisms. That is to say,
they will include protest against the center, the status quo, liberal theology and
globalizations. For the lord of the church is the Christ who resists. The lord is
the one who was flung to the margins of empire by empire. This is the locus for
salvation and Christian practice. Consequently, Christ's lordship, sometimes
through mimicry/mockery, subverts all who would dominate by force from the
top or from the center, including Christ's own professed agents. The Bible is,
then, read in open (porous) communities alert to power relations within the
texts and between interpreters. Networks of resistance (churches) are centered
in Jesus, and because of that, margins are not borders to police, but in the power
of the Spirit of Christ they are thresholds to participation in the (kenotic)
mission of God.

Part One

MISSION AND
METANARRATIVE

··· ⚉ ···

Origins and Articulations

INTRODUCTION TO PART ONE

Mission and Metanarrative
Origins and Articulations

x

THE EVANGELICAL REVIVALS THAT SWEPT through the United States and the United Kingdom in the late eighteenth and nineteenth centuries generated a missionary movement of unprecedented magnitude. Mission agencies deployed countless men and women to bring the light of Christ to unreached peoples and deliverance from the bonds of darkness. The missionary vision promised salvation not only from sin and satanic oppression but also from ignorance, superstition and savagery. The unquestioned premise of the missionary movement held that God had providentially raised up the United States and the United Kingdom to fulfill the Great Commission and that the extension of their empires also extended the benefits of Christian civilization for the good of the entire world. Evangelizing therefore went hand in hand with "civilizing" (or "assimilating" or "improving") indigenous converts and separating them from their cultures, which were regarded as primitive, backward or even demonic. The biblical narrative of salvation thus fused with the Enlightenment metanarrative of emancipation to explain and justify evangelical missions.

The chapters in this section explore the mixed legacy of evangelical missions in North America, India and sub-Saharan Africa, and the role of the Bible in extending Euro-American hegemony. L. Daniel Hawk and Richard L. Twiss render an account of missionary collusion with the US government's civilization program and the racialized interpretation of the Bible that facilitated it. Gregory L. Cuéllar and Randy S. Woodley then expand the scope of the story to encompass the whole of the missionary enterprise in the United States. They interrogate the way Christian mission is marked and remembered, and press for a new paradigm that accords indigenous people the lead in rendering the narrative of missions. Jayachitra Lalitha focuses on the missionary legacy in India and how colonial oppression played out in control and discrimination of subjects in terms of gender and caste as well. Her study of the interactions between white missionary and native women reveals how the Bible, and its interpretation, constituted both an instrument of colonial hegemony and a source of empowerment for low-caste women. Victor Ifeanyi Ezigbo and Reggie L. Williams offer a third variation on the theme of missionary colonization of minds and peoples with a reflection on the white Christ the missionaries presented and the "biblical Christianity" they attempted to instill. In response they elaborate the contours of a postcolonial African Christology that overcomes the colonial mentality, fosters African theological self-identity and autonomy, and makes a substantive contribution to global theological discourse.

1

From Good: "The Only Good Indian Is a Dead Indian"

to Better: "Kill the Indian and Save the Man"

to Best: "Old Things Pass Away and All Things Become White!"

An American Hermeneutic of Colonization

L. Daniel Hawk and Richard L. Twiss

.... ☥ ....

IN 1820 SECRETARY OF WAR JOHN CALHOUN sent the Reverend Jedidiah Morse on an intelligence-gathering mission to the Indian tribes living within the domain of the United States. Calhoun directed Morse "to ascertain the actual condition of the various tribes" for the purpose of "devising the most suitable plan to advance their civilization and happiness."[1] The mission was stimulated by the passage, in the previous year, of the Civilization Fund Act, which authorized the distribution of funds to benevolent societies for the purpose of educating Indian peoples "in the habits of civilization." Congress had passed the act as a means of "providing against the further decline and final extinction of the Indian tribes," which, in the prevailing opinion of the time, the inexorable advance of settlement rendered inevitable without gov-

---

[1]Jedidiah Morse, *A Report to the Secretary of War, On Indian Affairs....* (New Haven, CT: S. Converse, 1822), pp. 12, 11.

ernment intervention.[2] Most of the funds were subsequently disbursed to Christian denominations and mission agencies, which were regarded as essential for "laying the foundations for [the Indians'] civil, social, and religious improvement" and imparting "the blessings of civilization and Christianity."[3]

Morse was one of the leading intellectual, civic and religious figures of his time and had become troubled by the "blots" on the "character of our ancestors, and of our nation," specifically

> the manner in which we have, in many, if not most instances, come into possession of their lands, and of their peltry: also, to the provocations we have given, in so many instances, to those cruel, desolating, and exterminating wars, which have been successively waged against them; and to the corrupting vices, and fatal diseases, which have been introduced among them, by wicked and unprincipled white people.[4]

These "national sins," he believed, should be redressed by extending "the blessings of civilization and Christianity" to the Indians.[5]

Morse's report includes the manuscript of a speech he delivered to a gathering of Ottawas at Michillimackinac. It offers a revealing snapshot of Christian perspectives at this pivotal juncture in white America's interaction with indigenous nations. Morse begins with encouraging words: "Your fathers, the christian white people . . . are devising plans for your happiness. The Congress of the United States, the Great Council of our nation, feel for you, also, and have put money into the hands of your Father, the President, to promote the welfare of the Indians."[6] There follows a long account of the decline of Indians to the east and south due to pestilence, the loss of hunting grounds and the settlements of the white people. The Indian way, Morse avers, will not survive, for the time is past when Indians can "associate with white people, as their equals." White people are increasing, Indian lands are being lost and, bereft of game to hunt and furs to trade, Indians "will give themselves up to idleness, ignorance, and drunkenness, and will waste away, and by and bye, have no posterity on

---

[2]"Civilization Fund Act," in *Documents of United States Indian Policy*, ed. Francis Paul Prucha, 3rd ed. (Lincoln: University of Nebraska Press, 2000), p. 31.

[3]Morse, *Report to the Secretary of War*, pp. 2-3.

[4]Quoted in the American Society for the Promotion of the Gospel, *The First Annual Report of the American Society for the Promotion of the Gospel* (New Haven, CT: S. Converse, 1824), p. 66.

[5]Ibid. We use the term *Indian* here to accentuate the white colonial perspective.

[6]Morse, "Appendix," in *Report to the Secretary of War*, p. 9.

the face of the earth."[7] Morse assures his listeners, however, that Indians may yet become partakers in the blessings that all whites enjoy. To help them, he declares, "your christian fathers, will send among you, at their own expense, good white men and women, to instruct you and your children, in every thing that pertains to the civilized and christian life." Indigenous peoples stand at a precipice: "*Civilization* or *ruin*, are now the only alternatives of Indians."[8]

Morse continues,

> Among the means for your civilization, in addition to what have already been mentioned, we will bring you the best, the only *effectual*, means of making you truly happy—we will bring you the Bible, the best of all Books. We will teach you to read and understand it. This book is a revelation from God, and contains the words of eternal life. It reveals the true character of God, the Great Spirit, in whom you profess to believe, and of man, and the relation and duty of man to his Maker, and to his fellow men. It maketh wise to salvation, by revealing a Saviour, the Lord Jesus Christ, and the way of salvation by him. It contains the doctrines and precepts of the Christian religion. This book causes the wide difference which exists, as you see, between the white man and the Indian. We will bring you this blessed book. We will teach your children to read it, that they may be happy, and comfort you; that they may know how to live, and do good; and how to die, and to live forever.[9]

WHITE MAKES RIGHT

Morse's speech manifests the assumptions and ideology that have defined white thinking and practice in relation to the indigenous peoples of the continent throughout America's history. The framework of this thinking is as follows: Anglo-Saxon civilization represents the pinnacle of human development and progress. It has been founded on Christian principles, which articulate the highest vision for human well-being and happiness. As is manifest by the burgeoning white population, the nation's inexorable advance westward and its victories over resistant Indian nations, the future belongs to the white race, which is establishing a new society in the United States.[10] Anglo-Saxon civili-

---

[7]Ibid, p. 11.

[8]Ibid., pp. 13-14 (emphasis original).

[9]Ibid.

[10]See, for example, Reginald Horsman, *Race and Manifest Destiny* (Cambridge, MA: Harvard University Press, 1981); Anders Stephanson, *Manifest Destiny* (New York: Hill & Wang, 1995); and Richard T. Hughes, *Myths America Lives By* (Urbana: University of Illinois Press, 2004).

zation and Christianity merge in the New World, rendering the United States the apex and engine of human advancement, achievement and liberty. The indigenous peoples of the continent, by contrast, are part of a past that is rapidly fading away. Indigenous peoples and their way of life are headed toward extinction. Indian culture is primitive, simplistic and savage—a vestige of the human past that will be swept away by the ineluctable advance of civilization.

Guided by these ideas, Christian reformers like Morse were propelled by a sense of moral obligation to improve the condition of Indians. In practice this meant educating them into the civilized practices, lifestyle and modes of thought that enabled participation in the new human society that was emerging in the New World. Morse's words reveal the crucial role the Bible was to play in this program. Conceived as a compendium of principles and precepts, the Bible could be employed as the primary instrument for teaching indigenous peoples "how to live, and do good."

Against those who argued that Indians possessed an inferior intellect, Morse and other reformers asserted that their so-called savagery was the result of arrested social development. The reformers held that Indians were capable of improvement and civilization and so should be brought into the literate universe of which the Bible was the center. The Bible thus constituted both the cause of "the wide difference . . . between the white man and the Indian" and the means of eliminating the difference. Morse was confident that "civilization, and a knowledge of the scriptures, will doubtless dispel the mist which has so long hung over these nations, and show them not to be inferior to any other people."[11]

Morse's sentiments were rooted in a long history. John Eliot, the Puritan missionary whose work became the prototype for Protestant missions to the Indians, believed that civilizing the Indians was necessary for their successful conversion to Christianity. Eliot therefore suppressed indigenous religious practices and required that his converts adopt, among other things, English-style clothing, agricultural practices, monogamous marriage and English hairstyles.[12] Rigorous indoctrination in the tropes of Protestant thought and discourse brought about a corresponding inner transformation.[13] To protect his converts from the deleterious influence of indigenous ways, Eliot established Praying

---

[11]Morse, "Appendix," *Report to the Secretary of War,* p. 200.
[12]George E. Tinker, *Missionary Conquest* (Minneapolis: Fortress, 1993), p. 26.
[13]Ibid., p. 34.

Towns that separated Christian Indians from their families and communities.

This separatist sensibility derived from the internal boundaries the Puritans erected to differentiate themselves from the indigenous peoples. The Puritans regarded themselves as the visible community of God's elect and deeply valued their English cultural heritage.[14] Delivered from tyranny by a passage through the sea, they saw themselves as the people of God settling a new Canaan. They approached their "errand into the wilderness," however, with fear and trembling. The Indians' way of life struck the colonists as the very antithesis of godliness, moral restraint and civilized behavior. In Puritan eyes, Indians were lascivious, slothful and "undutiful." They did not hold ownership of property. They were "indulgent out of measure" with their children. They were bloodthirsty. They had no laws. They didn't wear pants.[15] They were, in the words of Cotton Mather, "doleful creatures who were the veriest ruins of mankind; who were to be found anywhere on the face of the earth."[16]

Worse yet, the Indians were agents of Satan. The new Canaan the Puritans settled was

A waste and howling wilderness,
Where none inhabited,
But hellish fiends and brutish men
That devils worshiped.[17]

Mather called the Indians Satan's "most devoted and resembling children"[18] and declared that "their whole religion was the most explicit sort of devil worship." When the Salem witch hysteria broke out, Mather suggested that the causes might lie with the Indians. "Their chief sagamores," he exclaimed, "are well known . . . to have been horrid sorcerers and hellish conjurers and such as conversed with demons." The Indians, in sum, constituted the "irreducible, satanic other" against which the Puritan community constructed its identity.[19]

---

[14]Charles M. Segal and David C. Stineback, *Puritans, Indians, and Manifest Destiny* (New York: Putnam, 1977), p. 33.
[15]James A. Morone, *Hellfire Nation* (New Haven, CT: Yale University Press, 2003), pp. 74-76.
[16]Quoted in Segal and Stineback, *Puritans, Indians, and Manifest Destiny*, p. 49.
[17]Michael Wigglesworth, "God's Controversy with New England," in *God's New Israel*, ed. Conrad Cherry, rev. and updated ed. (Chapel Hill: University of North Carolina Press, 1998), p. 42.
[18]Quoted in W. Scott Poole, *Satan in America: The Devil We Know* (Lanham, MD: Rowman & Littlefield, 2009), p. 16.
[19]Morone, *Hellfire Nation*, p. 76.

Informed by Puritan perspectives and practices, subsequent missions sought to obliterate the savage indigenous identity and replace it with a civilized Christian one. Early missionary John Sergeant described the objective as "the total eradication of all that marks them as native . . . to root out their vicious habits, and to change their whole way of living."[20] The association of "white" with civilization and Christianity, and "Indian" with savagery and idolatry, constituted the unquestioned framework of American thought and policy well into the twentieth century—effectively rendering indigenous cultures incompatible with Christian faith and practice. "The truth is," declared a prominent mission agency in 1856, "that Christianity has little affinity with the indolent, migratory, nomadic habits of the Indians. The two cannot abide together."[21] Education would bring about the transformation of indigenous identities, with instruction in the Bible as the linchpin of the curriculum.

MIGHT MAKES WHITE

Christian mission agencies constituted the de facto arm of the US government's civilization project throughout the nineteenth century. The reported success of mission schools early in the century suggested a promising partnership between government and Christian bodies. In 1818 a House committee declared,

> One of two things seems to be necessary; either that these sons of the forest should be moralized or exterminated. . . . Put into the hands of their children the primer and the hoe, and they will naturally, in time, take hold of the plough; and, as their minds become enlightened and expand, the Bible will be their book, and they will grow up in habits of morality and industry, leave the chase to those whose minds are less cultivated, and become useful members of society.[22]

Upon passage of the Civilization Act a year later, Secretary of War Calhoun sent a circular to mission agencies offering substantial federal grants for the construction and operation of new schools.[23]

---

[20]Quoted in Hilary E. Wyss, *Writing Indians: Literacy, Christianity, and Native Community in Early America* (Amherst: University of Massachusetts Press, 2000), p. 92.

[21]Society for Propagating the Gospel among the Indians and Others in North America, *Report of the Select Committee of the Society for Propagating the Gospel Among the Indians and Others in North America* (Boston: John Wilson and Son, 1856), p. 34.

[22]Quoted in Jon Reyhner and Jeanne Eder, *American Indian Education: A History* (Norman: University of Oklahoma Press, 2004), p. 43.

[23]Ibid., pp. 43-45.

Religious instruction was an integral part of the curriculum at these schools. The day commonly began with Bible readings, prayer and hymn-singing, and the Bible constituted the primary reading textbook in the classes that followed.[24] Instruction in Bible history drew students into the explanatory narrative of white America and displaced indigenous identities articulated through tribal myths and stories. Instruction in Scripture, centered on correct doctrine and moral precepts, colonized indigenous minds into a European qua Christian way of thinking. All instruction was conducted in English, as assimilation into this new humanity required fluency in the vernacular of white America. No one articulated the project more succinctly than the American Board of Commissioners for Foreign Missions, which aspired to establish a mission school for each tribe "so as gradually, with the divine blessing to make the whole tribe English in their language, civilized in their habits, and Christian in their religion."[25]

Missionary collusion with government civilization programs became even closer with the establishment of President Ulysses S. Grant's Peace Policy in 1874. A key plank of the policy was a short-lived and disastrous plan to assign government supervision of tribes to Christian denominations, which served as "duly subordinate and responsible" Indian agents to the United States Department of the Interior. The outcome was a fiasco, but the plan to give Indians "the Bible and the plow" continued unabated.[26] In 1882 then-commissioner of Indian affairs Hiram Price reported on the positive effects of the ongoing partnership between church and state: "One very important auxiliary in transforming men from savage to civilized life is the influence brought to bear upon them through the labors of Christian men and women as educators and missionaries. Civilization is a plant of exceeding slow growth, unless supplemented by Christian teaching and influence."[27] The "liberal encouragement" spoken of by Price would soon bring about a sinister and brutal transformation in Indian education: the forcible removal of indigenous children from their families to residential schools, where the curriculum followed the philosophy of Captain

[24]Robert F. Berkhofer Jr., *Salvation and the Savage* (New York: Atheneum, 1972), p. 31.
[25]American Board of Commissioners for Foreign Missions, *First Ten Annual Reports of the American Board of Commissioners for Foreign Missions* (Boston: Crocker and Brewster, 1834), pp. 135-36.
[26]Robert H. Keller Jr., *American Protestantism and United States Indian Policy, 1869-82* (Lincoln: University of Nebraska Press, 1983), p. 157.
[27]Hiram Price, "Report on the Mission Indians of California," in Prucha, *Documents*, p. 157.

Richard Henry Pratt at the Carlisle Indian Industrial School: "Kill the Indian. Save the Man."[28]

The combined efforts of federal policy and Christian missions epitomized what Steven Newcomb describes as "some huge Christian European re-clamation project metaphorically conceiving American Indians as needing to be 'reclaimed' or 'recalled from wrong or improper conduct.'"[29] By equating salvation from sin and new life in Christ with white, European Christianity and thus requiring native peoples to reject their God-given identities, missionaries rejected the *imago Dei* among the native peoples. By demonizing indigenous customs and beliefs, missionaries turned converts against their cultures, foisted an alien identity on them and "generated a sense of low self-worth . . . from which Indian people have not yet recovered."[30]

COLONIZATION, EVANGELIZATION AND ASSIMILATION

The historical record of missions among the First Nations of North America has been a saga filled with enormous potential but great failures and sadness—potential, because the people had a pervasive belief and faith in a monotheistic Creator; the Spirit of the Lord was already in North America revealing the God of Abraham, Isaac and Jacob to them prior to contact; grief, because so many of the early missionaries were unable to recognize and embrace the intrinsic, God-given value of the people to whom they went, blinded by the way they perceived the world to be. For the most part, few recognized—or were willing to recognize—the fundamental clash in worldview assumptions that lay at the root of their interactions. Their paternalistic assumptions produced a deep-rooted case of ethnocentrism in American Christianity, an instance of what Craig Storti refers to as "the ethnocentric impulse" or "phenomenon of cultural conditioning."[31] When the Native people exhibited behavior that violated values fundamental to European identity and self-esteem, the missionaries rejected that behavior. New negative categories had to be created.

---

[28]See Richard H. Pratt, "The Advantages of Mingling Indians with Whites," in *Americanizing the American Indians: Writings by the "Friends of the Indian" 1880–1900*, ed. Francis Paul Prucha (Cambridge, MA: Harvard University Press, 1973), pp. 260-71.
[29]Steven. T. Newcomb, *Pagans in the Promised Land: Decoding the Doctrine of Christian Discovery* (Golden, CO: Fulcrum, 2008), p. 13.
[30]Tinker, *Missionary Conquest*, p. 40.
[31]Craig Storti, *The Art of Crossing Cultures* (Yarmouth, ME: Intercultural Press, 1990), p. 67.

COLONIALISM AND IDEOLOGY

The work of Jean and John Comaroff, who write of the British colonial efforts among the Tswana people of South Africa, is germane to our discussion. They demonstrate that woven throughout the "philosophical construct" of colonialism are two dynamic realities, hegemony and ideology; and they define and expose the roles that hegemony and ideology played in the colonial campaigns of Europe, specifically the distinctive variety that emerged in the 1600s that was fueled by the British penchant for discovery, expansionism and evangelistic fervor.

Comaroff and Comaroff assert that the final objective or target of colonization is consciousness: the establishment of control and rule by replacing one way of seeing and being with the axioms, images and aesthetics of another, culturally foreign way.[32] The epistemological assumptions of the age shaped the development of the social, philosophical, scientific and economic ideologies and evangelistic efforts of the missionaries. African scholar Ngugi Wa Thiong'o describes this reality from the point of view of the colonized.

> The biggest weapon wielded and actually daily unleashed by imperialism . . . is the cultural bomb. The effect of a cultural bomb is to annihilate a people's belief in their names, in their languages, in their environment, in their heritage of struggle, in their unity, in their capacities and ultimately in themselves. It makes them see their past as one wasteland of non-achievement and it makes them want to distance themselves from that wasteland. It makes them want to identify with that which is furthest removed from themselves; for instance, with other peoples' languages rather than their own. Possibilities of triumph or victory are seen as remote, ridiculous dreams. The intended results are despair, despondency and a collective death-wish.[33]

Thiong'o asserts that "the real aim of colonialism was to control the people's wealth, what they produced, how they produced it."[34] The way control was introduced and managed was by deconstructing the people's sense of self and replacing it with that of the colonizer. This would occur when a people's perception of themselves and their world was overthrown. He continues,

---

[32]Jean Comaroff and John Comaroff, *Of Revelation and Revolution*, vol. 1, *Christianity, Colonialism, and Consciousness in South Africa* (Chicago: University of Chicago Press, 1991), p. 4.
[33]Ngugi Wa Thiong'o, *Decolonizing the Mind: The Politics of Language in African Literature* (Oxford: James Currey, 2009), p. 3.
[34]Ibid., p. 16.

Colonialism imposed its control of the social production of wealth through military conquest and subsequent political dictatorship. But its most important area of domination was the mental universe of the colonized, the control, through culture, of how people perceived themselves and their relationship to the world. To control a people's culture is to control their tools of self-definition in relationship to others. For colonialism this involved two aspects of the same process: the destruction or the deliberate undervaluing of a people's culture, their art, dances, religions, history, geography, education, orature and literature, and the conscious elevation of the language of the colonizer. The domination of a people's language by the languages of the colonizing nations was crucial to the domination of the mental universe of the colonized.[35]

Comaroff and Comaroff offer a case study of this process through a discussion that demonstrates and differentiates the "colonization of consciousness" of the Tswana people and their "consciousness of colonization."[36] Missionary language of European ethical and cultural universalism impressed on native people their notion of difference. Through the rhetoric of contrast, missionaries attempted to depreciate the unique qualities that made native people and their world distinct but inferior in European eyes. African scholar John S. Mbiti describes this reality:

> Christianity from Western Europe and North America has come to Africa, not simply carrying the Gospel of the New Testament, but as a complex phenomenon made of western culture, politics, science, technology, medicine, schools and new methods of conquering nature. It is necessary to draw a distinction between the Gospel and Christianity, which are not synonymous at certain points.[37]

Conversion, the ultimate goal of the missionary agenda, was a process of removing native differences and distinctives and assimilating indigenes into the European moral economy and civilization as measured against a single value that claimed to be absolute truth. Over time this process would not efface human differences but would slowly try to absorb them into a kind of homogenized European system, a single scale of social, spiritual and material inequality.[38] It was in this climate of technical optimism and rational idealism

---

[35]Ibid.
[36]Comaroff and Comaroff, *Of Revelation*, p. 26.
[37]John S. Mbiti, *African Religions and Philosophy* (Portsmouth, NH: Heinemann, 1999), p. 212.
[38]Comaroff and Comaroff, *Of Revelation*, pp. 244-45.

that the stage was set for a perceived "humane imperialism."[39] These observations made by the Comaroffs about Africa are in fact the same ones First Nations people have experienced both then and today; the hegemonic realities of colonialism are deeply embedded in the ethos of American Christianity. Only now, they are carefully cloaked in the neocolonial "constructs of modernity" and the ideologies of fundamentalism or conservative evangelicalism. The effect, however, is the same: the imposition of a consciousness that negates and denies the lived reality—hence the identity and value—of indigenous people.

TWISS: RESISTING COLONIZATION IN MY LIFE

In 2002 Jerry Yellowhawk prayed over me in a Lakota naming ceremony where I was given the name *Taoyate Obnajin*, "He Stands With His People," and Vincent Yellow Old Woman gifted me with his eagle feather war bonnet to confirm the name and Creator's gifting in my life. It was a defining moment in my journey as a Lakota follower of Jesus that further clarified and enforced the need for contextualized communication.

I am glad I embraced Jesus the Christ all alone on a beach in Maui, Hawaii, during a drug overdose. In 1974 I just yelled, "Jesus if you're real, save me; come into my life." I did not find faith in Jesus in a church building or institution. It spared me from having then to become Baptist right away; I didn't have to become a Presbyterian, Anglican, Pentecostal, Methodist, Christian Reformed, Wesleyan, Catholic or Quaker right away either. I just became a follower of Jesus. Soon after my commitment to Jesus, however, I learned I needed to become a Christian too. And from there I became a Calvinist, Wesleyan, Lutheran, dispensationalist, Arminian, Pentecostal, fundamentalist and evangelical. And then I learned that I had to decide on a Bible to read—the RSV, NASB, NRSV, KJV, NIV, CEV, NKJV—and that some English speakers believed only English speakers could have a Bible that was "Authorized" by God.

Somehow when Jesus came into my life and overwhelmed me with his love and kindness I wanted nothing more than simply to follow him because he truly saved me from a life of addiction, abuse, self-destruction and likely a premature death. While following Jesus seemed one thing, becoming a

---

[39]Ibid., p. 309.

Christian seemed quite another thing. The church told me God loved me a lot but that God didn't like me much, at least culturally.

As the years passed I began to resist the pressure to accept interpretations of the Bible that said, "Old things had passed away and all things had become white" (cf. 2 Cor 5:17) regarding my following Jesus in the context of my Native cultural ways, music, dance, drumming, ceremony and culture. In reference to my Native culture I was informed that the Bible said, "Touch not unclean thing," or "Come out from among them and be separate," or "What fellowship is there between light and darkness?" (see Is 52:11; Lam 4:15; 2 Cor 6:17; 2 Cor 6:14). This meant I needed to leave my Indian ways behind me, because I had a new identity in Christ, and it *was not* Indian. The Bible was used to demonize just about everything important to our cultural sense of being one with God and creation. So, while Jesus found me, the church began to lose me.

As the years went by and I visited my reservation to attend the funerals of relatives, my heart began to remember how I felt during the days when I had been active in the American Indian movement and how good it felt to "be home." Soon Jesus began to enter those areas of identity that had sat idle. My internal journey of self-realization brought me face-to-face with how my faith in Jesus fit with my Lakota culture, long before I heard the word *contextualization*.

The founders and leaders of the United States credited America's growth to God's favor or blessing. They considered the country's origins "inspired" by biblical notions, recharged through the Reformation, of the predestined, redemptive role of God's chosen people in the Promised Land, with the Anglo-Saxon race identified as God's chosen and America identified as that Promised Land. So Anders Stephanson notes, "The world as God's 'manifestation' and history as predetermined 'destiny' had been ideological staples of the strongly providentialist period in England between 1620 and 1660, during which, of course, the initial migration to New England took place. Any genealogy, in short, must begin with the religious sources."[40] I remember reading about Manifest Destiny in grade school, and the narrative only contributed more to the conflict in my soul. I was the Native guy in that story being crushed under the lady angel's foot as she blessed wagonloads of pioneers flooding from St. Louis to settle the Wild West and kill Indians—the bad guys.[41] Manifest Destiny,

---

[40]Stephanson, *Manifest Destiny*, p. 5.
[41]See the lithograph by John Gast titled *American Progress* (1872). This popular depiction of Ameri-

as a pseudo-biblical ideology, carried the weight of providence and privilege. It became thoroughly institutionally embedded, politically and religiously, part of America's self-identity as a Christian nation and/or nationalism. That ideology has supported the myth that the nation was founded by Christian leaders under the guidance of the Spirit of God, on biblical truth, and with a sense of divine calling to establish the kingdom of God.

COLONIZED MINDS

The ideologies and philosophies we identified throughout this chapter are not the archaic beliefs of a bygone era. They live on today and, sadly, have become firmly entrenched in Native American ministry. Many of the most vocal critics of cultural appropriation, redemption or contextualization today are Native American pastors, denominational leaders and Christians. As cases in point, we cite two documents authored by Native Christians. The first was issued by a group of Native leaders in 1998. It begins,

> 1. In the light of the resurgence of Native religious traditionalism, the coming of the peyote movement (Native American Church), the influx of New Age philosophy, and questions concerning Native spirituality and Biblical truth, we as Native believers in Christ, from a score of tribes (and evangelical denominations) and with hundreds of combined years of experience in tribal ministry among us, have gathered together to speak with one voice on these subjects to the body of Christ at large, basing our responses on the clear statements of the revealed Word of God.

Two of the document's seven affirmations directly challenge contextualization efforts.

> 2. We believe that Christ should have pre-eminence and permeates all aspects of our lives and, through us, all aspects of our cultures, to promote the glory of God. God will not share His glory with anything in creation. To do so is idolatry. To combine elements of Native religion and Biblical truth is syncretism. We must renounce and avoid any form of idolatry and syncretism, because they are forbidden in Scripture.

> 3. We believe our salvation is in the finished work of Christ and that we cannot

---

can westward expansion portrayed settlers moving west, guided by the angelic "Columbia" who personified American civilization, http://en.wikipedia.org/wiki/File:American_progress.JPG.

add anything to that work to improve our relationship with God. As believers, we should not, therefore, use or attach any spiritual value to items regarded as sacred such as tobacco, cedar smoke, sweet grass, peyote, prayer feathers, fetishes, masks, drums, dances, etc., to places regarded as sacred such as mother earth, kivas, mountains, sweat lodge, longhouse, or other traditional religious places of worship etc., or to spirit beings such as kachinas, skin walkers, animal and nature spirits, etc.[42]

The second document directly defines "evangelical" practice and consensus over against Native practices.

Over the years, there seems to have been a consensus among the evangelical denominations, mission organizations and independent native Christian churches that true believers should break completely with all animistic practices. Recently, there has been introduced in the native evangelical church community the concept that drums, rattles, and other sacred paraphanelia [sic] formerly used in animistic worship can be "redeemed" for use in Christian worship. This position does not enjoy consensus among native evangelical church leaders.[43]

These documents demonstrate that the condemnation of indigenous cultures that began with the Puritans persists today, even among Native Christian leaders. They manifest the effects of a centuries-long project to erase indigenous identities and assimilate Native peoples into a mangled vision of Christianity that equates biblical faith with white civilization. Christian denominations, institutions and agencies still advance theologies that oppress, marginalize and exclude Native peoples. We conclude by asking: When did you last listen to a lecture, or invite a Native Christian scholar, professor or author to lecture for you? How often do you include Native perspectives in your studies, lectures and teaching, not as exotic anthropological examples of mission or romanticized spirituality, but as coequal voices in shaping theology and mission? Are you willing to welcome Native followers of Jesus as real Christians and Native people as real human beings? It's time to tear down the corral, run off the sacred cows and rescue theology from the cowboys!

---

[42]CHIEF, Inc. "A Biblical Position by Native Leaders on Native Spirituality," www.indianbible.org/about-us/spiritualism.html.

[43]Craig Stephen Smith, *Boundary Lines: The Issue of Christ, Indigenous Worship, and Native American Culture* (Glendale, AZ: Native American District of the Christian and Missionary Alliance, 2000).

2

NORTH AMERICAN
MISSION AND MOTIVE

Following the Markers

Gregory Lee Cuéllar and Randy S. Woodley

.... ♀ ....

INTRODUCTION

Understanding the constructed nature of heritage sites in the North American landscape is particularly important for understanding how a society remembers its past.[1] Many nationally significant sites read a specific mythology into their past, wherein issues of power and oppression are often rendered unseen. When we examine heritage sites in the United States we see a clear public representation of ways that the United States inscribes its colonial heritage in its visible memorials. Heritage sites like John Quincy Adams Ward's *The Indian Hunter* (1864), Thomas Ball's *Freedman's Memorial to Lincoln* (1876), Horatio Greenough's *George Washington* (1841) or David Adickes's *A Tribute to Courage* (1994) reproduce power relations and create boundaries that separate "us" and "them." Just as these emblematic structures of North American national culture "persist over time" and "stay in the same place,"[2] so do the power relationships inscribed within them.

North American public monuments engender a shared experience that often comes at the expense of the silenced Other. Thus David Lowenthal writes, "Treasuring heritage as authentic history, we blind ourselves to our own legacy's

---

[1]Paul A. Shackel, introduction to *Myth, Memory, and the Making of the American Landscape*, ed. Paul A. Shackel (Gainesville: University Press of Florida, 2001), p. 5.
[2]Thomas A. Markus and Deborah Cameron, *The Words Between the Spaces: Buildings and Language* (New York: Routledge, 2002), pp. 138-39.

biased limits. We acclaim heritage as a universal requisite, yet disdain and derogate legacies that differ from or compete with our own."[3] Visitors of North American public monuments are often asked to uphold false notions of the past in order to nurture national identity.[4] The similar alliance between national identity and North American Christianity often finds expression in missionary strategies and practices. As such, to examine the ideological messages inscribed in our national monuments is to examine the ideologies that often underlie our approaches to missions. It also allows us to reconsider our values and ideologies in light of the gospel.

How does North American Christianity memorialize its past? What values and ideologies configure this operation? The underlying legacy of empire and colonization in the North American missionary enterprise, in which the subjugation, exploitation and erasure of the indigenous Other are still present mechanisms, easily goes unnoticed. In the words of Susan George, "Western colonialism, throughout much of the world, confused 'religion' with 'culture,' and imposed values . . . that were not intrinsically Christian or even religious."[5] This missionary enterprise continues to have a one-way, north-south directional flow wherein the indigenous Other is still viewed as a savage in need of civilization. As Rowan Williams observes, "Even when the old colonialisms have vanished, we in the Western world are still prone to think as if there were one narrative for Christianity, in which we continue to set the pace."[6] The unexamined residue of an imperial value system on contemporary North American missionary practices only perpetuates relationships of dependency.

Especially pertinent here are the important questions posed by Joerg Rieger: "But have we truly overcome our colonial legacies? Do we even understand what the basic problems of colonial Christianity were? Is this case really closed?"[7] Consequently the present but absent story is not only the hideousness of our colonial heritage but also the permutations of colonialism in the North

---

[3]David Lowenthal, *The Heritage Crusade and the Spoils of History* (Cambridge: Cambridge University Press, 1997), p. xv.

[4]Shackel, *Myth, Memory*, p. 11.

[5]Susan George, *Religion and Technology in the 21st Century: Faith in the E-world* (London: Idea Group, 2006), p. 115.

[6]Rowan Williams, foreword to *Mission in the Twenty-first Century: Exploring the Five Marks of Global Mission*, ed. Andrew Walls and Cathy Ross (Maryknoll, NY: Orbis, 2008), p. xi.

[7]Joerg Rieger, "Theology and Mission Between Neocolonialism and Postcolonialism," *Mission Studies* 21 (2004): 202.

American Christian missionary enterprise today. In this vein Philip Wickeri observes, "Despite the rhetoric of democratic liberalism, Third World theologians charge that patterns of sharing continue to be undemocratic and patronizing."[8] Hence overcoming colonizing tendencies begins with a critical acknowledgment of the nefarious side of the Christian missionary heritage in North America and its ongoing manifestations. Interrogating this religious legacy from a counterposture requires exposing this mandated suppression of the story of non-Western and indigenous Others.

HISTORICAL ROOTS: SPANISH CATHOLIC CONQUEST OF THE NEW WORLD (SOUTHWESTERN UNITED STATES)

As Christian T. Collins Winn and Amos Yong will elaborate in chapter seven, the story begins with the Spanish conquest of the New World. Its most visible heritage sites are the edifices and monuments of former Spanish missions throughout the region that was referred to by Spanish colonizers as the *Gran Chichimeca*, or "land of uncivilized dogs."[9] Other memorials include the statue of Franciscan missionary Francisco Tomas Hermenegildo Garcés in Bakersfield, California,[10] and the bronze plaque in the garden of San Gabriel Mission honoring Father Garcés and other victims of the Yuma Massacre of 1781. These last two sites encourage visitors to venerate the Spanish settlers who lost their lives at the hands of the Yuma Indians. However, this memorialization process operates within the framework of a negative dialectic, wherein ideological strategies override the harsh impact of the Spanish conquest on the Yuma's agrarian structure, household economy, kinship organization and community life.[11] These Spanish American memorial sites not only reflect particular configurations of power but are also based on the appropriations of a colonial history infused with social and racial barriers.

By the end of the seventeenth century the Catholic Church and the Mexican Inquisition were actively involved in the spiritual conquest of New

---

[8]Philip L. Wickeri, *Partnership, Solidarity, and Friendship: Transforming Structures in Mission: A Study Paper for the Presbyterian Church* (USA) (Louisville, KY: Worldwide Ministries Division, 2003), p. 2.
[9]Martha Menchaca, *Recovering History, Constructing Race: The Indian, Black, White Roots of Mexican Americans* (Austin: University of Texas Press, 2001), p. 78.
[10]The statue stands at the intersection of Old Highway 99 and Chester Avenue in Bakersfield, California.
[11]Laurie Burgess, "Buried in the Rose Garden: Levels of Meaning at Arlington National Cemetery and the Robert E. Lee Memorial," in Shackel, *Myth, Memory*, p. 167.

Spain's northern frontier. The Mexican Inquisition entered the eighteenth century with its usual zeal for ridding the viceroyalty of heresy. Among the heretical threats to the Iberian Catholic worldview in Spanish America were Judaism, Protestantism, Islam, Enlightenment philosophy and freemasonry.[12] With a heightened concern about the spread of heresies, the Inquisition and the church established new policing initiatives, the most notable being the *Propaganda Fide*. The first apostolic missionary college of *Propaganda Fide* in northern New Spain was commissioned in 1682.[13] This unique college would prepare Franciscan missionaries, who were already experts with conversion and official inquisitors (*comisarios* or *calificadors*), to evangelize unreached nomadic indigenous tribes and to reform many wayward Spanish Christians (i.e., *ovejas perdidas*) in New Spain's northern frontier.[14] This first apostolic college to be established outside of the Iberian Peninsula was considered a center for theological education.[15] It represented a new period in Franciscan missionary practice, which consisted of the reformation of Christian apostates, many of whom had settled in remote ranches and haciendas in the northern frontier (*Boca de Leónes*).[16] A second northern missionary college was established in 1704, *El de Ntra. Sra. De Guadalupe de Zacatecas*. This new phase in missionary education gave a renewed vigor to the spiritual influence of the Franciscan order in northern New Spain.[17] In the words of R. S. Sugirtharajah, "The voice of God blended with the voice of

---

[12]Richard Greenleaf, "The Mexican Inquisition and the Enlightenment 1763–1805," *New Mexico Historical Review* 41 (1966): 181-83.

[13]Antoni Picazo Muntaner, "El ideario de fray Antoni Llinás, OFM, para la creación del primer colegio de Propaganda Fide de América," *Archivo Ibero-Americano* 60 (2000): 437-38; Fray Isidro Felix de Espinosa, *Crónica de los colegios de Propaganda Fide de la Nueva España*, ed. Lino G. Canedo, new ed. (1746; repr., Washington, DC: Academy of American Franciscan History, 1964), p. 155.

[14]Muntaner, "El ideario," p. 437; Espinosa, *Crónica*, p. 156.

[15]León Lopetegui and Felix Zubillaga, *Historia de la Iglesia en la América española: Desde el descubrimiento hasta comienzos del siglo XIX, I: México, América Central, Antillas* (Madrid: BAC, 1965), p. 861.

[16]Hermenegildo de Vilaplana, *Vida portentosa del americano septentrional apostol el V.P. Fr. Antonio Margil de Jesús, fundador y exguardian de los Colegios de la Santa Cruz de Querétaro, de Christo Crucificado de Guatemala, y de Nuestra Señora de Guadalupe de Zacatecas* (Mexico City: En la imprenta de la Biblioteca Mexicana, 1763), p. 153; see also Armando C. Alonzo, *Tejano Legacy: Rancheros and Settlers in South Texas 1734–1900* (Albuquerque: University of New Mexico Press, 1998), pp. 30-31, 74.

[17]Rocío Cázares Aguilar and Francisco Mejía Sánchez, *Notas para la Historia del Colegio Apostólico de Propaganda Fide de Cholula* (Puebla: Universidad de las Américas, 2006), http://ciria.udlap.mx/franciscana/archivos/Cholula.pdf, p. 2; Lopetegui and Zubillaga, *Historia de la Iglesia*, p. 613.

the invader."[18] The damaging effects of this Spanish missionary enterprise have been masked and celebrated in the form of heroic veneration, as David Lowenthal notes: "Historical hindsight tidies chaos into order often into predestined sequence, as though things could not have happened otherwise."[19] Spanish colonial power went hand in glove with the theological authority claimed by the Franciscan missionaries.[20]

The Historic Disconnect Between Mission and Conquest in North America (English Protestants in the Eastern United States)

As L. Daniel Hawk and Richard L. Twiss noted in chapter one of this volume, English Protestant missions were also implicated in colonialism. Although the stated intent of some of the earliest English settlers in America was to do missionary work among the indigenous peoples, the usual pattern was similar to the Spanish: first, establish military superiority over the inhabitants; then, share a gospel heavily laden with White-European or US colonial cultural assumptions. Such was the case in the two earliest American colonies: their charters clearly stated that, along with performing Christian mission among the indigenous inhabitants, they would bestow what they considered to be human civility. Words in the Virginia Charter betray the imperial-missional prejudice already ingrained in the minds of the settlers toward Native North American spiritual matters. "Such people," it states, "as yet live in Darkness and miserable Ignorance of the true Knowledge and Worship of God."[21] In the colonizers' opinions the culture and values of the inhabitants of the land had little or no significance.

Because of this, Christian missions invariably attempted to assimilate the indigenous peoples into mainstream society. R. Pierce Beaver, former director of the Overseas Ministries Study Center, summarized most missionaries' views regarding Native North Americans in the three prior centuries: "Missionaries during this period believed that teaching primitive people about a 'better' way

---

[18]R. S. Sugirtharajah, *Bible and Empire: Postcolonial Explorations* (New York: Cambridge University Press, 2005), p. 89.

[19]David Lowenthal, *The Heritage Crusade and the Spoils of History* (New York: Cambridge University Press, 1996), p. 115.

[20]Rieger, "Theology and Mission," p. 203.

[21]"The First Charter of Virginia; April 10, 1606," *The Avalon Project: Documents in Law, History and Diplomacy*, http://avalon.law.yale.edu/17th_century/va01.asp.

of living was part of the Gospel message. Evangelization and civilization could not be separated. You could tell if an Indian was being saved from Hell by the way he or she began to live like the English."[22] Put simply, settler worldviews assumed that all indigenous spirituality was evil. Thus Jonas Michaelius, an early Dutch missionary in Manhattan, New York, wrote, "As to the Natives of this country, I find them entirely savage and wild, strangers to all decency, yea, uncivil and stupid as garden poles, proficient in all wickedness and godlessness; devilish men, who serve nobody but the Devil."[23] Representations in historical literature abound that attest to early European immigrants' beliefs that Native North American values and ways of life were inferior to European ones, which they assumed were inherently blessed by God. William Bradford describes one massacre: "Those that escaped the fire were slaine with the sword; some hewed to peeces, others run through with their rapiers. . . . It was a fearful sight to see them thus . . . but the victory seemed a sweet sacrifice, and they gave the prayers thereof to God, who had wrought so wonderfully for them, thus to inclose their enemies in their hands."[24] In contrast, a minority of the newcomers displayed respect for North America's indigenes. People such as Bartolomé de Las Casas, Thomas Mayhew, Roger Williams, William Penn, Evan Jones and Isabel Crawford are noteworthy exceptions to the majority of missionaries. They stood out as points of light compared to those who employed the conventional attitudes of their day. Conversely these examples provide a great indictment against the body politic that they represented, which generally persecuted this minority for their pro-Native tendencies.

COLONIAL VALUES AND MISSION POLICY

One cannot easily discount the influence of strong anti-Indian sentiment from the government and its citizenry on the missionary endeavor. In the 1820s–1840s this sentiment dominated US Indian policy and precipitated the removal and relocation of indigenous populations. The height of anti-Indian sentiment and its influence on Native mission in the early nineteenth century reached its

---

[22]R. Pierce Beaver, *Introduction to Native American Church History* (Tempe, AZ: Cook Christian Training School, 1983), p. 49.

[23]Quoted in Edwin S. Gaustad, *A Documentary History of Religion in America: To the Civil War* (Grand Rapids: Eerdmans, 1982), p. 83.

[24]Quoted in Howard Zinn, *A People's History of the United States: 1492–Present* (New York: Harper-Collins, 2003), p. 15.

peak under the influence of US president Andrew Jackson, who initiated the Indian Removal Act. After Jackson's election in 1828, the fate of the eastern tribes was sealed. In the American West, frontier sentiment supporting Indian removal was justified in the writings of Christian denominations and their missionaries to Native Americans.

In 1827 Isaac McCoy wrote a book endorsing Indian removal and colonization. His concept of an "Indian Canaan" was "heartily endorsed" by Andrew Jackson, who, in any case, had little concern for the indigene.[25] Many Anglo-Americans considered Indians incapable of improvement or civilization. Henry Clay's treatise against Indians, published in 1827 while he was US secretary of state, epitomizes this view: "It is impossible to civilize Indians. There was never a full-blooded Indian that ever took to civilization. It is not in their nature. They are a race destined for extinction. . . . I do not think they are, as a race, worth preserving."[26] Deep-seated racism was one main impetus for the mistreatment Native Americans received, whether by the US government or through colonial missions.

Christian denominations with missionaries in the Indian field around the time of Indian removal generally supported the policies of the US government. For example, during the Cherokee removal, even though individual missionaries resisted removal of Cherokees, all denominations active in Cherokee mission supported a policy of removal.[27] As a result of the Indian Removal Act many thousands of Native Americans lost their lands, their livelihoods and even their very lives. By the time of the opening of the Oregon Trail in 1847, the pressure to treaty and the subsequent resettlement of Native Americans on reservations was common practice. Those indigenous nations already located in the American West were either removed from their traditional homelands or squeezed onto nearby reservations, which constituted a sliver of their original boundaries.

By the twentieth century a small number of Native American Christians had emerged. These indigenous believers were systematically forced to adopt the culture of the dominant society or else pay a heavy price in the way of social torment, physical punishment or even death.

---

[25]William G. McLoughlin, *Champions of the Cherokees: Evan and John B. Jones* (Princeton, NJ: Princeton University Press, 1990), p. 119.

[26]Ibid., frontispiece.

[27]After their initial decision for removal, the American Baptists reversed and supported Cherokee sovereignty under the influence of Evan Jones.

This was particularly the case in the late nineteenth and twentieth centuries, when the government-funded and mission-administered residential boarding school system emerged. The supposed civilization process for indigenous children included compulsory attendance at residential boarding schools. Common tales of boarding-school coercion include spiritual and emotional manipulation, the threat of cutting off food rations to families who would not send their children and even outright kidnapping. There was often additional pressure from the missionaries who worked in conjunction with the government.[28]

Activists and scholars have named this a system of both ethnocide and genocide.[29] When calculating the end result, it makes little difference whether lives or cultures were destroyed because the two are so intricately intertwined. Don Trent Jacobs illustrates the point.

> A culture's destruction is not a trifling matter. . . . If a people suddenly lose their "prime symbol," the base of culture, their lives lose meaning. They become disoriented with no hope. As social disorganization often follows such loss, they are often unable to ensure their own survival. . . . The loss and human suffering for those whose culture has been healthy and is suddenly attacked and disintegrated are incalculable.[30]

Even when Indians accepted both Christianity and "civilization" on their own terms, it was not enough to satisfy the American Western capitalistic assumptions. For example, the Cherokee concept of redistribution of wealth was in direct opposition to the individualistic materialism found in dominant US culture. Remarkably, even after removal from their homelands, the Cherokees were able to retain their communal values. After touring Indian Territory in 1887, Senator Henry Dawes described the Cherokees in the following way: "There is not a pauper in that nation, and the nation does not owe a dollar. It built its own capitol . . . and built its schools and hospitals."[31]

Precolonial Native American patterns of thinking about the land developed

---

[28]I (Randy) have heard many elders who are victims of the boarding school policies reinforce these same themes.

[29]George Tinker, introduction to *Kill the Indian, Save the Man: The Genocidal Impact of American Indian Residential Schools*, by Ward Churchill (San Francisco: City Lights, 2004), has called it genocide.

[30]Don Trent Jacobs, a.k.a. Wahinkpe Topa (Four Arrows), *Unlearning the Language of Conquest: Scholars Expose Anti-Indianism in America* (Austin: University of Texas Press, 2006), p. 221.

[31]Quoted in Scott L. Malcomson, *One Drop of Blood: The American Misadventure of Race* (New York: Farrar, Straus & Giroux, 2000), p. 15.

over tens of thousands of years and millions of experiences to create a sense of harmony between the people and the land. This balance maintained the health of both land and people until the onslaught of European colonialism.[32] Misconceptions about indigenous cultures and the forced imposition of Euro-American values informed US Christian denominations well into the present era. G. E. E. Lindquist, in a 1951 missionary handbook, demonstrated this consistent lack of concern—or at least naiveté—among mission agencies concerning any possibility of utilizing native values in doing mission. He discouraged even the most basic cultural values of language: "Do not spend too much time trying to learn the language. . . . If the Indians among whom you are to work do not speak English, they will soon do so."[33] Ultimately the goal of Christian mission in the mid-twentieth century still reflected the government's goals of assimilation.

In the post–World War II era US government policies, now labeled *relocation* and *termination*, still encouraged assimilation of Native Americans. During this era Native American claims to special status, control over their reservations and access to public services were targeted. Government policies forced over 100,000 Native Americans to urban areas away from reservations for job training and placement.[34]

Tragically these same values and principles, which both explicitly and implicitly promoted assimilation in the past, continue today among mission-sending agencies to Native North America. The results of this entrenched missionary movement have been a paltry collection of Christian Indian converts. Most of these converts have been obligated to forsake their own Native American cultures and theologies. They have been compelled to take on the dominant culture's values and theologies in order to be accepted by the wider Christian community. These values and theologies, and their resultant methods, have proven to be ineffective and deeply destructive.

---

[32]Native values of sharing were more similar to the Christians in the New Testament. See 2 Cor 8:15, "Those who gathered a lot had nothing left over, and those who gathered only a little had enough" (NLT).

[33]G. E. E. Lindquist, *New Trails for Old: A Handbook for Missionary Workers Among the American Indians* (New York: National Council of Churches of Christ, Division of Home Mission, 1951), p. 33.

[34]Melanie A. Stansbury and Angela A. Gonzales, "Indian Gaming and the Rise of A New Nation-Building Era in Tribal U.S. Relations," Department of Development Sociology, Cornell University, 2011, http://aip.cornell.edu/outreach/tiwp/loader.cfm?csModule=security/getfile&PageID=267749, last modified 2011.

WHOSE VOICE LEADS THE CURRENT NARRATIVE?

Those ethnocentric assumptions, held primarily by the dominant Euro-American Christian mission enterprises concerning mission *to* others, have resulted in the inability of the enterprises to represent the broader sense of who Christ is *among* indigenous peoples. We cannot discount the survival instinct of the settlers as a major factor in shaping mission and colonial goals. But beyond the obvious need, which could have been met with equity, there was often a missional attitude reflecting racial superiority among Euro-Americans that has not been thoroughly addressed in today's missional conversations. In some very real ways Native North Americans are far worse off from having had contact with Christian mission.

The most serious flaw of the modern mission has been the missing indigenous voice. Without non-Western and indigenous peoples in places of governance and decision making, the same conversations concerning colonial and neocolonial mission strategies continue to take precedence over the actual work of the indigenized gospel. Indigenous peoples have a critical perspective and deserve *the lead voice* in missional conversations. The missionary enterprise in the American West cannot afford to lose the input and observations of indigenous peoples. Unfortunately, there is little expectation of a conversation that garners critical participation with lead roles taken by America's First Nations peoples. In his seminal project setting the stage for the East-West-South mission conversation, Phillip Jenkins has noted how "the center of gravity in the Christian world has shifted inexorably southward, to Africa, Asia, and Latin America."[35] Yet Jenkins makes no mention of North American indigenous voices. To be sure, compared to the sheer numbers of Christians in the Global South and East, the aboriginal American voice might seem insignificant, but that is exactly the problem. Such attitudes still express the imperial-missional zeitgeist. By and large, much of Christianity in the Global South and East still reflects colonial cultures of the West, cultures that have caused incalculable damage.

Adrian Jacobs (Cayuga) comments regarding the missionary enterprise,

> I don't want your expertise. I don't want your wisdom. I don't want your competence. I don't want your money. I don't want your pity. I don't want your sweat

---

[35]Phillip Jenkins, *The Next Christendom: The Coming of Global Christianity* (New York: Oxford University Press, 2002), pp. 1-2.

and advice. I don't want you to reach down to me. I don't want you to look down on me. I don't want your perfect image. I don't want your unsullied testimony. I don't want your perfection. I want your heart.[36]

Jacobs compares the inability of Western missionaries to appreciate aboriginal culture, worldview and frame of reference to a relational sense akin to autism. He argues that modern missions ask the wrong questions, which usually position the indigene as the problem. According to Maori author Linda Tuhiwai Smith,

> Both "friends of the Natives" and those hostile to indigenous peoples conceptualized the issues of colonization and European encroachment on indigenous territories in terms of a problem of the Natives. The Natives were, according to this view, to blame for not accepting the terms of their colonization. . . . The belief in the "indigenous problem" is still present in the western psyche.[37]

In contrast, Jacobs says, "We are not your problem, we are your cure."[38]

WHAT ARE THE RESULTS OF COLONIAL MISSION?

The results of the combined efforts of the US government and Christian missionary efforts to advance Native North Americans, whether through health, education or religion, are bleak and demoralizing to both the non-Native and the Native. As a people Native North Americans are still suffering from ill health brought on by colonialism and colonial missions, with Native Americans' health being disproportionately poorer than the rest of society.[39] American Indians and Alaska Natives (AI/ANs) frequently contend with issues that prevent them from receiving quality medical care, including cultural barriers, geographic isolation, inadequate sewage disposal and low income.

Some of the leading diseases and causes of death among AI/ANs are heart disease, cancer, unintentional injuries (accidents), diabetes and stroke. AI/ANs have a high prevalence of mental health diagnoses and suicide, obesity, sub-

---

[36]Adrian Jacobs (Cayuga), "Mitigating Missionary Autism: A Proposal for an Aboriginal Cure" (paper presented at the North American Institute for Indigenous Theological Studies Annual Symposium, Calgary, AB, June 10, 2011).

[37]Linda Tuhiwai Smith, "Problematizing the Indigenous Is a Western Obsession," in *Decolonizing Methodologies: Research and Indigenous Peoples* (London: Zed Books, 1999), pp. 91-92.

[38]Jacobs, "Mitigating Missionary Autism."

[39]"American Indian/Alaska Native Profile," U.S. Department of Health and Human Services, Office of Minority Health, last modified September 17, 2012, http://minorityhealth.hhs.gov/templates /browse.aspx?lvl=2&lvlID=52.

stance abuse, sudden infant death syndrome (SIDS), teenage pregnancy, liver disease and hepatitis. All of these maladies are, in a very real sense, markers of the colonial enterprise.

It cannot be denied that, though not always intentional, disease contributed to the near holocaust of Native Americans and to the ill health of America's indigenes. In fact, in and of itself, the waning Native population helped to reinforce colonial attitudes of superiority. Thus William Bradford stated, "The good hand of God . . . favored our beginnings, sweeping away great multitudes of the Natives . . . that he might make room for us."[40] Charles Mann concurs with reports of the scope of the devastation: "More than fifty of the first colonial villages in New England were located on Indian villages emptied by disease."[41] Shortly after the colonists arrived, disease introduced by foreigners spread at unimaginable rates, leaving the indigenous civilizations in ruin. Most of the colonists were immune to the European diseases, but the effect on Native Americans was cataclysmic: "Throughout the Americas, diseases introduced with Europeans spread from tribe to tribe far in advance of the Europeans themselves, killing an estimated 95 percent of the pre-Columbian Native American population . . . even before Europeans themselves made their first settlement on the Mississippi River."[42]

Health and well-being is just one indicator of colonial mission's ongoing impact on America's indigenes, but it is a major factor, directly affecting indigenous values and culture. John C. Mohawk comments,

> Colonization is the greatest health risk to indigenous peoples as individuals and communities. It produces the anomie . . . that underlies the deadly automobile accidents triggered by alcohol abuse. It creates the conditions of inappropriate diet which lead to an epidemic of degenerative diseases, and the moral anarchy that leads to child abuse and spousal abuse. Becoming colonized was the worst thing that could happen five centuries ago, and being colonized is the worst thing that can happen now.[43]

Given the higher health status enjoyed by most Americans, the lingering health

---

[40]Quoted in Charles C. Mann, *1491: New Revelations of the Americas Before Columbus* (New York: Alfred A. Knopf, 2005), p. 56.

[41]Ibid.

[42]Jared Diamond, *Guns, Germs, and Steel: The Fates of Human Societies* (New York: W. W. Norton, 2005), p. 78.

[43]John C. Mohawk, "The Tragedy of Colonization," *Indian Country Today*, http://indiancountry todaymedianetwork.com/node/89858, last modified January 23, 2004.

disparities of AI/ANs are troubling. While mission organizations often care for the "soul" of the Indian, too often their physical health has not been taken seriously. This issue is particularly disturbing because Native North American worldviews do not make vast distinctions between physical and spiritual well-being, tending to view physical and spiritual problems in symbiotic relationship with one another. Embracing the holistic healing process of indigenous peoples' lives might concern missiologists for the sake of the indigene. They also might see it, as noted earlier by Adrian Jacobs, as the "cure," or "salvation," of the colonial missions enterprise itself. The story must first be recapitulated and then understood in the indigenous voice in order for modern missions to understand it.

CONTEMPORARY NATIVE AMERICAN MISSION EFFORTS

This survey of the historical record shows the duplicity that existed in the dominant culture's past practices of undertaking Native American mission. Although individual missionaries have attempted and continue to attempt to do mission in more humane ways, being a part of the dominant society and its influence, they still end up doing mission primarily from a place of power and, therefore, presumed racial superiority. Without regard for Native North Americans' equality as human beings and their place in leading missional conversations, there is inadequate appreciation for indigenous values. Mission, by its nature, demands a sense of equality for all. Jesus came to all humanity, emptying himself of his superiority over us, while he became one of us. Mission among America's indigenous people must be done from a place of indigenous values.

CONCLUSION

In the midst of continued centuries of harmful mission policy, Native North Americans are still fighting for their survival. This is true physically, regarding health and welfare, but it is also true in the realm of public perception, which still affects mission. Racism, stereotypes, mascots and hate crimes—often perpetrated by Christians—are just a few of the attitudinal pressures faced by Native Americans. This pattern of disregard for Native North American values by the dominant Euro-American society remains evident by the markers elucidated above.[44] In spite of this historical backdrop, aboriginal cultures still

---

[44]An Internet search on April 11, 2010, of eleven major denominations under the broad subject of Native American mission and policy changes yielded no statements concerning methods of mission

reflect their core Native North American values in significant ways. Now many Native Americans are asserting a decolonizing process that affirms the value of their customs and traditions. For example, Taiaiake Alfred writes,

> We can, of course, choose to ignore these realities [of white encroachment] and simply accede to the dissolution of our cultures and nations. Or we can commit ourselves to a different path, one that honours the memory of those who have sacrificed, fought and died to preserve the integrity of our nations. This path, the opposite of the one we are on now, leads to a renewed political life and social life based on our traditional values.[45]

Nevertheless, caution is warranted for any proposal of renewal. Even when these systems are replaced with indigenous forms, they can remain laden with the values of the dominant society. Alfred uses education as an example.

> Even if such education resembles traditional Native American systems on the surface . . . an education that is not based on the traditional principles of respect and harmonious coexistence will inevitably tend to reflect the cold, calculating and coercive ways of the modern state. *The whole of the decolonization process will have been for nothing if indigenous education has no meaningful indigenous character.* Worse, if the new education does not embody a notion of power that is appropriate to indigenous cultures, the goals of the struggle will have been betrayed. Leaders who promote non-indigenous goals and embody non-indigenous values are simple tools used by the state to maintain its control.[46]

The same is true of mission. In spite of their bereaved history, ill health, poor education, inadequate housing and marginalization, the Native Americans' residual set of values are a repository of true wealth. These values have the potential to produce new mission models resulting in real well-being for Native Americans. For such a model to find footing in Indian country, a missional paradigm shift must occur. The Native North American decolonized indigenous voice must be the lead voice and itself serve as a new marker on the landscape of future missions.

---

that included the incorporation of Native American core values. Policies were mostly justice oriented, affirming native rights, statements of repentance for wrongs done and statements of full acceptance of natives into the mainstream of denominational life.

[45]Taiaiake Alfred, *Peace, Power, Righteousness: An Indigenous Manifesto* (Don Mills, ON: Oxford University Press, 1999), p. xii.

[46]Ibid., p. xiv (emphasis added).

3

Postcolonial Feminism, the Bible and the Native Indian Women

Jayachitra Lalitha

.... ⚸ ....

BORN IN POSTINDEPENDENT INDIA, I learned about British colonial rule in India through the pages of history textbooks and in the movies. The English education initiated by the colonial government and missionaries to "civilize" the native Indians has benefited me to speak and write a "powerful language," which, although I had never thought of it ironically, is also a powerful tool to critically analyze the very "civilization" English education has brought in. Until I went to a theological seminary in 1996, I had not sensed any residue of British colonialism governing my day-to-day life. During those four years of graduate theological studies, Western philosophies, systematic theologies and hermeneutical tools that were heavily influenced by Western biblical scholarship governed the curriculum. The sparing inclusion of Indian philosophy and Indian Christian theologies, moreover, did not critically engage Western, philosophically based theologies or develop an interactive theological model.

It was only when I started reading more Western biblical commentaries that I began to sense disturbing comments against the cultures of the rest of the world. I soon realized my mind was profoundly molded by the overarching impact of Western theories and theologies, which have colonized my mind unduly beyond repair! My undertaking of a master's in theology specializing in New Testament only reiterated to me my uncritical submission to Western academia, as all the books I read were predominantly written by

Western European and American New Testament scholars who never instilled a need to look for alternate Indian hermeneuts and hermeneutics. I had already begun to read the Bible through a feminist lens, but I soon realized that the patriarchal values embedded in biblical texts are so intertwined with colonial ideology that a simple feminist reading would not be hermeneutically sufficient.

How could I decolonize my mind of Western interpretations of the Bible? What is the significance of postcolonializing feminist hermeneutics? How does a postcolonial feminist hermeneutic differ from other feminist hermeneutics? Is India truly postcolonial? If so, will it affect the way one does a feminist reading of the Bible? Did not patriarchy exist before colonial powers took over India? Did patriarchy not continue even after British colonizers left the country? Was not patriarchy in colonial and postcolonial India safeguarded by casteism? These questions make me curious as to how colonial hegemony has intersected with the caste-bound patriarchal ideology of colonial India to create a complex hegemonic identity of colonial patriarchy. What is the legacy of such a colonial patriarchy in a neocolonial India?

PART ONE

In a world scenario of developing countries dominated by the American and Eurocentric global economy, gender discourse alone cannot adequately address the sexual differences perceived in the form of a monolithic notion of patriarchy. Western feminist assumptions about women in developing countries lie on the shaky ground of assuming those women already to be a constituted and coherent group with identical interests and desires, regardless of class, caste, race, ethnicity, age, colonial state, geographical location or their place in the global economy. It is futile to make any attempt to engage in feminist discourses without situating oneself critically in a globalized cultural, political and economical framework. Any such effort otherwise would lead to a reductive, homogeneous construction, which Chandra Talpade Mohanty calls "third-world difference." She elaborates,

> It is in the production of this "third-world difference" that Western feminisms appropriate and colonize the constitutive complexities which characterize the lives of women in these countries. It is in this process of discursive homogenization and systematization of the oppression of women in the third world that

power is exercised in much of recent Western feminist writing and this power needs to be defined and named.[1]

Defining and naming power that determines a race-gender nexus is inevitable for exploring the possible biblical resources for indigenous women's liberation. Postcolonial feminist biblical interpretations challenge the scriptural authority claimed by colonial/patriarchal texts and institutions and critique how the Bible has been used as a weapon against women in the past.[2] The degree of oppression varies in relation to the sociocultural context of the women. In this way, even if a white woman and a brown woman approach the Bible on the common ground of male domination, their aspirations and struggles differ, as the white woman may comparatively enjoy a more privileged position in her own society than a brown woman does. This may or may not have resulted as part of the aftermath of colonialism and imperialism in world history. In essence, the experience of each woman in her particular sociocultural context has to be taken into account for a postcolonial feminist interpretation of the Bible.

In a predominantly patriarchal Indian society[3] it is unfortunate that the Bible is used in Christian families to legitimize male domination. The Bible seems to have failed to address the issues of women due to one-sided approaches to it in Indian churches by interpreters and preachers, who are largely men. Many times the Bible has not been able to offer solutions to Indian women's struggles for self-respect and human dignity. S. J. Samartha highlights that the books of the Bible were shaped in a male-dominated world, the canon was determined by councils of men, and it was male theologians and interpreters who expounded and interpreted the androcentric biblical passages over the centuries. Eventually it becomes difficult to challenge those interpretations in order to highlight God's concern for the

---

[1]Chandra Talpade Mohanty, "Under Western Eyes: Feminist Scholarship and Colonial Discourses," in *Feminist Postcolonial Theory: A Reader*, ed. Reina Lewis and Sara Mills (Edinburgh: Edinburgh University Press, 2003), p. 51.

[2]Elisabeth Schüssler Fiorenza, "The Will to Choose or Reject: Continuing Our Critical Work," in *Feminist Interpretation of the Bible*, ed. Letty M. Russell (Oxford: Basil Blackwell, 1985), p. 129.

[3]Interestingly, even in matrilineal communities like that of the Khasi tribe in Meghalaya, where the youngest daughter in a family inherits the lion's share of ancestral property, all matters and decisions regarding lands and properties fall under the authority of maternal uncles and brothers and finally have to be approved by the clan/family council. As custodians of the family properties, women shoulder family responsibilities without having access to equivalent power.

whole of humanity.[4] In such a context it is highly crucial that such androcentric, authoritative interpretations of the Bible are critiqued from the
perspective of other sociocultural contexts—here, that of a postcolonial
Indian feminist.

Mostly, Christians of scheduled castes and scheduled tribes constitute the
churches in India.[5] People belonging to scheduled castes are the outcastes in
the hierarchical social system of casteism. They are called the Dalits and face
caste discrimination even within the churches. Dalit women are the "Dalit of
Dalits," as they suffer discrimination on account of their gender, caste and
class.[6] The experiences of rural and urban Dalit women are different. Caste-
based oppression is severe for the rural Dalit women but milder for the edu-
cated, urban Dalit women, because there is more space to interact with dominant caste women in an urban setting.[7] Similarly, as Solomon Rongpi
comments, though the percentage of Christian tribal women in Northeast
Indian churches is high, they continue to play traditional, low-status roles in
churches and lack positions of leadership.[8] The percentage of dominant caste
women is much lower in Indian churches. Nevertheless, there are differences
between their experiences and those of the Dalit, or tribal, women in the Indian
church scenario. All this suggests that a postcolonial feminist perspective
cannot be developed without seriously interacting with such ongoing struggles
of women within Indian churches.

In a pluralistic country like India, the cultural ethos and social values
have been molded by various Scriptures of many faiths, including Christianity. In fact, Christianity and the Bible are of comparatively recent origin
compared to other faiths like Hinduism, which was prevalent long before
Christianity originated. In India the females, Sita, of the *Ramayana*, or
Draupati, of the *Mahabharata*, may call for a wider impact than Eve of the

---

[4]S. J. Samartha, *The Search for New Hermeneutics in Asian Christian Theology* (Bangalore: The Senate
of Serampore College, 1987), pp. 33-34.
[5]Sanjay Paswan and Paramanshi Jaideva, eds., *Encyclopaedia of Dalits in India* (Delhi: Kalpaz, 2002),
1:297.
[6]Monica J. Melanchthon, "The Indian Voice," *Semeia* 78 (1997): 155.
[7]S. T. Shirke, "A Study of the Status of Dalit Women," in *Indian Woman*, ed. C. M. Agrawal (Delhi:
Indian Distributors Publishers, 2001), p. 29.
[8]Solomon Rongpi, "Empowerment of Women: A North East Indian Perspective," in *Transforming
Theology for Empowering Women: A Theological and Hermeneutical Reflection in the Context of North
East India*, ed. R. L. Hnuni (Jorhat: Women's Studies Eastern Theological College, 1999), p. 119.

Bible. Nevertheless, in Christian families and churches in India the primeval biblical woman character, Eve, plays a significant role in determining the role and position of women. In most Indian churches the ministerial involvement of women (ordained ministry, theological teaching ministry, etc.) is forcefully limited by men. This is mainly due to the traditional interpretation of the Bible that women are of secondary importance because Eve was made from Adam and was the primary cause for the entry of sin and death into the world. Aruna Gnanadasan affirms that the task of Indian Christian women is to transform the liberating Word of God from a boring book, which has submerged women into silence and submission, into a challenging book that will bring new life and energy to women, motivating them to participate with God in cocreating a new and living community.[9] Such an effort will enhance the visibility of women in biblical religion and in Christian families and churches, so that "freedom from spiritual male control"[10] will be achieved.

The biblical narratives evolved from people's colonial experiences, whether Assyrian, Babylonian, Persian or Greco-Roman.[11] Empire building and colonialism shaped biblical texts, canonization and interpretation. Until the late nineteenth century, empire was considered to be "a humanitarian enterprise where an amiable form of civilization was pressed upon the hapless and ignoble races."[12] The predatory nature of imperialism/colonialism became vividly clear, however, as economic and political propaganda began to unfurl in the colonized territories. Postcolonial theory thus originally emerged as a resistance discourse of the colonized to interrogate the dominant knowledge systems of the colonizers and neocolonizers.

R. S. Sugirtharajah comments that postcolonial biblical interpretations emerging from the once-colonized peoples highlight the historical and cultural reality of colonialism, the effects of colonization and colonial ideals on interpretative works, the possibilities of reconstructive readings from the per-

---

[9]Aruna Gnanadasan, "Towards an Indian Feminist Theology," in *We Dare to Dream: Doing Theology as Asian Women*, ed. Virginia Fabella and Sun Ali Lee Park (Maryknoll, NY: Orbis, 1989), p. 123.

[10]Elisabeth Schüssler Fiorenza, *Bread Not Stone: The Challenge of Feminist Biblical Interpretation* (Boston: Beacon, 1984), p. 7.

[11]Kwok Pui-lan, "Postcolonialism, Feminism and Biblical Interpretation," in *Scripture, Community and Mission*, ed. Philip L. Wickeri (Hong Kong: CCA & CWM, 2002), p. 271.

[12]R. S. Sugirtharajah, *Postcolonial Criticism and Biblical Interpretation* (Oxford: Oxford University Press, 2002), p. 24.

spective of postcolonial concerns, and the dubiousness, not only of the colonial past, but also of the contemporary world order in the form of globalization and its neocolonizing tendencies.[13] Against this backdrop Sugirtharajah adopts Edward Said's words to elaborate postcolonial criticism "as life-enhancing and constitutively opposed to every form of tyranny, domination, and abuse; its social goals are noncoercive knowledge produced in the interests of human freedom."[14] Therefore, what postcolonial critical theories aim at is to enhance de/reconstructive readings of texts that highlight the struggles and resistance in different colonial contexts.[15] In a postcolonial India, postcolonial hermeneutics can open up new vistas for the biblical interpretative process by broadening the scope and relevance of the Bible for contemporary, neocolonial challenges.

The uniting/coinciding factor between postcolonial and feminist criticisms is their resistance to any form of oppression. "They [both] seek to uncover the subjugation of both men and women in colonial texts, and the modes of resistance of the subjugated, and expose the use of gender in both colonial discourse and social reality."[16] Postcolonial feminism points to the impact of Western imperialism on women's identity formation in their particular sociocultural locations. The initial discussions approached patriarchy and imperialism as two parallel systems of oppression; however, in later research, they have been recognized as social systems to be analyzed in an integrated manner.[17] Three issues were identified in these early attempts at postcolonial feminist discourse: first, postcolonial feminists demonstrated how male-centered postcolonial discourse overlooked and underplayed gender differences and women's concerns (held by women of both developed and developing countries); second, feminists of developing countries, in solidarity with their male counterparts, questioned male colonial tendencies of developed-world biblical scholarship; third,

---

[13]R. S. Sugirtharajah, *Postcolonial Reconfigurations: An Alternative Way of Reading the Bible and Doing Theology* (London: SCM Press, 2003), p. 103.

[14]Edward Said, *Orientalism* (London: Penguin, 1985), quoted by Sugirtharajah, *Postcolonial Criticism and Biblical Interpretation*, p. 14.

[15]Kwok Pui-lan, "Making the Connections: Postcolonial Studies and Feminist Biblical Interpretation," in *The Postcolonial Biblical Reader*, ed. R. S. Sugirtharajah (Oxford: Blackwell, 2006), p. 46; R. S. Sugitharajah, *The Bible and the Third World: Precolonial, Colonial and Postcolonial Encounters* (Cambridge: Cambridge University Press, 2001), pp. 251-53.

[16]Sugirtharajah, *Postcolonial Criticism and Biblical Interpretation*, p. 29.

[17]Elisabeth Schüssler Fiorenza, *Wisdom Ways: Introducing Feminist Biblical Interpretation* (Maryknoll, NY: Orbis, 2001), pp. 62-63.

developing-world feminists complained that developed-world feminists had overlooked the colonial contexts of biblical texts and compromised with the colonial agenda embedded in them.[18]

In such a complex methodological situation, exploring possibilities for critiquing power relations among women themselves as colonizers and colonized calls for sincere engagement. Therefore, a postcolonial feminist perspective not only facilitates a reevaluation of the way "third-world women" have been homogenized in colonial discourses but also reviews the relationships of power between women as colonizers and colonized. The analysis of gender intersections with respect to colonialism and patriarchy unfolds complex realities of women acting in favor of the same ideologies that they in fact attempt to fight against.

PART TWO

Jane Pilcher and Imelda Whelehan remind us that when women are "associated with the colonizers they are neither 'other' nor holders of means to power, but they are implicated in and act as reinforcers of power relations as well as being appealed to as the moral centre of the colonizing will."[19] This applies to both colonizing and colonized women. I will demonstrate this power differential in describing an account of the white women missionaries of the London Missionary Society (hereafter LMS) and the brown, native Bible women of South Travancore in the nineteenth century. It was in a complex context of retaining "European purity" that the women missionaries of LMS initiated their ministry among native Indian women. Pilcher and Whelehan explain, "Women had an ideological role to play in colonialism as guardians of the 'race,' in the face of moral panics about miscegenation or compromising the perceived 'purity' of the European woman and these fears have also had an impact on the depiction of the non-European colonized woman."[20] Indian Bible women, the initial products of the European women's missionary activities, became the mediators between the local women and themselves, thus allowing the European women to maintain their perceived "purity."

Originally initiated as the "women's work" of the wives of missionaries of the London Missionary Society in South Travancore, the work among women

---

[18]Sugirtharajah, *Postcolonial Criticism and Biblical Interpretation*, p. 29.
[19]Jane Pilcher and Imelda Whelehan, *Fifty Key Concepts in Gender Studies* (London: Sage; 2004), p. 103.
[20]Ibid.

began to expand when the LMS recruited single women as missionaries from England, breaking through "the confining domestic world of married women."[21] The single women missionaries later outnumbered even the male missionaries. They joined with married women missionaries and began to negotiate with their privileged colonial identity, breaking the image of their roles as being confined to that of "the mothers of the missionaries," or even wives of the missionaries, and establishing new roles as active agents in the mission movement by starting a school for native Indian girls. Thus the presence and activities of the single women missionaries influenced the married women, resulting in the married white women moving away from being part of their husbands' missionary roles. They started establishing their own identities as independent and active agents by making appeals for native Indian women's education.[22]

Nevertheless, while white women missionaries found freedom from their patriarchal bondage in this way, they created further oppression for native Indian women. The native women's oppression could be understood in terms of triple colonization on the basis of race, caste and gender. Caste is an addition that was left out in the formulation of "double colonization" by the African women in the 1980s,[23] but it is an additional burden of internal apartheid for Indian women. This burden is evident in the rationale provided for introducing white women missionaries into the LMS: "The aim of female education was thus to produce the good wives and mothers deemed essential if the converts of the male missionaries were to establish solid Christian families and communities as the critical bulwark against 'heathenism.'"[24] Here "heathenism" could refer to all the social evils of Hinduism, which held native women under the bondage of caste and patriarchy in various forms such as child marriage, widow immolation and denial of rights to the "low caste" Channar (Nadar) women to wear upper clothes/jackets or to cover their breasts.[25]

---

[21]Jane Haggis, "White Women and Colonialism: Towards a Non-Recuperative History," in Lewis and Mills, Feminist Postcolonial Theory, p. 167.

[22]Ibid.

[23]The concept of double colonization became popular in the 1980s, when African and African American feminists/womanists proposed that women are colonized twice, first by the European colonizers and second by the patriarchal custodians of their native societies.

[24]Haggis, "White Women and Colonialism," p. 168.

[25]In the nineteenth century in South Travancore, Channar (Nadar) women were restricted from wearing the upper cloth to cover their breasts in front of casteist Nayar people. After a long-fought struggle, on July 26, 1859, the King of Travancore sanctioned their right to wear the upper cloth on the condition that they would not imitate the dress code of upper caste women.

The founding of the Society for the Propagation of Female Education in the East (SPFEE) in 1834 in London further institutionalized the triple colonization of native Indian women. The SPFEE never wanted to start new mission fields but only sent single women to assist wives of the LMS missionaries on demand. By this arrangement both British colonial patriarchy and Indian caste-bound patriarchy extended their grip over the native Indian women, which resulted in the intensifying of triple colonization. The women converts predominantly belonged to the then–"low caste" of *Channars* or *Nadars*. The role of white women in the triple colonization of Indian women did not guarantee those white women freedom from being "othered" in their own, patriarchal British society, however. As Jane Haggis suggests,

> The ambiguities between wife and lady worker were resolved by portraying the missionary wife as the critical grass-roots actor, defining, initiating and over-seeing the work, thus conforming to the properties of gender. This portrayal was predicated on the existence of women's work as a separate sphere of organization and endeavour which allowed the female agency, married or single, to operate outside the immediate structures of a masculine world.[26]

Strangely enough, their female agency did not dismantle the masculine world of British Empire. Empire was and is a patriarchal enterprise, and the women played a predominantly supporting role to further imperial interests, either as colonizers or colonized. Here the women missionaries played the colonial role so successfully that they were able to channel conversion of the "low caste" women to Christianity; however, they did not alter the caste status quo.

The greatest achievement of these committed women missionaries, both married and single, by the end of the nineteenth century was the addition of a large number of converts to Christianity from the "low caste" people and the women pupils in the schools run by them. However, their attitude to evangelizing these low caste women exhibited their racial prejudice against people belonging to different races and religions. This is evident from the letter of Ellen Horton, a missionary aspirant to India, who wrote to the LMS Ladies Committee[27] in 1881 that "the thought of those poor women in India, their darkness and ignorance; the greatness of the work & the need of workers makes

---

[26]Haggis, "White Women and Colonialism," p. 169.
[27]LMS recruited women as lady missionaries along with setting up the Ladies Committee of LMS supporters in 1875.

me feel I could do anything or give up anything to save and help them."[28] This letter illustrates how, for many British young women, the motivation for their volunteering was to save Indian women and girls from the brunt of a "heartless" Hinduism. This kind of response was the result of the LMS and SPFEE portraying native Indian women and girls as the most pathetic victims of heathenism to their British supporters.

The mission of *Zenana* visitation to high caste homes was introduced in the 1860s by the SPFEE to gain access to the *Nayar* women with Christian teachings while simultaneously carrying out the mission of "civilizing low caste" women, who converted in masses. Since it was difficult for white women missionaries to have direct interaction with the local women, especially the "high caste," *Nayar* women, they instead took the help of enthusiastic *low caste* Bible women. This newly found social agency of the Bible women in reaching out to the caste women manifested the transformation brought by Christianity. By undertaking their own identity struggles for equality among native Indian men and the caste system, *native* women also resisted colonial hegemony from the ruling British political powers. Nevertheless, the division that the missionaries accepted between the castes reiterated the triple colonization that the Bible women particularly encountered during the British colonial period. However, experiences of colonized women in their native land and those of colonizing women in their foreign colonies are certainly different. On this Sara Mills comments, "British women's travel writing in colonized countries, together with the accounts of British women in outpost situations, by their very presence alone in the public sphere destabilize notions of a clear female-private/male-public sphere divide."[29] The ruling or dominant voice in the society decides what the norms in relation to gender and space will be. When the dominant voice is that of a political invader, then their culture is treated as superior to the native culture, and gender gets alienated (as in the case of the Bible women) in the resultant power discourses. As far as the women missionaries of LMS were concerned, their active role in the evangelistic as well as social mission to native Indian women opened up new vistas of blurring the boundaries between public and private spheres

---

[28] The letter of Ellen Horton, quoted by Jane Haggis and Margaret Allen, "Imperial Emotions: Affective Communities of Mission in British Protestant Women's Missionary Publications c 1880–1920," *Journal of Social History* (Spring 2008): 695.

[29] Sara Mills, "Gender and Colonial Space," in Lewis and Mills, *Feminist Postcolonial Theory*, p. 699.

between themselves and their white male counterparts. However, that could not guarantee them freedom to dismantle the patriarchal notions of British colonialism itself, which targeted them too as subjects of colonial patriarchy. Further, their marital status also mattered, as married women missionaries remained in the shadow of their husbands, while single women were more forceful in penetrating the local cultures. In the case of native women, they had to fight for fraternity and unity among their native men against colonial powers. Nevertheless, their interactions with women missionaries motivated them to stage public protests against *Nayar* men, as in the Upper Cloth Movement.

In such a complex matrix of colonial, casteist and patriarchal hegemony, would it not be unduly harsh to attempt to decode the mission activity of white women missionaries as colonial artifices in a way that "would reveal the missionary women as racist agents of an imperial state"?[30] Here the endeavor is only to highlight how white women missionaries represented a category of people who were trapped in an intricate web of race, class and gender that underpinned the age of empire. It would be appropriate to observe that "white women were not the hapless onlookers of empire, but were ambiguously complicit both as colonizers and colonized, privileged and restricted, acted upon and acting."[31] Therefore, these two systemic forces—colonialism and patriarchy—function not as two extreme poles of realities, but rather as part of the intricate web of hegemonic effects of oppressive forces. Thus the gender category in a colonial worldview helps us to analyze how women act in favor of and against colonialism.

The power analysis of the missionary activities of white women missionaries in South Travancore provokes the question about the role of the Bible in the lives of the *native* Bible women of colonial patriarchy, who were caught between the ideological power of the colonizers and the native, caste-bound, patriarchal ideological systems. How did these indigenous women perceive the Bible as a tool for their social emancipation? How did they interpret the Bible? Did they interpret it through the perspective of the white women missionaries or through their own perspectives and interests, which were to attain social emancipation from their patriarchal oppressors? Missionaries invariably por-

---

[30]Haggis, "White Women and Colonialism," p. 172.
[31]Anne McClintock, *Imperial Leather: Race, Gender and Sexuality in the Colonial Context* (New York: Routledge, 1995), p. 6, quoted by Pilcher and Whelehan, *Fifty Key Concepts*, p. 103.

trayed the Bible as a symbol of modernity and civilization to the indigenous communities. The Bible was the resource book for the white women missionaries to educate the local women with both Christian faith and modern civilization. They trained the Bible women to conduct Bible study for the local women in their own languages. Eventually they translated the Bible into indigenous languages and interpreted it for those cultures. Generally in the colonies missionaries encouraged individualistic and intimate relations between native converts and their newly found God, mainly through providing the Bible in the languages of the indigenous peoples. Therefore the colonial intentions of both Christianization and modernization were channeled through the translation of the Bible into local languages.[32] This worked in favor of native women, as owning the Bible in their native languages helped them to develop a hope for commonly acclaimed evangelical Protestant values such as universal fraternity, "equality before God, and the potential for self-improvement."[33] On the 26th of July, 1859, the Upper Cloth Movement secured the native women's right to wear the upper cloth/jacket after long years of struggle. However, after the official proclamation, it took a few more years to establish a peaceful situation in which women could exercise their right over against the former dress restrictions. Indigenous Indian women's struggles to gain equality among their own caste men and among men of other castes continue until today, even after India historically and politically moved into a postcolonial state. This indicates the long reach of colonialism and the longer reach of gender and caste discrimination in general.

CONCLUSION

In British colonies, especially in India, gender inequalities were considered essential in maintaining the structure of colonial racism and British imperial authority. The management of white women missionaries' sexual activity, reproduction and celibacy was controlled by imperial authority to signify its power in maintaining distinctions between the colonizers and colonized. Postcolonial feminist hermeneutical approaches to the use of the Bible in missionary endeavors have unearthed the larger cultural and political contexts in

---

[32]Anna Johnston, "The Book Eaters: Textuality, Modernity, and the London Missionary Society," in *Semeia* 88 (January 2001): 24.

[33]Ibid., p. 29.

which Indian Christianity defined its existence in negotiation with the imperial and casteist social norms. Such critical readings have also underscored how missionary agencies have often collaborated with the colonial regime by acting as a buffer between the colonizers and the people. As an example, the triple colonization of native Indian women under hegemonic categories of race, caste and gender was endorsed by the Christian evangelistic teachings of LMS missionaries, including its women. In this way Christian missionaries reinforced Indian women's general discrimination as colonial subjects and specific double discrimination as "low caste" women. The continuing struggle of native Indian women against casteism and patriarchy in postcolonial India further reiterates that these oppressive forces have not ceased to exist. Because of this, native Indian women's experiences need to be taken into account in any postcolonial analysis of multiple oppressions in postcolonial India, especially those examining the intersection of caste, gender and coloniality.

4

CONVERTING A
COLONIALIST CHRIST

Toward an African
Postcolonial Christology

Victor Ifeanyi Ezigbo and Reggie L. Williams

.... ⚹ ....

AFRICA, FROM THE EARLIEST DAYS of Christianity, has contributed to Christianity's theological identity. The works of prominent African theologians like Tertullian, Arius, Athanasius, Cyril and Augustine are among the many Christian scholars who continue to inform theological discussions in numerous Christian communities. Contemporary African Christianity continues in this great theological tradition. African theologians continue to reimagine Jesus' identity and significance in light of contemporary social, religious, economic and political situations in postmissionary and postcolonial Africa. Many of these theologians share the vision to rethink the Christologies of the Western missionaries who evangelized Africa in the colonial and decolonized eras on the grounds that (1) the missionaries' Christologies did not exhaust the significance, or knowledge, of Jesus Christ, and (2) most of the Christologies failed to present Jesus Christ in a way that steered clear of Western colonial agendas and derogatory views of indigenous Africans.[1]

In this essay we examine the theological implications of the way of Jesus for a discussion about Christology in postcolonial Africa. We argue that an African Christology is *postcolonial* if it meets the following three, interrelated

---

[1]See Kwame Bediako, *Theology and Identity: The Impact of Culture upon Christian Thought in the Second Century and Modern Africa* (Oxford: Regnum, 1992), pp. 225-444.

requirements: (1) it overcomes the shackles of the modern colonial mentality, (2) it fosters the theological self-determination of African Christianity and (3) it contributes to the development of global Christian theology.

COLONIAL CHRISTIANITY AND THE WHITE, IMPERIALIST CHRIST

African Christianity is deeply influenced by imperialism and colonialism. Thus we will begin our examination of Christianity in Africa with a question: What has been the role of the modern colonial mentality in the Western Christian worldview? We may begin to understand the colonial distortion of Christianity by paying attention to the way that modern, imperialist Europeans saw themselves in relation to non-Europeans. Walter Mignolo recounts early Spanish cartographers' division of the world into three parts, assigning each of the known continents to a son of Noah.[2] The corresponding, partitioned world, a European Christian geopolitical construct, invented a connection between the continents based on the contemporary theological understanding of geography and its inhabitants, primarily drawing from the biblical characters of Shem, Ham and Japheth.[3] Early Christian explorers borrowed from Augustine, who claimed that Shem was important as the ancestor of Semitic peoples, through whom Christ was born, while the destiny of Ham was marked by a curse and Japheth was destined to expand.[4] Spanish cartographers assigned Asia to Shem, Africa to Ham and Europe to Japheth.[5]

---

[2]Walter Mignolo, *The Idea of Latin America*, Blackwell Manifestos (Malden, MA: Blackwell, 2005), p. 24. This division of lands occurred prior to the 1494 Treaty of Tordesillas, according to which Pope Alexander VI divided the newly discovered lands between the Portuguese and the Spanish respectively. The early division by Spanish cartographers is a prototype of that later division. A worldview derived from the theological notion of orders of creation was normative in Germany, especially among the Christian groups who sought to synchronize German Protestant congregations with the Nazi government under Hitler and the Führer principle.

[3]The "Curse of Ham" myth is a misrepresentation of Gen 9:20-27, in which Noah pronounces a curse on his grandson Canaan, the son of Ham. The distortion came to be understood as a biblical curse on black people, since Ham was mythologically understood as the father of the darker races where the climate is hotter. If the curse was upon Canaan, as the passage is written, it could not be read as a patriarch's curse on African people and thus could not have become the biblical endorsement of perpetual, race-based slavery. See Stephen R. Haynes, *Noah's Curse: The Biblical Justification of American Slavery* (New York: Oxford University Press, 2007); and George M. Fredrickson, *Racism: A Short History* (Princeton, NJ: Princeton University Press, 2002), pp. 42-45.

[4]See Augustine, *City of God* 16.2.650, as quoted in Mignolo, *Idea of Latin America*, p. 28.

[5]Mignolo illustrates the famous "T-in-O" map that was published in the ninth-century edition of Isidore of Seville's *Etymologies*. The map demonstrates an obvious tripartite division, with Asia occupying the top part of the circle (in an emerging interpretation of the shape of the Earth), and Europe and Africa dividing among themselves the bottom half. See figure 1. This early division of

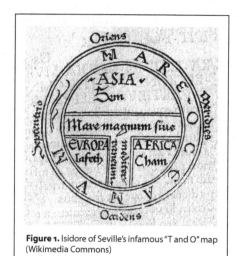

Figure 1. Isidore of Seville's infamous "T and O" map
(Wikimedia Commons)

The European "discovery" of Africa, the Americas and Asia corresponds with the Christian cosmology of modern imperialism, in which Japheth was destined to expand into non-European lands, subjugate the inhabitants and assimilate them into the European Christian imagination. This was the beginning of what was to become a process of racializing continents. For Mignolo, the racialization of continents corresponds with this curse-of-Ham narrative, in which people of color—typically of African descent—are destined to be subjugated, and the role of Japheth is that of the blessed one to whom Ham's descendants are subjected. Mignolo argues that after the sixteenth century this Christian geopolitical perspective was understood as the natural way the continents fit together, with all of their subdivisions.

This Christian narrative of racially divided continents included a racialized, European, imperialist Christ who gave privileges to Europeans by becoming the divine representation of their superiority over others. In addition, modern, imperialist Europeans replaced traditional connections native peoples made with their geography as a way to identify themselves with European-defined self-understandings. Traditions connected to geography were stripped from people who came to know themselves, instead, by physical features, like skin color. Europeans derived their rights to take creative liberties with the humanity of other people from a supersessionist worldview that understood Christian Europe, not Israel, to be the center of God's salvific purpose in the world.

The marker of membership in God's chosen people was based on similarity to white European bodies, as Willie Jennings explains: "Before there was any notion of race as a scientific concept, a social principle, or a fully formed racial

---

the world, prior to the discovery of further continents, provides the rationale for the later interpretation that the world is naturally divided into four continents—Asia, Africa, Europe and America. See Mignolo's description of the ninth-century Spanish T-in-O map in *Idea of Latin America*, p. 23.

optic on the world, it was a theological form—an inverted, distorted vision of creation that reduced theological anthropology to commodified bodies."[6] Thus, in the age of discovery, people groups were "discovered," brought into existence and classified according to racial phenotypes in relation to "model" white, European humanity. Armed with this distorted curse-of-Ham geopolitical cosmology and its corresponding racialized interpretation of human beings, European imperialist Christians created people as they created maps and discovered lands. Theirs was an imitation of Christ that did not follow the suggestion of Thomas à Kempis; their imitation of Christ was an impersonation of God. In the practice of colonialism they sought to create the world in their own image. To be sure, their christological claim was also an invitation, albeit by force, to discipleship; salvation and inclusion into the community of God's chosen people, the European body of Christ, was commensurate with the "gift" of salvation that was demonstrated by the resemblance of the "discovered" body to white European bodies and culture. Europe was more than a geographical location as such; Europe became a process that created people, inventing them socially and physically, from an imposed nonexistence and perceived savagery, into the white European imagination of a "civilized" human being. Israel was replaced by Europe as the community of God's chosen people, and Christ became white.

African Christology and the Colonial Mentality

A colonial mentality is a mindset that institutionalizes the colonizer as the arbiter of self-determination, civilization and all truths. In many theological communities such a mindset has helped to sustain the idea that "Western theological writings and reflection . . . represent normative, universal Christian reflection whereas non-Western theology is more localized, and ad hoc and contextual."[7]

Many Christians in Africa have remained in the shackles of a colonial mentality. This is evident in some practices of missionary churches that see the missionaries' theologies as the universal judge of true Christianity. To cite one example, many of the missionary churches have continued to encourage the

---

[6]Willie James Jennings, *The Christian Imagination: Theology and the Origins of Race* (New Haven, CT: Yale University Press, 2010), p. 58.

[7]Timothy C. Tennet, *Theology in the Context of World Christianity* (Grand Rapids: Zondervan, 2007), p. 11.

practice of adopting Western names during baptism. In many cases the Western names function as the mark of a Christian's identity. What many of these churches have failed to acknowledge is that the majority of the earliest Western missionaries required Christian families and Christian converts to adopt foreign names on the grounds that African names were rooted in pagan cultures, which were not conducive to proclaiming the Christian message in Africa. Like most Westerners in the 1400s through the 1800s, the majority of the missionaries presented to Africans portraits of Jesus that included derogatory perceptions of Africans. Also, many of the missionaries viewed missions as a divine call to preach Christ as a means of extending the territorial boundaries of their respective countries. The nineteenth-century Scottish missionary Thomas Pringle articulated this understanding of missions when he wrote, "Let us enter upon a new and nobler career of conquest. Let us subdue and salvage Africa by justice, by kindness, by talisman of Christian truth. Let us thus go forth, in the name and under the blessing of God, gradually to extend moral influence, the territorial boundary also of our colony, until it shall become an empire."[8]

These missionaries and colonial administrators had an ambivalent relationship; both sometimes collaborated to bring an imperialist Christ to sub-Saharan Africa. Even when the missionaries' relationships with the imperial powers were frosty, the missionaries, like the imperialists, operated with a colonial mentality that stigmatized and degraded Africans. Roy Bridges's assessment of the relationship between the evangelical missionaries and the colonial administrators who worked in East Africa in the nineteenth century highlights this ambivalence.

> There were changing patterns of interaction between missions and lay authority. While the instinct of evangelicals was usually to avoid association with state authority, class identities between missionaries and officials and a dismissive attitude to other cultures may have brought officials and missionaries to cooperate; there was a confusing set of ambiguities and uncertainties.[9]

In the story of the Western colonization and Christianization of Africa, Western missionaries and explorers spread a Christian message about Jesus

---

[8]Thomas Pringle, *African Sketches* (London, 1834), p. 479.
[9]Roy Bridges, "The Christian Vision and Secular Imperialism: Missionaries, Geography, and the Approach to East Africa, c. 1844–1890," in *Converting Colonialism: Visions and Realities in Mission History, 1706–1914,* ed. Dana L. Robert (Grand Rapids: Eerdmans, 2008), p. 45.

that was merged with the colonial system, resulting in the creation of the "colonial Christ," whose goal was to colonize and civilize Africans. They characterized Africa as savage and uncivilized in order to sustain and justify their claims about the Africans' need to be colonized. For the missionaries and colonialists, Africans were intellectually inferior and spiritually godless people destined to remain under the tutelage of the West in order to be made civil and authentically human.[10] Hence the missionaries did more harm than good to the image of Christianity. For many indigenous Africans, slavery and apartheid became associated with Christianity. Even the good works of the missionaries and colonialists (such as the providing of medicine, Western education and the proclamation of the Christian gospel) were overshadowed in the minds of the Africans by the derogatory attitudes that Westerners displayed toward them.

Africans have long fought against colonialism and neocolonialism on the fronts of religion and politics. Some African elites in the early years of decolonization and nationalist movements were critical of the colonial elements embedded in the teaching and lifestyle of the missionaries. On the political front, the Nigerian Nnamdi Azikiwe, one of the key leaders of the nationalist movement of the 1930s through the 1950s, sternly rejected any democratic rule that excluded the participation of Africans in the administration of the country.[11] On the ecclesial front, K. O. K. Onyioha, the founder of the National Church, was also deeply dissatisfied with the missionaries' exclusion of Africans in important leader positions within the church.[12] Jomo Kenyatta, the first president of Kenya, bemoaned the missionaries' condemnation of African customs, dances, ceremonies and feasts.[13] The missionaries' replacement of African customs and dances with Western musical instruments and music (such as hymns) in African churches, in the guise of promoting and maintaining authentic Christianity, has been most intriguing. Many mission churches, until

---

[10]See Kari Miettinen, *On the Way to Whiteness: Christianization, Conflict and Change in Colonial Ovamboland, 1910–1965* (Helsinki: SKS, 2005).

[11]Nnamdi Azikiwe, "Religious Toleration," *West African Pilot* 21, no. 1 (1939): 4.

[12]Patrick J. Furlong, "Azikiwe and the National Church of Nigeria and the Cameroons: A Case Study of the Political Use of Religion in African Nationalism," *African Affairs* 91 (1992): 433-52; see also Michael Crowder, *West Africa Under Colonial Rule* (Evanston, IL: Northwestern University Press, 1968), pp. 365-69. The National Church was founded in 1948.

[13]Jomo Kenyatta, *Facing Mount Kenya: The Tribal Life of the Gikuyu* (1938; repr., New York: Random House, 1962).

the recent past, have been reluctant to allow indigenous African dance steps and tunes during church services.

The founders of African Independent or Instituted Churches (AICs) have led African Christianity in the quest to express the Christian message with Africa's vernaculars and indigenous religious beliefs. Since the 1800s many African Christians have fought with varying degrees of intensity and tact against the imposition of Western Christianity on Africans. The Nigerian Samuel Ajayi Crowther (ca. 1807–1891), the first African bishop in the Anglican Church, began a movement that sought to establish indigenous churches. Crowther's aim was to help African Christianity become self-supporting, self-propagating and self-governing. Crowther's experience at Fourah Bay College and Sierra Leone, and his contact with Henry Venn of the Church Missionary Society (CMS), inspired him to imagine and pursue these daunting tasks.[14] Crowther died a frustrated and broken man, as he lived long enough to see the leaders of CMS repudiate his efforts. The seed he planted, however, grew in due course, with its roots spreading in different directions, one of which led to the birth of several African Independent Churches.

Christology and Africans' Theological Self-identity and Autonomy

Can Africans become Christians without embodying "Western" as a prefix or as baggage? Can they worship God, through Jesus Christ and in the power of the Holy Spirit, in African languages and with African indigenous religious thoughts, without being haunted by the claims that they are betraying the Christian gospel? Many studies conducted on contemporary African Christianity—sub-Saharan Christianity in particular—have shown that Christians there tend to read and apply the Bible through indigenous lenses that view the spiritual and human worlds as being in mutual relationship.[15] Some Christians secretly consult the priests of local deities to find the causes and solutions to their misfortunes. African theologians cannot afford to ignore these practices if they aim to develop Christologies that are both relevant to the experiences

---

[14]See Andrew F. Walls, *The Cross-Cultural Process in Christian History* (Maryknoll, NY: Orbis, 2002), pp. 155-64.

[15]See Kwame Bediako, *Jesus and the Gospel in Africa: History and Experience* (Maryknoll, NY: Orbis, 2004); Diane B. Stinton, *Jesus of Africa: Voices of Contemporary African Christology* (Maryknoll, NY: Orbis, 2004).

of African Christians and faithful to the Christian Scriptures. To ignore such practices is to repeat the mistake of the missionaries who sought to decontextualize the gospel and force all Christianity to be read through European lenses. African theologians face the task of addressing the issue of Christianity in Africa without making the same mistake of the missionaries and without being unfaithful to the biblical testimony about God's action in the person and work of Jesus Christ.

Many members of the missionary churches continued to contend that they had encountered an undistorted, "biblical Christianity" in the gospel proclamation of the missionaries. Two problems with this assumption are noteworthy. First, the notion of "biblical Christianity" can be misleading. In the New Testament we find different forms of Christianity professed by Syriac, Hebraic, Hellenistic and Greco-Roman communities that sought to appropriate the event of Jesus Christ to their contexts from their own cultures, histories and experiences. The varied Christologies in the New Testament were the earliest Christians' responses to Jesus' invitation to his followers to interpret and appropriate his person and work from their own histories and social locations (see Mk 8:27-29). Jesus' invitation, it should be noted, extended to all people who would come to believe in him through the ministry of his disciples. The second problem is that Western missionaries proclaimed Christologies and different forms of Christianity that were wrapped in garbs of their cultures and disparate theologies. Recognizing this will embolden Africans to view the theological and ecclesiastical heritage of the missionaries more critically. The missionaries' quest for the expansion of imperial, Western, "Christian" territories became a hermeneutical lens through which they interpreted and applied all Scripture. Their error conferred on their readings of the Scriptures the status of an objective and universally relevant criterion for assessing alternative interpretations. As an example, they presented to Africans a Jesus who required Africans to wash away their *Africanness*—their names, traditions, cultures and identities—before they could become his followers.

What do Africans living in Africa *hear* when Jesus Christ is proclaimed to them as God's good news? Given that the story of Christianity's presence in sub-Saharan Africa is rarely told without highlighting its connection with Western missionaries and colonialists, it is to be expected that the majority of African Christians *actually* hear a whitewashed Jesus, a Jesus wrapped in

Western cultures. Because of this, for most Africans, "the image of Jesus was and still is that of a blue-eyed, blond, white male, whose benevolent face, along with similar white faces of his disciples, still grace our churches today."[16] The mission of the modern colonial Jesus was to "civilize" Africans and to send them on the way to "whiteness."

But does the colonialist Jesus faithfully represent the Jewish Jesus of the New Testament who opposed domination and oppression (see, for instance, Lk 4:16-21)? Africans' reactions against the imperialist Christology and Christianity of the West have varied. Some have rejected Christianity, viewing it as a tool of domination. Others accepted it because they construed it as the only way to survive the suffocating presence of foreign powers.[17] Others today refuse to throw away the "baby" (Christian message) with the "bathwater" (Western understandings of the Christian message).

Two approaches separate the Christian message from the Western understandings of the message. The first is the *culture-oriented* approach, which questions and resists the colonial entanglements present in Western missionaries' stories of Jesus Christ. This approach is critical of the colonial Christologies that relegate Africa's indigenous cultures and religions to the sphere of the uncivilized, irreligious and demonic. Theologians that use this approach argue that African cultures and indigenous thoughts can be used to communicate the gospel effectively in African communities. They employ several terms, like ancestor and traditional healer, to explain the identity and significance of Jesus.[18] The culture-oriented approach helps African Christians to see Christianity as the religion they can appropriate in their own communities, as their *own* religion, and not as a foreign religion that opposes all African cultural values.[19] The second is the *liberation-oriented* approach, which unearths the imperial setting in which Western Christologies flourished in Africa. This approach exposes the Christologies that present Jesus of the Christian Scriptures as an imperialist and a racist whose salvific work only extends to Africans at the

---

[16]Musa W. Dube, "Toward a Post-Colonial Feminist Interpretation of the Bible," in *Hope Abundant: Third World and Indigenous Women's Theology*, ed. Kwok Pui-lan (Maryknoll, NY: Orbis, 2010), p. 89.

[17]Okot p'Bitek, *African Religions in Western Scholarship* (Kampala: East African Literature Bureau, 1970).

[18]See Robert J. Schreiter, ed., *Faces of Jesus in Africa* (Maryknoll, NY: Orbis, 1991); Ben E. Udoh, *Guest Christology: An Interpretative View of the Christological Problem in Africa* (Frankfurt am Main: Peter Lang, 1988).

[19]See Ogbu U. Kalu, J. Hofmeyr and P. J. Marit, eds., *African Christianity: An African Story* (Pretoria: University of Pretoria Press, 2005).

expense of Africans' freedom to determine their own sociopolitical situations. Some African female theologians have adopted this approach in their critique of both African and Western cultures that oppress women.[20] South African theologians have also employed this approach in their construction of Christologies that confront the horror of apartheid.[21]

Between the 1950s and 1990s African Christianity witnessed the flourishing of theological treatises that aimed "to achieve some integration between the African pre-Christian religious experience and African Christian commitment in ways that would ensure the integrity of African Christian identity and selfhood."[22] Some African theologians, however, were suspicious of any attempt to promote the idea of a symbiotic relationship between African indigenous religions and Christianity.[23] Many of those theologians did not consider themselves worthy to question, critique or, when necessary, correct Western theologies. Sadly this mindset continues to reverberate in African Christianity.

However, many African theologians are critical of the meanings and values Western missionaries assigned to Jesus Christ during the great Western missionary expeditions in Africa. They are asking why the missionaries viewed such meanings and values as central, important and the most adequate ways of interpreting and appropriating Jesus Christ in a foreign context. They are making the story of Christianity their own story by using their history and experience to interpret their encounter with Jesus Christ. They are also rediscovering the theological import of the gospel's universality and its capacity to resist any attempt by a single human culture to encapsulate it.

AFRICAN CHRISTOLOGY AND GLOBAL CHRISTIANITY

Christianity is desperately in need of a new theological landscape where the formerly colonized and colonizers see each other as learners as well as educators who are willing both to teach and be taught. A postcolonial Christology imagines the "universality" of Jesus Christ in a way in which both the (de)

---

[20]See Mercy Amba Oduyoye and Musimbi R. A. Kanyoro, eds., *The Will to Arise: Women, Tradition, and the Church in Africa* (Maryknoll, NY: Orbis, 1992).

[21]See Leonard Sweetman, ed., *Black and Reformed: Apartheid, Liberation, and the Calvinist Tradition* (Maryknoll, NY: Orbis, 1984).

[22]Kwame Bediako, "Understanding African Theology in the 20th Century," in *Issues in African Christian Theology*, ed. Samuel Ngewa, Mark Shaw, and Tite Tiénou (Nairobi: East African Educational, 1998), p. 56.

[23]See Byang H. Kato, *Theological Pitfalls in Africa* (Kisumu: Evangel, 1975).

colonized and colonizer have mutual conversations to construct a new global Christian identity. The "universality" of Jesus Christ should not be confused with the *universalizing* of a particular Christology. The universality of Jesus' significance is only truly realized when each local community *contextually* imagines and interprets his life and teaching incarnationally, within the lived context of a present discipleship community and outside of the theological parameters created by colonizers or the imperial powers. African theologians who use postcolonial theory to construct Christology must set free the Jesus of the Christian Scriptures who has been buried under the rubble of the colonization of Africa and colonial mentality so that he can speak God's gospel, or good news, to Africans.

The demographic shift in the center of Christianity's gravity from the West to the non-Western world represents a watershed moment in the history of the expansion of Christianity in the twenty-first century. It will take several years to unravel the theological implications of this phenomenon. What is clear is that the business of theology can no longer be conducted in the old ways, as when Western forms of Christianity wielded "Christian" hegemony over other forms. An African postcolonial Christology is truly born when its interpretation and appropriation of the event of Jesus Christ enjoys the theological autonomy to engage and critique the history and experience of Africans and Westerners who have internalized colonial mentalities.

What christological models can successfully achieve this daunting task? Some of the Christologies developed by Africans since the mid-1970s provide helpful resources for the construction of postcolonial African Christologies.[24] The "Revealer Christology" model developed by Victor Ezigbo reimagined Jesus Christ in a way that follows the three requirements for an African postcolonial Christology we outlined in this essay.[25] The requirements are overcoming colonial mentality, fostering the theological self-determination of African Christianity and contributing to the development of theologies that are beneficial to churches beyond Africa. We will highlight some of the central

---

[24]See John S. Mbiti, "Some African Concepts of Christology," in *Christ and the Younger Churches*, ed. G. F. Vicedom (London: SPCK, 1972), pp. 51-62; Kofi Appiah-Kubi and Sergio Torres, *African Theology en Route* (Maryknoll, NY: Orbis, 1979); Schreiter, *Faces of Jesus in Africa*; Udoh, *Guest Christology*.

[25]Victor I. Ezigbo, *Re-imagining African Christologies: Conversing with the Interpretations and Appropriations of Jesus Christ in Contemporary African Christianity* (Eugene, OR: Pickwick, 2010).

arguments of the Revealer Christology model and also demonstrate how it contributes to the discussion on postcolonial Christology in Africa.

The Revealer Christology model sees Jesus Christ as a *revealer* of divinity and humanity. The word *revealer* is used in both communicative and hermeneutical senses. In the *communicative sense* Jesus functions as the one who conveys and expresses divinity and true humanity. As God's self-revelatory act Jesus Christ embodies both God's presence and true humanity in the world. In Jesus, therefore, a person encounters and is invited into God's fellowship.

Most important for our purposes, however, is the *hermeneutical sense* of this model. In this sense Jesus functions as the one who critiques, judges and re-molds our preconceived notions of divinity and humanity. As a divine *hermeneutical act* the event of Jesus Christ interprets, critiques and reforms "human beings' preconceptions of God, other spirit beings, and humanity."[26] To put it differently, Jesus is the lens through which African Christians can assess the knowledge of God and humanity that they gained from both the indigenous religions of Africa and Western forms of Christianity.

African Christians who search for God's purposes for their lives and the causes of their misfortunes, and who sometimes visit the shrines of native doctors to hear from the ancestors, need not do so in a manner that excludes Jesus' critique. A Revealer Christology helps us to see that being a Christian requires committing to the solution and critique of Jesus Christ. Rather than ignoring this situation, however, the Revealer Christology model situates Jesus within the core of African indigenous religious experience. Jesus does not merely fulfill the aspirations of African peoples; the Revealer Christology model presents Jesus simultaneously as "questioner" and "solution" to the experiences and religious quests of Africans. That is, the Jesus of the Revealer Christology model does not simply provide the answers to the questions Africans are asking about their lives. This Jesus also shapes and informs the questions African Christians are asking about the spiritual and human worlds. For example, the Jesus of the Revealer Christology interrogates African Christians who assume, because of their colonial mentality, that they are either incomplete human beings or are cursed by God or evil people when, for instance, they are unable to have children. This "questioning" by Jesus will help such Christians

---

[26]Ibid., p. 154.

to rediscover Jesus' teaching on the values and dignity of all human beings as God's creatures (see Mt 6:25-32).

Another contribution of the Revealer Christology model is that it subjects all christological models produced both in the West and non-Western worlds to critical scrutiny, allowing the work and person of Jesus to create an elastic boundary for the construction of Christology. To be sure, Francis Watson rightly argues that to

> be a Christian is, among other things, to care about the way that Jesus is represented, and to do so because the reality is so supremely important that misrepresentations are bound to be deeply damaging. To celebrate the limitless proliferation of images of Jesus, not caring about their adequacy as representations of reality, is only possible on non-Christian premises.[27]

A Revealer Christology indeed cares about the representation of Jesus but challenges the culturally and colonially bound representations of Western Christianity. In the Revealer Christology model, the criteria for determining an adequate representation of Jesus Christ lie in the "spirit," and not the "letter," of the different biblical images of Jesus. While the "letter," that is, the collection of images of Jesus in the New Testament, can point us to him, enrich our understanding of the significance of his work and guide us in the construction of Christology, it does not encapsulate or exhaust the significance of the life and work of Jesus Christ. The "spirit" of the christological inquiry of the biblical writers ought to inspire us to imagine the person of Jesus Christ afresh as we draw insights from them and from our own encounters with Jesus Christ. So, for instance, African Christians who identify with ancestor Christologies because of the mediatory roles of ancestors in indigenous Africa acknowledge that (1) it is within their epistemic and theological rights to explain Jesus' person and work with African thoughts; (2) their understandings of Jesus should not be in contradiction with the Christian Scriptures; and (3) it is Jesus Christ, and not African ancestors, that define the lives of Christ followers.

CONCLUSION

African theologians tend to be intentionally "local" and "global" in their theo-

---

[27]Francis Watson, "The Quest for the Real Jesus," in *The Cambridge Companion to Jesus Christ*, ed. Markus Bockmuehl (New York: Cambridge University Press, 2001), p. 157.

logical activities. Christianity is not truly "global" by its mere presence in many countries of the world though. It is truly global when two criteria are met. First, the local communities of the world's nations are given the freedom to rethink and reexpress Christianity's teaching about God's relationship with the world through Jesus Christ. And second, the local communities see themselves as equals, conversing and critiquing each other and contributing theologically to Christianity's long tradition.

The "colonialist Christ" undercuts these two criteria. A postcolonial mentality is required to liberate African Christianity from the colonial mentality that holds captive many of the mission churches. By "postcolonial mentality" we mean the mindset that rethinks colonial history and mentality in light of the experiences of the colonized. A postcolonial mindset does not erase colonial history; it does, however, empower the colonized or the formerly colonized to imagine a new identity that accounts for colonial history, on the one hand, and moves beyond colonial cultural and cognitive frameworks, on the other. A postcolonial Christology is not oblivious to colonialist and neocolonialist interpretations of Jesus Christ. Instead it critically interacts and questions colonialism and neocolonialism in its own construction of the meaning, significance and relevance of Jesus Christ.

Part Two

THE STORIES BEHIND
THE COLONIAL STORIES

··· ⚓ ···

Introduction to Part Two

The Stories Behind the
Colonial Stories

✴

IN PART TWO TERI MERRICK AND KURT ANDERS RICHARDSON examine
grand stories—narratives and metanarratives. Metanarratives are the overarching, all-encompassing dramas that purport to explain who we are and
where we stand in the cosmos and in history as well as to set the terms for what
accounts for knowledge. Metanarratives have come under scrutiny in recent
decades. By nature a metanarrative purports to explain and collapse all of
human events in a comprehensive history. Recent philosophers have argued
that they are reductive, coercive, racist, colonialist and sexist in their choices
of which narratives to include and which to erase. Those erased are the very
real stories of people groups whose accounts do not reinforce the myth that the
metanarrative puts forward.

Merrick examines the ways that Kant and Hegel successfully propounded
such a metanarrative in their Enlightenment myth of the hero of knowledge
who defines the terms of rational thought and objective knowledge—a myth
that is still widely assumed today. She then details how this metanarrative has
underwritten the tragic violence that has occurred in the modern era. Finally,
she urges postcolonial thinkers to consider whether, despite its historic use in
legitimizing violence, Kantian objectivity is worth salvaging.

Richardson focuses on the narrative myth of "American exceptionalism,"
which has underwritten much of our public discourse and which, as he shows,
is deeply beholden to religious mythic themes. This myth animates and inspires,
on the one hand, but also self-consciously masks, occludes and suppresses
stories that do not support it, on the other. Hence the cost to maintain the myth
is high and involves loss of life, suppression of culture and denial of autonomy

to those who stand in the way of the supposed mythic destiny of the powerful.

Richardson concludes that, once the benefits and costs are weighed, the myth of American exceptionalism for Christians is, in the end, "false prophecy." It presupposes an inevitable link between salvation, military conquest and national interests, and replaces traditional biblical concerns for the outcast with contemporary concerns focused on national interests alone.

5

Tracing the Metanarrative
of Colonialism and Its Legacy

Teri R. Merrick

Introduction

In 1979 French philosopher Jean-François Lyotard published a report commissioned by the Quebec government on "the condition of knowledge in the
most highly developed societies."[1] *The Postmodern Condition: A Report on
Knowledge* is now considered the authoritative text on the meaning of the
oft-used terms *metanarrative* and *postmodern*. For Lyotard a metanarrative
is a "grand recit," or grand story, that legitimates a source of knowledge and
the rules for acquiring or disseminating that knowledge. "The postmodern
condition" refers to late twentieth-century skepticism or "incredulity" concerning such stories.[2]

While Christian philosophers debate whether postmodern incredulity applies to any legitimating grand story, including the biblical narrative,[3] there is
no disputing the fact that Lyotard intended so-called Enlightenment metanarratives to fall under the suspicious eye of the postmodern critic. He claimed
that, despite obvious differences, the metanarratives of modern philosophers
like Immanuel Kant, G. W. F. Hegel, Karl Marx and Adam Smith contain the
same basic plot: "The hero of knowledge works toward a good ethico-political

---

[1]Jean François Lyotard, *The Postmodern Condition: A Report on Knowledge*, trans. Geoff Bennington
and Brian Massumi (Minneapolis: University of Minnesota Press, 1984), p. xxiii.
[2]Ibid., p. xxiv.
[3]See James K. A. Smith, "A Little Story About Metanarratives: Lyotard, Religion and Postmodernism
Revisited," *Faith and Philosophy* 18 (2001): 353-68.

end—universal peace."[4] This end is achieved by forging a univocal, unanimous consensus "between rational minds."[5]

Who are these heroes of knowledge, and why have Enlightenment metanarratives rightly come under suspicion? To answer that question, in this chapter I focus on the metanarrative coauthored by Kant and Hegel. Since the hero of knowledge in their grand story is the would-be objective knower, in the first section I unpack Kant's concept of objectivity. We will see how this concept serves to confer legitimacy on Western modern science as *the* institution tasked with producing, disseminating and verifying objective knowledge claims. Here I argue that this places an undue burden of proof on non-European indigenous peoples to prove that *their* perceptions and judgments must be considered when attempting to forge a consensus on issues of joint concern. The second section introduces additional traits that Kant and Hegel ascribe to the would-be objective knower. The goal here is to show that, regardless of their intent, Kant and Hegel cowrote a racialized, Eurocentric metanarrative that authorized interpreting and perceiving exploitive colonial enterprises as civilizing messianic missions of the West.[6] I conclude that until English-speaking evangelical institutions reexamine and modify the concept of objectivity permeating their speech and practice, they will continue to perpetuate the system of epistemic injustice[7] inherited from their predecessors.

KANT'S ENLIGHTENMENT HERO: THE WOULD-BE OBJECTIVE KNOWER

To understand what Kant means by "objectivity," we must see where it sits in a family of contrasting concepts. Note first that Kant maps the distinction between subjectivity and objectivity onto the contrast between particularity and universality. Subjective perceptions are perceptions referring to and grounded on an individual's experiences. Subjectively valid judgments are judgments re-

---

[4]Lyotard, *Postmodern Condition*, p. xxiii.

[5]Ibid., pp. xxiii-iv.

[6]Thomas McCarthy, *Race, Empire, and the Idea of Human Development* (Cambridge: Cambridge University Press, 2009), p. 64.

[7]See Miranda Fricker's *Epistemic Injustice: Power and the Ethics of Knowing* (New York: Oxford University Press, 2007) for my use and understanding of this concept. "Epistemic injustice" refers to the well-documented phenomena where someone's testimony or knowledge claims are discredited as unreliable or irrelevant due to prejudice on the part of the hearers. Fricker cites Harper Lee's *To Kill a Mockingbird* for a fictional account of this phenomenon, which is an all-too-real part of our past and present knowledge-gathering efforts.

ferring to and grounded on the contingent particularities of a knowing subject.[8] When I assert a subjectively valid judgment, I am asserting a judgment about my particular situation or mental state, and the judgment's truth or scope of validity extends no further than for those in that situation or state. By contrast, objectively valid perceptions and judgments purport to represent an object or state of affairs that is potentially knowable or cognizable by any human being. When asserting an objectively valid judgment, we expect it "to be valid for us and for everyone else."[9]

For an example of Kant's distinction between asserting subjectively valid and objectively valid claims, consider a disagreement that my husband and I had about where we parked the car. At the end of a basketball game we came out of the arena and did not immediately remember where we had parked the car. I said, "It is over there," and pointed to the right. Jeff said, "No, it's over there," and pointed to the left. We were with a friend and so kept on talking about other things as we walked to the car. Once we were in the car, one of us said, "See, it was where I said it was." The other immediately responded, "What are you talking about? It was where *I* said it was." We asked our friend to settle the matter, he wisely declined, and we continued to argue about who was right for the entire twenty-minute drive home. Once we got home my husband decided it was high time that I was confronted with my stubborn refusal to ever admit I am wrong. So he drew a map of the parking lot oriented by the door where we had come out. Directly north of the door was twelve o'clock, and each of us then had to state where we remembered the car being parked. I said one o'clock and he said eleven o'clock. Believe it or not, we drove the entire way back in the pouring rain to see who was right.

It is important to note that both Jeff and I ascribed objective validity to our recollected perceptions. Neither of us said, "Oh, I remember the car being there, but your recollection must differ from my own." Rather, both of us insisted that we had *correctly* perceived where the car was, expecting that the other's perceptions and assertions should match our own. According to Kant, people are not entitled to treat their perceptions and judgments as objectively

[8]Immanuel Kant, *Critique of Pure Reason*, trans. and ed. P. Guyer and A. Wood (Cambridge: Cambridge University Press, 1998), A320/B376-7.
[9]Immanuel Kant, *Prolegomena to Any Future Metaphysics*, trans. and ed. G. Hatfield (Cambridge: Cambridge University Press, 2004), 4:298.

valid without subjecting them to mutually recognized principles or proce-
dures that confer the requisite universality. For many of us, a well-recognized
procedure for settling disputes about the spatial location of an object observed
in the past is to return to that location in order to jog our respective memories.
Therefore, this is the procedure that Jeff demanded we both perform. Notice
what Jeff did not do. He did not pat me on the head and smile, as one sometimes does with a child, and say, "I am sure that the car *appeared* to you as if
it were on the right." For my part, I would prefer being dragged out in the
pouring rain at ten o'clock on a Wednesday night and thus respected as a possible purveyor of objective knowledge.

Whenever I cite this example my audience wants to know where the car was,
and I hesitate to tell them because it distracts from my point. The point is not
about who was right, but about what it means to hold someone accountable to
norms of objectivity.[10] According to North American philosopher Robert
Brandom, the "crowning achievement" of Kant and Hegel's philosophy is their
account of human beings as "normative, rational, free, self-consciously historical animals."[11] As Brandom explains, holding others accountable to normative principles for ascribing objective validity to perceptions and assertions
is tantamount to recognizing them as fellow rational beings: "Taking something to be subject to appraisals for its reasons, holding it rationally responsible
is treating it as some*one*: as one of *us* (rational beings)."[12] Miranda Fricker, in
her groundbreaking work on epistemic injustice, also argues that routinely
failing to take people's testimony seriously or failing to see them as possible
purveyors of objective knowledge is treating them as less than fully human: "To
be wronged in one's capacity as a knower is to be wronged in a capacity essential to human value."[13]

The problem is that the conditions that Kant and Hegel establish for recognizing individuals and peoples as would-be objective knowers practically guarantee that only "scientifically minded," white, male, Christian Europeans will
be treated as one of *us*. In *Critique of Pure Reason*, Kant asks what entitles us

---

[10]If my reader must know, the car was parked directly north of the entrance, at twelve o'clock on the map. We were each one "hour" off.
[11]Robert Brandom, *Reason in Philosophy: Animating Ideas* (Cambridge, MA: Harvard University Press, 2009), p. 17.
[12]Ibid. p. 3.
[13]Fricker, *Epistemic Injustice*, p. 44.

to bridge the gap between the subjectively valid and objectively valid. "How does the representation . . . go beyond itself and acquire the objective signifi-cance in addition to the subjective significance that is proper to it as a determi-nation of the state of mind?"[14]

The entire post-Kantian philosophical tradition can be read as developing, defending or challenging his answer to this question. For our purposes it is enough to know that Kant argues for a complete, nonrevisable set of concepts and principles that serve as universal and necessary conditions that any sub-jectively valid representation must satisfy in order to be granted objective sig-nificance. He also argues that the picture of nature represented in Newtonian mechanics meets these conditions.[15] Despite the fact that Hegel and subsequent philosophers sought to historicize or modify Kant's set of objectifying condi-tions, they did little to supplant his conclusion, namely, that Western, modern, mathematical physics is the gold standard of objective knowledge.

Historians of science Lorraine Daston and Peter Galison confirm that Kant's formulation of the distinction between the subjective and the objective "rever-berated with seismic intensity in every domain of nineteenth-century intel-lectual life, from science to literature."[16] Adopting this formulation and the high value placed on "the objective" was crucial to the nineteenth-century Eu-ropean construction of the scientific self. Kant's imperative to reason objec-tively thus became an imperative that everyone reason like a modern Western scientist, and this imperative reverberated throughout European culture, just as European expansionism was at its height.

Kant's Eurocentric metanarrative still operates today. Even contemporary scholars intending to demonstrate the cognitive achievements of colonized indigenous peoples invoke Western science as the measuring rod of rational, objective thought. In *Latin American Thought: Philosophical Problems and Ar-guments*, Susana Nuccetelli argues that the history of Latin American phi-losophy should be included in the curriculum of North American universities. She begins by challenging the assumption that native Latin Americans were less rational than the Europeans who killed or conquered them. But consider how she frames this challenge: "The first two chapters consider the questions

[14]Kant, *Critique of Pure Reason*, A197/B242.
[15]Michael Friedman, *Kant and the Exact Sciences* (Cambridge, MA: Harvard University Press, 1992).
[16]Lorraine Daston and Peter Galison, *Objectivity* (New York, Zone Books, 2007), p. 205.

whether the Mayans, one of the major traditional cultures of Latin America, could be said to have developed intellectual skills, such as critical thinking and a rational understanding of the natural world that is comparable to those of Western culture."[17] She then argues that Mayan astronomy is on a par with the predictive success expected from modern Western scientific theories. Nuccettelli's argumentative strategy illustrates that, for her, Kant's description of the would-be objective knower as someone subscribing to the methods and goals of modern Western science is still a widespread assumption. She employs a strategy that assumes that unless colonized peoples can show that their knowledge-gathering practices resemble those endorsed by North American and Western European institutions, their testimony can be discounted when it comes to obtaining objective knowledge about the world.[18]

Consider too that although North American evangelical universities routinely encourage undergraduate students to pursue study-abroad programs in Africa and South America, the expected learning outcome is rarely conceived as participating in a collective pursuit of knowledge. Instead, these outcomes are couched in terms of ministering to the people who live there or listening to them so as to better appreciate the perceptions and values particular to their culture. In sum, people often assume that previously colonized peoples are locked within their subjectivity in a way that previously colonizing peoples are not.

The burden placed on indigenous peoples to show that their testimony is compatible with that of Western science even extends to facts concerning the sex, race and ethnicity of their children, a burden only recently called into question. In 2009 South African runner Caster Semenya won the women's 800 meters at the World Track and Field Championship. Afterward, several competitors demanded that she undergo genetic testing determining her sex. Ariel Levy, staff writer for *The New Yorker*, reports that South Africans were "appalled by the idea of a person who thinks she is one thing suddenly being told that she is something else."[19] Leonard Chuene, president of South Africa's gov-

---

[17]Susana Nuccetelli, *Latin American Thought: Philosophical Problems and Arguments* (Boulder, CO: Westview, 2002), p. xvi.

[18]Nuccetelli is aware of the problematic assumption underlying her argumentative strategy, but employs it nonetheless (ibid., p. 50). I am indebted to the students in my Latin American philosophy course for raising this objection against Nuccetelli's argument.

[19]Ariel Levy, "Either/Or: Sports, Sex and the Case of Caster Semenya," *The New Yorker*, November 30, 2009, www.newyorker.com/reporting/2009/11/30/091130fa_fact_levy?currentPage=all.

erning agency for track and field competition, told reporters, "We are not going to allow Europeans to define and describe our children. . . . The only scientists I believe in are the parents of this child."[20] Chuene's refusal to defer to the testimony of "European scientists" was echoed by Semenya's aunt: "I know what Caster has got. . . . I've changed her nappies."[21]

The postmodern incredulity expressed by Chuene and Semenya's relatives toward Western biomedical practices is not unwarranted. Beginning with the Population Registration Act of 1950, teams of white people were tasked with classifying the races of South Africans, a classification that would determine the scope of their educational, vocational, residential and marital opportunities. Levy concludes: "*Taxonomy is an acutely sensitive subject*, and its history is probably one of the reasons that South Africans—particularly black South Africans—have rallied behind their runner with such fervor."[22] In the next section I argue that Kant and Hegel are responsible for this history of constructing gendered and racialized taxonomies, rightly provoking postmodern incredulity, not just for black South Africans but for anyone.

KANT'S MASCULINIZED, RACIALIZED ENLIGHTENMENT HERO

In the essay "What Is Enlightenment?" Kant boldly answers, "Dare to use your own understanding."[23] He argues that exercising this autonomy requires cultivating the intellectual virtues of diligence and courage: "Laziness and cowardice are the reasons why such a large proportion of men . . . gladly remain immature for life."[24] He goes on to develop another conceptual contrast related to the distinction between subjectivity and objectivity, the contrast between heteronomy and autonomy.

> If I have a book to have understanding in place of me, a spiritual advisor to have a conscience for me, a doctor to judge my diet for me, and so on, I need not make any efforts at all. I need not think, so long as I can pay. . . . Others will soon enough take the tiresome job from me. The guardians who have kindly taken upon themselves the work of supervision will soon see to it that by far the largest

---

[20]Ibid.
[21]Ibid.
[22]Ibid.
[23]Kant, *Political Writings*, trans. and ed. H. S. Reiss (Cambridge: Cambridge University Press, 1991), p. 54.
[24]Ibid.

part of mankind (including the entire fair sex) should consider the step forward
to maturity not only as difficult but also as highly dangerous.[25]

For Kant, acting and reasoning autonomously is acting and reasoning according to laws or norms that we would legislate as binding on ourselves and
other rational beings. Acknowledging the capacity of human beings to reason
autonomously when formulating scientific, political and ethical propositions
is equivalent to expressing the dignity that is their due.

> Every rational being, as an end in itself, must be able to regard himself as also
> giving universal laws with respect to any whatsoever to which he may be subject;
> for it is just this fitness of his maxims for giving universal law that marks him out
> as an end in itself; it follows that this dignity (prerogative) he has over all merely
> natural beings brings with it that he must always take the point of view of himself,
> and likewise every other rational being.[26]

The autonomous reasoner respects the autonomy of all natural rational
beings, a respect manifested in bringing as many perspectives to bear as possible on matters presumed to have objective significance. By contrast, the heteronomous reasoner forsakes this responsibility and operates as if she were a
machine that must be programmed by the thinking of another.

Although Kant acknowledges that the sociopolitical structures of his day make
it especially difficult for women ("the entire fair sex") to incur the risks and responsibilities of thinking and speaking for themselves, he never engages in a
sustained critique of those structures. Indeed, he and Hegel subscribe to what we
now call a complementarian account of male and female virtues that reinforces
these structures.[27] Generally speaking, complementarian accounts hold that God
or nature intend for men and women to fulfill different, complementary social
roles. Typically women are assigned the roles of childbearers, child-rearers, care-
givers, homemakers or managers. Men are assigned the roles of providers, pro-
tectors, decision makers and leaders for the family or society as a whole. Since
males and females are designed for different functions, they ought to develop
different, complementary virtues enabling them to best perform these functions.

---

[25]Ibid.

[26]Immanuel Kant, *Groundwork of the Metaphysics of Morals*, trans. and ed. Mary Gregor (Cambridge:
Cambridge University Press, 1997), 4:438.

[27]Lawrence Blum, "Kant's and Hegel's Moral Rationalism: A Feminist Perspective," *Canadian Journal
of Philosophy* 12, no. 2 (1982): 287.

Even though Kant and Hegel repeatedly insist that human nature resides in a free, rationally motivated will that cannot be adequately viewed through the empirical lens of biology and cultural anthropology, their own writings often undercut this thesis. In his anthropological works Kant writes as if men and women have differing natures or at least differing natural aptitudes.

> Since nature also wanted to instill the finer feelings that belong to culture— namely those of sociability and propriety—it made [the female] sex man's ruler through her modesty and eloquence in speech and expression. It made her clever while still young in claiming gentle and courteous treatment by a male, so that he would find himself imperceptibly fettered by a child through his own magnanimity, and led by her, if not to morality itself, to that which is its cloak, moral decency.[28]

Kant adds, "Feminine virtue or lack of virtue is different from masculine virtue or lack of virtue, not only in kind but also as regards incentive—She should be patient; he must be tolerant. She is sensitive; he is sentimental. . . . The man has his *own* taste, the woman makes herself the object of *everyone's* taste."[29] Notice that the virtues and moral feelings that Kant identifies as characteristically feminine are impediments to exercising the intellectual virtues of courage and fortitude, which he associates with rational maturity. How is this oft-repeated and specific injunction to *women* that they ought to exercise modesty and gentility in speech supposed to encourage them to participate in a rigorous public critique of the reasoning expressed by culturally authorized texts and "kindly guardians"?

Consider too the fact that Kant calls women to cultivate complaisance. "Complaisance" is Kant's term for the inclination to conform ourselves to the dispositions of significant others and to acquiescence to their demands.[30] He denies that complaisance is a "true virtue," given that it can hinder us from taking a more universal perspective and, if left unchecked, easily gives rise to vice.

> For without even considering that this complaisance towards those with whom we associate is often an injustice to those who find themselves outside of this little circle, such a man, if one takes this impulse alone, can have all sorts of vices, not

---

[28]Immanuel Kant, *Anthropology, History and Education*, ed. G. Zöller and R. Louden, trans. M. Gregor et al. (Cambridge: Cambridge University Press, 2011), AK 7:306.
[29]Ibid., AK 7:307-8.
[30]Ibid., AK 2:216.

because of immediate inclination but because he gladly lives to please. From affectionate complaisance he will be a liar, an idler, a drunkard, etc.[31]

Still, Kant maintains that complaisance is a moral feeling that nature has especially accorded to women, and he encourages wives, unlike men, to develop it, since this "beautiful" and "charming" feeling can be checked by the "sublime" and truly virtuous character of their husbands.[32]

Kant and Hegel go on to coauthor a story about the progressive development of humanity wherein these same feminine inclinations and feelings are identified as inherited racial characteristics as well. The result is a metanarrative that promises progressively equitable and emancipatory sociopolitical institutions while presuming and perpetuating a racialized taxonomy. Accordingly, women and non-Anglo-Europeans are encouraged or expected to function as heteronomous, particularistic reasoners capable of silently influencing those within their private sphere. Thus Kant and Hegel assume both that their heroes of knowledge will be Anglo-European males and that forging the consensus of rational minds, which is a prerequisite for working toward cosmopolitan peace and justice, will not require bringing other perspectives to bear on these matters.

Consider the last work published in Kant's lifetime: "A Renewed Attempt to Answer the Question: Is the Human Race Continually Improving?" Here he argues that a sufficiently rational, albeit conjectural, yes depends on writing a history of progressively civilized societies appearing on the world stage. The goal is to detect the working of divine providence despite and even through the violence, selfishness and folly marking much of human history. He insists that this history must aim at universality, taking as its subject matter all peoples and their recorded histories, but only if these histories were authenticated in the writings of the ancient Greeks. That is, Kant insists that the beginning of a providentially guided history of humanity becoming more civilized starts in ancient Greece with "the first page of Thucydides."[33] Miranda Fricker analyzes two types of epistemic injustice: (1) testimonial injustice, which occurs between individual speakers and their hearers; and (2) hermeneutical injustice, which is a function of cultural inheritance. In the second case, an individual cannot

---

[31]Ibid., AK 2:217.
[32]Ibid., AK 2:218.
[33]Kant, *Political Writings*, p. 52.

make her experiences understandable to others or even herself because the metanarrative supplying the culture's interpretive resources is insufficient to accommodate those experiences. Given Fricker's analysis, it should be obvious that Kant's proposal, whether he realized it or not, proposes to rob the cultures of ancient peoples of any interpretive resources used to make sense of their experience that are unauthorized by late eighteenth-century European readings of the ancient Greeks.

Kant may have proposed writing such a history, but Hegel infamously completed it. During this same period, Kant and Hegel were formulating the modern conception of race, the idea that "racial" characteristics are biologically inherited and permanent.[34] Their metanarrative of a progressively developing human race, where each stage is supposedly marked by observable, inherited racial characteristics, allowed whites of European descent to invoke an allegedly scientific natural history of the human race to justify the colonizing and "civilizing" enterprises imposed on the indigenous peoples of Africa, the Americas, Australia and portions of Asia throughout the nineteenth century.[35] Based on reports from European explorers, traders and missionaries concerning the bodily, behavioral and cultural characteristics of non-European peoples, Kant proposed four races: white, "Negro," "Hun" and "Hindu." Hegel split Kant's white classification into two: European Christian whites and Western Asiatic Mohammedan whites. Kant warned against the "speculative" nature of his own proposed racial taxonomy.[36] Nevertheless, he applied it for the purposes of collecting empirical data on the natural mechanisms that drive or impede the progressive development of humanity's rational capacities.

Kant maintained that the native inhabitants of extremely cold and extremely hot regions are naturally disposed to exhibit and biologically transmit laziness and cowardice. Recall that laziness and cowardice are intellectual vices keeping us from exercising the traits of the would-be autonomous objective knower. The

---

[34]Robert Bernasconi and Tommy Lee Lott, introduction to *The Idea of Race*, ed. Robert Bernasconi and Tommy Lee Lott (Indianapolis: Hackett, 2000), pp. viii-ix.

[35]In fairness, it should be noted that Kant explicitly denounced the African slave trade and colonial expansionism as immoral. Hegel also argues that racial differences provide no justification for denying the "implicitly rational" nature of differing human races. He concludes that denying non-European indigenous peoples their freedom and dominating them like animals is groundless (G. W. F. Hegel, "Anthropology," in *The Encyclopedia of the Philosophical Sciences*, in Bernasconi and Lott, *The Idea of Race*, p. 39).

[36]Immanuel Kant, "Of the Different Human Races," in Bernasconi and Lott, *The Idea of Race*, p. 22.

"natural disposition of the native American," claimed Kant, "reveals a half-diminished life force."[37] He adds that they are "too weak to work in the fields" and "lack ability and durability."[38] Likewise, he argued that climatic factors and the abundance of natural resources make the "Negro . . . lazy, indolent and dawdling."[39]

Hegel went further in incorporating this taxonomy into the Eurocentric metanarrative of progressively developing human reason.

> Negroes are to be regarded as a race of children who remain immersed in their state of uninterested *naïveté*. They are sold, and let themselves be sold, without any reflection on the rights or wrongs of the matter. . . .
>
> In the Asiatic race . . . mind is already beginning to awake, to separate itself from the life of Nature. . . .
>
> It is in the Caucasian race that mind first attains to absolute unity with itself. Here for the first time mind . . . achieves *self*-determination, *self*-development, and in so doing creates world history. . . .
>
> [Christian] Europeans, [in contrast to "Caucasian" Mohammedans], have for their principle and character the concrete universal, self-determining Thought. . . . In this religious conception the opposition of universal and particular, of Thought and Being, is present in its most developed form and yet has been brought back to unity.[40]

"Negroes," like unmarried, unchecked European women, exhibit a childlike complaisance, making them entirely too insensitive to matters of universal rights and wrongs. The moral of this story, for both Kant and Hegel, is that the discursive practices dominated by "Caucasian" European Christian thought constitute the most fully developed mode of objective reasoning.

Conclusion

Thomas McCarthy recaps Kant and Hegel's civilizing, emancipatory mission as follows: "In law and politics, art and science, European developments will set the pace and provide models for the rest of the world. Ethico-religious community, like legal-political union, will arrive not through some form of dialectical or dialogical mediation of differences, but through the global diffusion of

---

[37]Kant, "The Classification of Races," in Bernasconi and Lott, *The Idea of Race*, pp. 16-17.
[38]Ibid., p. 17n3.
[39]Ibid., p. 17.
[40]Hegel, "Anthropology," pp. 40-43.

Western ways."[41] This is why our postmodern and postcolonial brothers and sisters rightly urge us to cast a skeptical eye at the Enlightenment hero of knowledge with his message and methodologies of universal peace. We need to see how this metanarrative served to legitimate masculinized, racialized practices of European colonization.

So, what have we—Western evangelicals—done wrong? As I have shown, Kant and Hegel based their racialized taxonomies on the reports from European missionaries. Insofar as we are part of Christian denominations and traditions tracing back to these missional efforts, we bear the sins of our forefathers and foremothers. Moreover, as the other essays in this volume show, our institutions often perpetuate an assimilationist model of Western cultural hegemony.

Given the role that Enlightenment notions like objectivity played in establishing this hegemony, some postcolonial theorists have called for jettisoning these notions entirely.[42] I agree that we cannot accept Kant's original account of objectivity wholesale and must denounce its role in legitimizing Kant and Hegel's sexist, Eurocentric metanarrative of a progressively developing human race. Still, there are reasons why a would-be postcolonial evangelical philosopher like myself might want to retain some of what Kant says about holding people accountable to norms of objectivity. For one, it allows me to rebut a common objection to postcolonial critiques of objectivity.

A common objection to critiques of objectivity like the one that I have just written is that they are self-defeating. The objector argues as follows: If the postcolonial philosopher maintains that objective knowledge claims are discursive power plays on the part of an individual or a hegemonic culture, the same must be said of her own claims. Therefore, concludes the objector, the postcolonial philosopher is in no position to criticize the discursive power plays of others.

My rebuttal is as follows. Anyone alleging to assert an objectively valid claim should be held accountable to genuinely shared norms of objectivity, and Kant

---

[41]McCarthy, *Race, Empire, and the Idea of Human Development*, p. 57.

[42]For example, R. S. Sugirtharajah envisions a postcolonial mode of biblical interpretation built on "the conviction that modernist values . . . like objectivity and neutrality, are expressions of political, religious, and scholarly power." See his "Biblical Studies in India: From Imperialistic Scholarship to Postcolonial Interpretation," in *Teaching the Bible: The Discourses and Politics of Biblical Pedagogy*, ed. Fernando F. Segovia and Mary Ann Tolbert (1998; repr., Eugene, OR: Wipf & Stock, 2004), p. 293.

and Hegel's metanarrative violates Kant's own proposed norms. In the *Critique of Pure Reason*, Kant proposes what I call the public scrutiny test: "The touchstone of whether taking something to be true is conviction is therefore, externally, the possibility of communicating it and finding it to be valid for the reason of every human being to take it to be true."[43] The public scrutiny test is an "experiment" to see "if the grounds that are valid for us have the same effect on the reason of others."[44] This test does not guarantee that we will ever *possess* objective knowledge, but reminds us that *pursuing* objectivity is an inherently social practice. Authentically engaging in that practice implies ensuring that the plurality of human voices and perspectives are seated at the dialogical table. Clearly, Kant and Hegel never checked to see if their reasoning *about* women and non-European peoples was considered valid *by* those people. They thus failed to subject their alleged objectively valid claims to the public scrutiny test.

So why might a would-be postcolonial evangelical philosopher want to retain a modified, neo-Kantian notion of objectivity, despite its limitations? It enables her to show that Kant and Hegel's metanarrative of the would-be objective knower is internally flawed. It can also motivate her to expose and redress the epistemic injustices perpetuated by metanarratives of whatever age or kind.

And what can we twenty-first-century evangelicals make right? As would-be followers of Christ, the answer seems obvious—we need to repent, ask for forgiveness and work toward reconciliation, justice and peace. For that repentance and forgiveness to be authentic, we must first listen and learn from those whom we have infantilized and refused to seat at the table for mediating our differences. It is my prayerful hope that this volume is a step in that direction.

---

[43]Kant, *Critique of Pure Reason*, A820/B848.
[44]Ibid., A821/B849.

6

AMERICAN EXCEPTIONALISM AS
PROPHETIC NATIONALISM

Kurt Anders Richardson

.... ⚹ ....

*In the seventeenth and eighteenth centuries, Americans defined their
mission in the New World in biblical terms. They were a "chosen people,"
on an "errand in the wilderness," creating "the new Israel" or the
"new Jerusalem" in what was clearly "the promised land."*

SAMUEL P. HUNTINGTON[1]

The attribution of religious value to the American experience has led to
what is called civil religion and has become the source of a peculiar form
of nationalism—a form that we now often hear in public discourse referred to
as "American exceptionalism."[2] There are numerous "exceptionalisms" in the
world, and for many today the American version has become a shibboleth to
determine who is a "true American." American exceptionalism is a doctrine
based on Christian sources in biblical prophecy, ecclesiology, messianism and
"Christendom."[3] This ideology is now called "exceptionalism."[4] In this ideology,
redeemer nation and visionary republic mark America as superior above all

[1]Samuel P. Huntington, *Who Are We? The Challenges to America's National Identity* (New York: Simon & Schuster, 2004), p. 64.
[2]See Ronald Weed and John von Heyking, eds., *Rational Theology: Thomas Jefferson and the Foundation of America's Civil Religion* (Washington, DC: Catholic University of America Press, 2010).
[3]"Constantinianism," the notion that political and cultural Christian imperialism is rooted in Emperor Constantine's selection of Christianity as the official religion of Rome, is closely related to exceptionalism.
[4]Harold Bloom, *The American Religion: The Emergence of the Post-Christian Nation* (New York: Simon & Schuster, 1992); cf. Stephen Mennell, *The American Civilizing Process* (Malden, MA: Polity, 2007).

others. These Christian and biblical notions are then translated into civil religious discourse in order to create an ideology of an American "national character." As such, American exceptionalism is not necessarily a partisan doctrine, although political partisanship has indeed led to a radical veering to the political right in its current incarnation. Exceptionalist ideology in the United States has nevertheless been embraced by both parties and can be seen in notions of Manifest Destiny and the myth of a reluctant empire covenantally bound to spread the rule of law and democracy around the globe. Indeed, this was one of the original implications of the ways that congregational polity and democratic polity became correlated.[5]

In the United States, constitutional rights originated with a national vision of people who, at the same time, advanced slavery—based as much on the tenth commandment as anything—and colonization—based as much on the Great Commission (Mt 28:18-20) as anything. The signers of the American Constitution constituted a combination of traditional Christian groups, a variety of Christian dissenters and deists. In signing for their soon-to-be states, slaveholding and colonizing nationalisms merged legally, and to them naturally, with the rights and freedoms proclaimed by the Constitution. The New Testament view of the human—its anthropology—gave a portrayal of creaturely equality before the Creator. While there was no biblical warrant for Christian nationalism, over a millennium of political theology correlated emperors and their empires with messianic prophecy and apocalypse. This political experience shaped the founders' readings of Scripture.

To some this is evidence of a culture in no way exemplary of an exceptional moral force in the world. Although it is said that we live in a post-Constantinian age, we still hear rhetoric of Christian empire as perceived to be clashing with Islamic empire and other empires, whether real or imagined. This indicates how deeply the Constantinian imperial story has become embedded in US American Christianity. As an example, the US American tragedy of 9/11 was handled in conspicuously religious ways. The religious language and symbolism used, according to Mark Landau, functioned to allow traumatized US Americans to "assume mastery over nature and tragedy and uphold the cultural

---

[5]There is a connection from the beginning between constitutional democracy and theocracy; see Ran Hirschl, *Constitutional Theocracy* (Cambridge, MA: Harvard University Press, 2010).

meaning system that imbues individual lives with transcendent meaning, order, and permanence."[6] Religion and religious forms of meaning-making very quickly rose to the surface as a primary means by which US Americans were apprehending historical events. Monica Toft observes, "In that and subsequent events, the world has come to a stunned awareness that religion has massively extended itself in new ways."[7] Beginning largely in the 1980s there was a concerted move by many Anglo-American churches in the United States to embrace religious nationalism by intensifying identification with party politics, public policy battles, militarism and advocacy of serious curtailments of personal liberty.[8] In recent decades this redrawn set of contours of US American religious nationalism has developed into an overarching ideology. The ideology of exceptionalism is the heart of this nationalism and is advanced by the likes of popular current political voices such as Sarah Palin, who describes the ideology as essential to the American soul.[9] Djelal Kadir notes that in this ideological doctrine of exceptionalism, the nation adopts a perception of itself in accordance with "America's self-perceived godliness and infallibility,"[10] and it sees itself as possessing true virtue, by which it is morally bound to exert its influence on a global scale. Whether reacting to the religious extremism of 9/11 or tolerating new forms of racism and colonialism, exceptionalism adopts and ideologically undergirds nationalism from the perspective of a doctrine of biblical providence and divine inevitability.

With a prophetic form of exceptionalism abounding, Christian nationalism in America is free to do its own form of "civic theology," a phrase Augustine used to describe the public theology of Roman religion in *The City of God*. This is why in recent scholarship it also has been called "providentialist

---

[6]Mark J. Landau et al., "Deliver Us from Evil: The Effects of Mortality Salience and Reminders of 9/11 on Support for President George W. Bush," *Personality and Social Psychology Bulletin* 30, no. 9 (2004): 1136-50, cited in Robert Pirro, "Tragedy, Theodicy and 9/11: Rhetorical Responses to Suffering and Their Public Significance," *Thesis Eleven* 98 (2009): 22.

[7]See Monica Duffy Toft et al., *God's Century: Resurgent Religion and Global Politics* (New York: W. W. Norton, 2011), p. 19.

[8]See Robert Wuthnow, *Boundless Faith: The Global Outreach of American Churches* (Berkeley: University of California Press, 2009); see also Robert Wuthnow et al., "Religion and Altruistic U.S. Foreign Policy Goals: Evidence from a National Survey of Church Members," *Journal for the Scientific Student of Religion* 47 (2008): 204.

[9]Sarah Palin, *America by Heart: Reflections on Family, Faith, and Flag* (New York: Harper, 2010), p. 43; note her entire chapter devoted to American exceptionalism.

[10]Djelal Kadir, "America: Problematizing Global Knowledge: Genealogies of the Global/Globalizations," *Theory, Culture & Society* 23, nos. 2-3 (2006): 417-19.

exceptionalism."[11] A special, "exceptional" account of divine providence is superimposed on the nation so that its history is an extension of the prophetic history or metanarrative of the Bible as relayed by the ideological center. What the holy nation did when it acknowledged God or was delivered by God from its enemies and what it endures when divine disfavor chastises and punishes it are seen to be concordant with an elect nation, now reimagined in Christian terms. We can trace the beginnings of providentialist exceptionalism in US American historical literature from the eschatological, "new world" writings of Columbus, to the Puritan theocratic "New Canaan" in the vision of John Winthrop, through the nineteenth-century sense of divine mandate in Manifest Destiny, to the presidency of George W. Bush, who accorded himself the status of being divinely installed and guided.[12] Of course, while President Barack Obama's style is very different from Bush's, he did not surrender the ground that had been gained by utilizing these claims. If anything he has expanded them. In this way historical and political events evoke the theological terms of prophecy and fulfillment in which they were cast long ago by the Puritan John Winthrop and other religious advocates, thus embedding prophetic themes in the national discourse.

Belief in providence is basic to any version of orthodox Christianity: the church and its individual members share in affirming an overarching divine plan of salvation for the world, both eschatologically and in the immediate sense of its benefits in lived experience. But any nationalist exceptionalism goes a step further when it assigns biblical providence to itself as a national entity. This, ipso facto, is false prophecy. It must be said that exceptionalist tendencies are the stuff of many nationalist ideologies and theologies, from France to early twentieth-century Japan. I focus here, however, on the particularly US form of exceptionalism,[13] which concentrates and appropriates the notions of providence and election, including in its laws, in order to create a national prophetic tradition that transcends historic time and space. In this way it assigns to itself

[11]Ibid., p. 418.
[12]President Bush declared on a July 16, 2004, visit to an Amish community in Smoketown, PA, "God speaks through me." See Al Kamen, "George W. Bush and the G-Word," *The Washington Post*, October 14, 2005.
[13]See Seymour Martin Lipset, *American Exceptionalism: A Double-Edged Sword* (New York: W. W. Norton, 1996); cf., in response, Godfrey Hodgson, *The Myth of American Exceptionalism* (New Haven, CT: Yale University Press, 2009).

a kind of divine status that delegitimizes debate and self-critique.

For an example of this uniquely US form of exceptionalism, we have such American classical texts in mind as the Puritan John Winthrop's, particularly his famous sermon creating the new English tribe, its divine origin, blessing, purpose and warning.

> Now the onely way to avoyde this shipwracke, and to provide for our posterity, is to followe the counsell of Micah, to doe justly, to love mercy, to walk humbly with our God. For this end, wee must be knitt together, in this worke, as one man. . . . Wee shall finde that the God of Israell is among us, when ten of us shall be able to resist a thousand of our enemies; when hee shall make us a prayse and glory that men shall say of succeeding plantations, "the Lord make it likely that of New England." For wee must consider that wee shall be as a citty upon a hill. The eies of all people are uppon us.[14]

This vision continues to find reaffirmation and reframing into the present, as is widespread in the many Tea Party movements.[15] This text, often cited as an American standard, is not mere civil religion. It addresses the whole citizenry of the nation in a specifically Christian way that cannot be embraced by nonconformist Christians, members of other religions or nonreligious people. Instead, it is a translation of blessing and cursing narratives in Deuteronomy, specifically addressed now to the Puritan community and thus appropriated for the American context.

Seymour Martin Lipset, one of the definers of exceptionalism as an ideology, points to the claim of leadership and identity in the full range of social spheres: religion, politics and race. Lipset argues that many US Americans still see themselves as "the new nation," which liberated itself from empire. He writes that, for many US Americans, "there can be little question that the hand of providence has been on a nation which finds a Washington, a Lincoln, or a Roosevelt when it needs him."[16] But Lipset employs a scientific pretention that "exceptionalism" is just a neutral term which helps to signify the unique features of America; he makes no value judgment about it as an ideology.

---

[14]John Winthrop, *A Modell of Christian Charity*, Collections of the Massachusetts Historical Society, 3rd series (1630; repr., Boston: Massachusetts Historical Society, 1838), 7:31-48, here p. 33, http://history.hanover.edu/texts/winthmod.html.

[15]See Geoffrey M. Kabaservice, *Rule and Ruin: The Downfall of Moderation and the Destruction of the Republican Party, from Eisenhower to the Tea Party* (New York: Oxford University Press, 2012).

[16]Lipset, *American Exceptionalism*, p. 14.

The United State's most notable Reformed theologian, Jonathan Edwards, in many ways extended Winthrop's particularistic Christian interpretation of America by interpreting the religious revival he was instrumental in bringing about from 1740–1743 as reinforcing US American exceptionalism.[17] Acutely sensitive to free will and deist interpretations of the First Great Awakening, Edwards fashioned his own redemptive history of the world in which the events took place as a result of the special providence of God according to "his absolute sovereignty."[18] God's work in Edwards's United States was an illustration of "the great work and successive dispensations of the infinitely wise God in time"[19]—the result of special providence in history. Like Calvin's notion of creation as the theater of divine revelation, for Edwards the emerging historical consciousness of early modernity was no less divine as the providential sphere of all events in God's "order of time,"[20] the high point of which, for him, was the awakening. As through all history, the awakening of his days was evidence of the "rise and continued progress of the dispensation of grace towards fallen mankind."[21] As the Second Great Awakening on the American frontier erupted between 1800–1830, Edwards's writings became the guiding interpretation of events and the nation's own history. Anticipating a later theology of history that would measure all religious phenomena according to a hierarchy of truth, with Christianity at its summit, Edwards supplied an American framework.[22] What this meant was that whatever happened in terms of religious diversity in the nation, the greatest and most hallowed events must always be those that advanced its Christian, providential destiny and not those of any other religious tradition.

American scholars such as Myra Jehlen[23] and David Noble[24] have posed interpretations of American nationalism in which this notion of divine election is translated into a vision of a land of unlimited possibilities at the end of time.

---

[17] Avihu Zakai, *Jonathan Edwards's Philosophy of History: The Reenchantment of the World in the Age of Enlightenment* (Princeton, NJ: Princeton University Press, 2003), pp. 276-79.

[18] Quoted in ibid., p. 45.

[19] Quoted in ibid., p. 47.

[20] Quoted in ibid., p. 59.

[21] Quoted in ibid., p. 89.

[22] For a discussion of the history and ideology of this metanarrative of historical progress, see the chapter in this volume by Teri Merrick.

[23] Myra Jehlen, *American Incarnation* (Cambridge, MA: Harvard University Press, 1986); cf. Thomas Bender, *A Nation Among Nations: America's Place in World History* (New York: Hill & Wang, 2006).

[24] David Noble, *Death of a Nation* (Minneapolis: University of Minnesota Press, 2002).

At this point it is crucial to remind ourselves that the framers of the Constitution strongly and purposefully resisted any notion of creating a divinely inspired or religiously sanctioned document. This most secular of early modern legal foundations—the Constitution itself—is a testament to an aversion to false prophecy among our founders, particularly when it came to the realm of the political. This observation of what they did *not* invest in the American Constitution, given the religious rhetoric of the time, in itself constitutes a sharp critique of exceptionalism. It also reminds us that exceptionalism itself is a mythic metanarrative that causes us to forget history and to overlay it with only the events that reinforce the myth.

Max Weber's assessment of this myth is quite complex, and yet there is a ringing truth to it that is essential. He also regarded US political theology to be determined by the Puritanism of its original establishment, yet he argued that this cultural production was not positive but was characterized by unbrotherly and nonsalvific discourse. Weber wrote,

> As a religion of virtuosos, Puritanism renounced the universalism of love, and rationally routinized all work in this world into serving God's will and testing one's state of grace. . . . In this respect, Puritanism accepted the routinization of the economic cosmos, which, with the whole world, it devalued as creatural and depraved. This state of affairs appeared as God-willed, and as material given for fulfilling one's duty. In the last resort, this meant in principle to renounce salvation as a goal attainable by . . . everybody. It meant to renounce salvation in favor of the groundless and always only particularized grace. In truth, this standpoint of unbrotherliness was no longer a genuine "religion of salvation."[25]

Thus while indeed appropriating some biblical principles, exceptionalism did so at the expense of others, whether through the ways it legitimated slavery laws or through its colonization projects—projects carried out by US Americans who themselves were at one time colonized by others. What is crucial to observe here is that the soteriology of the Bible was subsumed under the false ideology of prophetic exceptionalism.

In other forms this exceptionalism was invoked to call for radical change.

---

[25]Max Weber, "Religious Rejections of the World and Their Directions," in *From Max Weber: Essays in Sociology*, ed. Hans Gerth and C. Wright Mills (New York: Oxford University Press, 1946), pp. 323-59.

When Lincoln formulated his Second Inaugural Address, he appealed to providence to explain the Civil War as the antidote to American slavery.

> If we shall suppose that American Slavery is one of those offenses which, in the providence of God, must needs come, but which, having continued through His appointed time, He now wills to remove, and that He gives to both North and South, this terrible war, as the woe due to those by whom the offense came, shall we discern therein any departure from those divine attributes which the believers in a Living God always ascribe to Him? Fondly do we hope—fervently do we pray—that this mighty scourge of war may speedily pass away. Yet, if God will that it continue, until all the wealth piled by the bond-man's two hundred and fifty years of unrequited toil shall be sunk, and until every drop of blood drawn with the lash, shall be paid by another drawn with the sword, as was said three thousand years ago, so still it must be said, "the judgments of the Lord are true and righteous altogether."[26]

Ready with scriptural allusions, Lincoln, who never joined a church, nevertheless had come to regard religious sources highly as the only way to interpret the world around him. The need for all the resources of humanity drove him into his own religiousness—a religiousness that borrowed from the discourse of exceptionalism.

This "double effect" of exceptionalism is telling, both for evil and for good, as Robert Bellah remarks about "public theology."

> Every movement to make America more fully realize its professed values has grown out of some form of public theology [a.k.a. civil religion], from the abolitionists to the social gospel and the early socialist party to the civil rights movement under Martin Luther King and the farm workers' movement under Caesar [sic] Chavez. But so has every expansionist war and every form of oppression of racial minorities and immigrant groups.[27]

One is a little hesitant of course regarding the entire legacy of civil religion, from Augustine on, and the public theology movement, although it tends to shy away from political theology, is ripe for revival. Religion is the tran-

---

[26]Abraham Lincoln, "With Malice Toward None (Second Inaugural Address)," in *The Political Thought of Abraham Lincoln*, ed. Richard Current (Indianapolis: Bobbs-Merrill, 1967), p. 316.

[27]Robert Bellah, "Afterword: Religion and the Legitimation of the American Republic," in *The Broken Covenant: American Civil Religion in Time of Trial*, 2nd ed. (Chicago: University of Chicago Press, 1992), p. 180.

scendent element that can go either way, depending on how it is instrumentalized. This means that neither conservative nor liberal values can be ends in themselves. Thus a critique of the theology of exceptionalism does not imply an unquestioning affirmation of liberalism. Liberalism itself is not the answer. James Morone makes this case when he states, "Liberalism protects our people from dangerous impulses, from discrimination and hate crimes. But it does not rouse people to win new rights, wider justice, and greater social equity. It does not dream big dreams about a better society."[28] No version of exceptionalism—whether supporting conservative *or* liberal political action—qualifies as true prophecy. Just as politics co-opts religious symbols because of their incomparable potency, liberal and conservative are twin opposites that require one another.

Although there is nothing particularly wrong with claiming a general providential advantage for Christian mission and service, it becomes apparent that a system moves into a new ethical realm when it claims for itself the kind of divine right, authorization or election that comes with special prophecy for a nation. The term *exceptionalism* signifies a divinely appointed existence for the nation. The idea of exceptionalism provides a guiding rationale and source of justification for the nation's grandest domestic and foreign policies. But since many other "Christian" nations have claimed the same status, the American iteration is just one of many examples of the so-called exceptionalist fallacy.[29] As the apostle states, there is "no distinction" among human beings before God since God is gracious toward all (Rom 10:12)—to think otherwise is fallacious, all the more of nations. Once a nation claims for itself a divinely ordained "exceptionalism" that arrogates to itself the duty to act in the sociopolitical realm, it implies the belief that there is an office or charisma that is above the law, exempt from natural justice or excepted from the demands of human obligation under certain self-defined circumstances.

Perhaps the best way to categorize exceptionalism is as a "para-ideology."[30]

---

[28]James Morone, *Hellfire Nation: The Politics of Sin in American History* (New Haven, CT: Yale University Press, 2002), 492.

[29]See Julian Go, *Patterns of Empire: The British and American Empires, 1688 to the Present* (Cambridge: Cambridge University Press, 2011); Ali Parchami, *Hegemonic Peace and Empire: The Pax Romana, Britannica and Americana* (New York: Routledge, 2009).

[30]"Ideologies" function to provide political and moral norms by which collective decision making, such as voting, can be carried out. A "para-ideology" trades on the same form of communication but without providing political and moral reasoning and argument.

Exceptionalism fits this category because it does not have the typical charac-teristics of a coherent ideological tradition. According to this ideology, what the United States has been since its founding and ever shall be is, in theological terms, a work of providence. There are of course many dimensions to what can be called "national" or "international" greatness and the ambitions and oppor-tunities that go with it, but there are also incalculable costs. While public dis-course has focused on the opportunities, it behooves US Americans also to consider the costs.

The costs are high. For one, once it has constructed the ideology of America as a redeemer nation, the United States then obligates itself to act on that claim.[31] Second, like other colonial powers, the United States employed the ideology of exceptionalism in a way that was destructive to the aboriginal other and its growing slave and immigrant populations. In this way, the United State's oppressive and exclusionary usage of exceptionalist language, itself drawn from the Bible of Jews and Christians, also undermined other, more central man-dates of the Judeo-Christian traditions from which it drew those symbols. As such, American exceptionalism, by violating many central biblical mandates, subjects itself to a delegitimizing theological critique as false prophecy.

Postcolonial theology provides here a helpful resource for conducting this critique of the ways that exceptionalism can be a form of theologically false prophecy. Paul Johnson states,

> The Civil War, like the Revolution, was the political and military expression of a religious event, the product of the second Great Awakening, just as the Revo-lution was the product of the first. Lincoln, like Washington, saw the Deity as the final arbiter of public policy, but in addition he articulated what I would call the most characteristic element in American political philosophy—the belief that the providential plan and the workings of democracy are organically linked.[32]

This connection between spiritual awakening and warfare is particularly powerful. It justifies armed conflict and binds up that justification for conflict with the justification of individual sinners. In this way religious revival en-genders national "salvation" by military means. "Salvation," then, a distinctly theological term, becomes indecipherable from national political interests—

---

[31]Ernest Lee Tuveson, *Redeemer Nation: The Idea of America's Millennial Role* (Chicago: University of Chicago Press, 1968).
[32]Paul Johnson, *Unsecular America* (New York: Center on Religion & Society, 1986), p. 103.

interests that in many cases require morally or theologically repugnant actions in order to maintain them.

We can see this demonstrated in film, one of the ways that American exceptionalism is perpetuated in contemporary society, which often takes the form of a secularized version of Judeo-Christian redemption models. The use of these salvific, redemption models, in turn, justifies the inevitable and necessarily radical violence often employed in these films. Violence is necessary to eliminate evil. This manifestation of exceptionalism also heightens the distinction between the "good" characters, who, because of their divine mandate, are justified in violating laws of jurisprudence in order to commit often egregious violence, against the "bad" characters, who represent a threat to the salvation and redemption of the "good."[33] On this development of such sharp ideological contrasts, Paul Johnson writes, "What we are seeing now is a fourth Great Awakening, and it too is proving divisive in some ways. In no period has American exceptionalism been more marked, have American religious patterns diverged more sharply from those of the West as a whole, than in the twentieth century."[34]

Are there US American antidotes to these new forms of exceptionalism? Notably the work of Mark Noll in historical theology provides us with clues that the ideology has been opposed in this country many times, often much earlier than we might have thought. Noll especially focuses on Abraham Lincoln, pointing to Lincoln's speech "Meditation on the Divine Will" (September 1862), during which Lincoln uniquely declared, "In the present civil war it is quite possible that God's purpose is something different from the purpose of either party."[35] Here Lincoln shows us that he had more insight as an unaffiliated religious person than did the theologians of the time. Noll declares that Lincoln embraced the theologians who emphasized God's "mysterious sovereignty"—theologians such as Augustine, Luther, Calvin, Pascal—over against those who claimed to understand divine sovereignty. For Lincoln the hiddenness of God's will on the human plane made fully embracing exception-

---

[33]Richard Slotkin, *Regeneration Through Violence: The Mythology of the American Frontier, 1600–1860* (Middletown, CT: Wesleyan University Press, 1973), pp. 14-24.

[34]Paul Johnson, "An Almost-Chosen People," *First Things* 164 (June/July 2007): 21.

[35]Abraham Lincoln, "Meditation on the Divine Will," in *The Collected Works of Abraham Lincoln*, ed. Roy Basler (New Brunswick, NJ: Rutgers University Press, 1953), 5:404, quoted in Mark A. Noll, *America's God: From Jonathan Edwards to Abraham Lincoln* (New York: Oxford University Press, 2002), p. 431.

alism impossible. Noll also highlights Emily Dickenson, whose solitary faith and "heart religion" (piety over intellect), private reading of Scripture, and intuitive insights about political events was far more "adequate" to reality. Noll also declares that, while he is an evangelical believer, as a scholar he has sought to have "as close to no opinion about the nature and destiny of the United States as it is possible to have."[36]

Although colonialism was not only an Anglo-American phenomenon, new centers of power—caused by population changes and the massive distribution of advanced weaponry—change the balance of power and influence throughout the globe. Economic colonization from China, for instance, is now rampant and only just beginning to be felt in a geopolitical way. Much of the national discourse in Britain and the United States is "declinist"[37] in orientation; that is, it describes or predicts significant decline of their respective global powers. Formerly colonized countries such as India are developing their own versions of global power and influence. Although culture and cultural consciousness take time to catch up with political and economic realities—and British and US declinism may only be a way of maintaining military readiness as superpowers—neocolonialism is definitely a present reality as China, India and other new powers step onto the global stage.

It must be understood that the United States does not need to propound a prophecy to undergird its national interests in order to achieve its influence for immense good in the world. The example of Christian witness in the formation of the United Nations High Commissioner for Refugees (UNHCR)[38] is a case in point.[39] The United States, along with the global community of nations, continues to be an agent in providing for the foundation of human rights collectively, rather than exclusively or unilaterally. This can and should occur without recourse to the doctrine of exceptionalism.

By way of conclusion, the contribution made here is to highlight first of all the prevalence of prophecy claims that are used to undergird—however ille-

---

[36]Mark Noll, "Mark Noll Responds," *The Journal of the Historical Society* 3, nos. 3-4 (Summer/Fall 2003): 467-68.

[37]See Arthur Herman, *The Idea of Decline in Western History* (New York: Simon & Schuster, 2010), pp. 109-10.

[38]See Niklaus Steiner, Mark Gibney and Gil Loescher, *Problems of Protection: the UNHCR, Refugees, and Human Rights in the 21st Century* (New York: Routledge, 2003).

[39]See John Nurser, *For All Peoples and All Nations: Christian Churches and Human Rights* (Washington, DC: Georgetown University Press, 2005), pp. 12-17.

gitimately—an immensely powerful and captivating para-ideology. This ideology of exceptionalism has had very tangible effects, particularly in foreign policy, where it has been used to justify American unilateralism.[40] There are other bases within our tradition, however, that can form a much sounder and more robust effort to contribute to the common good, both within our borders and abroad.

---

[40]See Charles Krauthammer et al., eds., *When Unilateralism Is Right and Just. Liberty and Power: A Dialogue on Religion and U.S. Foreign Policy in an Unjust World* (Washington, DC: Brookings Institution, 2004); Charles S. Maier, *Among Empires: American Ascendancy and Its Predecessors* (Cambridge, MA: Harvard University Press, 2006).

Part Three

REVISIONING
EVANGELICAL THEOLOGY

··· ☆ ···

Introduction to Part Three

Revisioning Evangelical Theology

ℛ

Parts one and two having analyzed how imperial metanarratives have legitimized colonialism-based mission strategies and how such means of mission have influenced the knowledge production of Western hegemony, part three now moves to develop postcolonial eschatologies, Christologies and pneumatologies and thus challenges forced assimilation of Christian theologies into imperial agendas.

Christian T. Collins Winn and Amos Yong, in their essay titled "The Apocalypse of Colonialism: Notes Toward a Postcolonial Eschatology," envision an evangelical postcolonial eschatology that is well grounded in Christology along with apocalyptic expectations. They pursue this goal by retrieving apocalyptic visions that are centered on the life, death and resurrection of Jesus, and on the pouring out of the Spirit of the resurrection on all flesh.

In "Jesus/Christ the Hybrid: Toward a Postcolonial Evangelical Christology," Joya Colon-Berezin and Peter Goodwin Heltzel identify how the high Christology fundamental to evangelical apologetics and ethics contributed to creating white supremacy. This contribution was characterized by the "inability to see the racism embedded in Christian triumphalism." Their proposal for Jesus/Christ as hybrid is a postcolonial imagination of refusing to accept Western-dominant ideas that have failed to address the Jewish embodiment of Jesus on earth.

Finally, in "Recovering the Spirit of Pentecost: Canon and Catholicity in Postcolonial Perspective," Megan K. DeFranza and John R. Franke use the same postcolonial critical tool of hybridity to question how Syriac Christian tradition has been lost in the Hellenistic imperial process of colonization. The Spirit of Pentecost, in their opinion, checks assimilation of imperial and patriarchal dominance on Christian traditions and theologies. The authors propose a valid mode of postcolonialism in which the Spirit in the trinitarian formula removes the binary of Father-Son and adds plurality, including gender plurality. Thus emerges a postcolonial pneumatology that "entails the resistance to hardened difference based on binary oppositions and the determined refusal to assimilate all difference into a universal hegemonic whole."

These essays certainly trigger a new mode of thinking in evangelical post-colonial studies, given the genuine attempts to engage with the difficult nexus of triumphalist evangelical theologies and critical postcolonial questions.

7

The Apocalypse of Colonialism

Notes Toward a
Postcolonial Eschatology

Christian T. Collins Winn and Amos Yong

.... ⚹ ....

Already I pointed out that for the execution of the journey to the Indies
I was not aided by intelligence, by mathematics or by maps. It was
simply the fulfillment of what Isaiah had prophesied.

Christopher Columbus[1]

THIS ESSAY IS AN ATTEMPT to understand the theological conditions that made it possible for Christians of various traditions not only to participate in but also to promulgate and initiate the colonial project that launched the modern age and, in many respects, continues to shape it. We focus on the theological locus of eschatology, as this proved to be significant for many of the actors who populated the fifteenth through the seventeenth centuries. Much has been written about the power of the Christian eschatological imagination to fuel political and social resistance.[2] Though true, this long-held judgment must also be accompanied by a realization that the Christian eschatological imagination has also been a major source in the construction of the modern

---

[1] *The* Libro de las profecias *of Christopher Columbus: An* en face *Edition*, trans. and ed. Delano C. West and August Kling (Gainesville: University of Florida Press, 1991), p. 111.

[2] See, e.g., *Radical Christian Writings: A Reader*, ed. Andrew Bradstock and Christopher Rowland (Oxford: Blackwell, 2002), which catalogs a number of examples of eschatologically inspired radical writings.

world and the colonial project that made that world possible.[3]

What follows is an attempt to diagnose the theological conditions of the colonial project in order to surface the specific form of apocalyptic eschatology assumed by various colonizing agents, with a focus on the *performative* apocalyptic of Joachim of Fiore (1135–1202). Joachim's apocalyptic scheme, through various mediations and mutations, was an important lens through which Christopher Columbus and the early Catholic missionaries interpreted the "discovery" and conquest of the Americas and was likewise influential in much of the Protestant world, especially among the Puritans of New England. What all of these different expressions shared in common was the belief that their colonizing endeavors were central in the drama of salvation, as understood by Joachimite, pseudo-Joachimite and related forms of apocalyptic—so central, in fact, that one could describe the respective colonial projects as forms of "apocalyptic mission." As Kathleen Davis has observed, "Apocalyptic claims, as well as those of the more radical millenarianism, are politically freighted bids to control history."[4] One can well understand how such a bid to control history would have been appealing and even determinative for the colonizing powers of the early modern period.

What is hoped is that this brief genealogical analysis will contribute to a future evangelical postcolonial eschatology that does not withdraw from apocalyptic modes of thought but rather seeks to ground Christian eschatology more resolutely in Christology, and in particular in the abject body and spirit of the Jew from Nazareth. It is our conviction that central to a reconstructed evangelical postcolonial vision will be the argument that the resurrection of the Crucified and the outpouring of the Spirit of Pentecost, in a very real sense, are the apocalypse of God, the events that mark the dawning of a new day that contains its own performative logic, though one quite different from the logic that animated the colonial projects of early modernity.

THE APOCALYPSE OF COLONIALISM

Apocalypse, apocalypticism, apocalyptic—these terms carried various meanings

---

[3]See Robert J. C. Young, *Postcolonialism: A Very Short Introduction* (Oxford: Oxford University Press, 2003), p. 98.

[4]Kathleen Davis, *Periodization and Sovereignty: How Ideas of Feudalism and Secularization Govern the Politics of Time* (Philadelphia: University of Pennsylvania Press, 2008), p. 114.

over the course of several millennia[5] and have come to be associated with other forms of discourse and thought in contemporary scholarship.

> In modern scholarship apocalypticism has also been related to other terms, especially "eschatology" (teaching about the last things), "millennialism" or "chiliasm" (belief in a coming better age on earth, such as that described in the thousand-year reign of Christ at the end of the book of Revelation), and "messianism" (hope for a heaven-sent savior who will usher in the better age).[6]

By *apocalypse* we mean a theological vision that includes the following: (1) a sense that the final outcome of history is either very near or upon us; (2) a belief that with the end of history a new time is about to emerge, often styled as a "new age"; and (3) a sharp juxtaposition between that which came before—that is, "the old age"—and that which has or is about to be revealed[7]—that is, "the new age." "Apocalyptic" visions of history, then, emphasize the disjunctive, radical undoing or dissolution of history in favor of an impending new time, new history, new world, often populated by a new humanity. As our narrative will show, various colonizing agents, including the official political powers that authorized the ventures in the first place, viewed their endeavors through an apocalyptic lens, which in turn shaped their interpretations of themselves and, perhaps even more importantly, the lands and peoples they encountered. Typical of this "apocalyptic hermeneutic" is the statement of Francisco López de Gómara, biographer of Hernán Cortés, who described the "discovery" of the Americas as "the greatest event since the creation of the world except for the birth and death of our Savior. That is why they call it the New World."[8]

Whatever the self-understanding of the various colonizing agents, it is undoubtedly true that the colonized—or those indigenes who were unfortunate enough to live through the events of "discovery" and conquest—experienced colonization as nothing less than an apocalypse, in the catastrophic sense of the term. As Aimé Césaire puts it, "The colonial enterprise is to the modern world what

---

[5]See Bernard J. McGinn, John J. Collins and Stephen J. Stein, eds., *The Continuum History of Apocalypticism* (New York: Continuum, 2003).
[6]Ibid., p. ix.
[7]In fact, the Greek term *apocalypsis* means "to reveal," "to unveil" or "to disclose."
[8]Francisco López de Gómara, *Hispanic Victrix, Primera y segunda parte de la historia general de las Indias*, t. 22 (Madrid: Biblioteca de Autores Españoles, 1852), p. 156; as quoted in Delano C. West, "Medieval Ideas of Apocalyptic Mission and the Early Franciscans in Mexico," *The Americas* 45, no. 3 (1989): 303.

Roman imperialism was to the ancient world: the prelude to Disaster and the fore-runner of Catastrophe."[9] Undoubtedly the arrival of Europeans in the Americas in the late fifteenth century signaled that nothing would ever be the same.

To be sure, nothing ever was. Tzvetan Todorov's description captures the disastrous results experienced by the indigenous peoples of the Americas.

> It will be recalled that in 1500 the world population is approximately 400 million, of whom 80 million inhabit the Americas. By the middle of the sixteenth century, out of these 80 million, there remain ten. Or limiting ourselves to Mexico: on the eve of the conquest, its population is about 25 million; in 1600, it is one million.[10]

The death of millions of people, interpreted and justified by appeal to apocalyptic categories, highlights the fact that theological ideas are not only affected by the social contexts in which they are articulated but also produce their own "history of effects" (i.e., *Wirkungsgeschichte*). Postcolonial theology is constituted in part by the attempt to think through the history of effects that Christian theology and theological discourse has had on the construction of the modern world, especially as it has affected and shaped the lives and histories of those who have lived on the "underside of modernity."[11] If evangelicals are really committed to the goodness of the "*good* news," then they need to begin asking questions about how and why the "good news" has actually been "bad news" for so many people in the modern world.

THINGS HIDDEN SINCE THE FOUNDATION OF THE (MODERN) WORLD

The postcolonial "criticism of modernity is suspicious of any attempt to find a conclusive and all-encompassing meaning for history. In other words, its suspicion is directed toward the Western eschatological conception—that all of history is funneled toward a point at which and when all meaning will be unveiled."[12] The eschatology of modernity finds its foundations in the late me-

---

[9]Aimé Césaire, *Discourse on Colonialism*, trans. Joan Pinkham (New York: Monthly Review Press, 2000), p. 74.

[10]Tzvetan Todorov, *The Conquest of America: The Question of the Other* (Norman: University of Oklahoma Press, 1999), p. 133.

[11]This is a central gesture informing the work of a number of postcolonial theologians. See, for example, Marion Grau, *Rethinking Mission in the Postcolony: Salvation, Society and Subversion* (London: T & T Clark, 2011); and Vítor Westhelle, *After Heresy: Colonial Practices and Post-Colonial Theologies* (Eugene, OR: Cascade, 2010).

[12]Westhelle, *After Heresy*, p. 65.

dieval period, particularly in the apocalyptic exegesis and schema of Joachim of Fiore. Joachim's apocalyptic eschatology became so influential that even during his lifetime he was visited by popes, emperors and kings.[13]

Born in Celico, Calabria, Joachim joined the Benedictine house in Corazzo, which later became Cistercian, and was raised to abbot before 1183. According to legend, Joachim had a pivotal spiritual experience while on pilgrimage in the Holy Land, in which he claimed to have received the gift of *intellectus spiritualis* (literally "spiritual understanding") or spiritual illumination whereby he was able to discern and expound the inner meaning of the Bible.[14] This experience was followed by two more, a biographical mark of the threefold symbolism that would be so important to his thought. To be clear, Joachim's spiritual illumination did not simply mean that he could understand the meaning of the biblical text; rather, it referred to his claim to have discerned the underlying pattern that organized the history of the two testaments in the Bible as well as the underlying dynamic of ongoing history. In other words, through spiritual illumination and careful study of the Bible, Joachim claimed to have unlocked the dynamics and inner-meaning of history itself, and in some detail. He worked out these theories in a series of biblical commentaries and illustrative *Figurae,* which also functioned as prophecies and apocalyptic interpretations of contemporary events.

Fully explicating the complexity of Joachim's schema is beyond the purview of this short essay. There are, however, three elements that should be highlighted: the principle of concordance, the threefold division of history and the *performative* dynamic of Joachim's apocalyptic. The principle of concordance refers to the hermeneutical gesture that underlies much of his thought: interpretation that is simultaneously allegorical/typological and historical. In his work *The Book of Concordance of the New and Old Testaments,*[15] Joachim attempted to show how the Old and New Testaments functioned as mirrors of one another, the Old Testament as the type and the New Testament as the

---

[13]For a discussion of Joachim's influence on his contemporaries see Marjorie Reeves, *The Influence of Prophecy in the Later Middle Ages: A Study in Joachimism* (Notre Dame: University of Notre Dame Press, 1993), pp. 3-15; and Brett Edward Whalen, *Dominion of God: Christendom and Apocalypse in the Middle Ages* (Cambridge, MA: Harvard University Press, 2009), pp. 100-124.

[14]Reeves, *Influence of Prophecy,* pp. 21-22.

[15]*Abbot Joachim of Fiore: Liber de concordia novi et veteris testamenti,* ed. E. Randolph Daniel (Philadelphia: American Philosophical Society, 1983).

fulfillment of that type. In Joachim's words, by following "this pattern, therefore, the persons of the one Testament and those of the other gaze into each others' faces. City and city, people and people, order and order, war and war, act in the same way, as well as any other things that are similarly drawn to each other by some affinity."[16] Allegorical interpretation was commonplace in the Middle Ages; what made Joachim's unique was his penchant for creating prophetic correspondences between historical events within the Old and New Testaments respectively.[17] For instance, Joachim argued that just as the Israelites had endured seven persecutions in the Old Testament, so also one could discern seven persecutions the church would have to endure. Joachim was careful, however, to argue that not all of the persecutions in the New Testament had yet come to pass.[18] One would not be far from the truth to say that Joachim was working with the idea that the "history" of the New Testament was an "open canon," so to speak. That is, the history of prophecy was still unfolding, a claim to which the "book of revelation" pointed and that led to the perception that patterns and events within the Bible foreshadowed and pointed to events that would happen on the stage of history.

Perhaps the greatest contribution, certainly the most unique, was Joachim's threefold division of history. He divided the history of the world into three ages or statuses, which correspond to the three members of the Trinity and whose respective beginnings and endings overlapped. The age of the Father began with Adam and ended with Christ, while the age of the Son began with King Josiah and, as Joachim calculated, would come to an end around 1260. Significantly, the age of the Spirit had begun with Benedict of Nursia in the fifth century, would become dominant with the end of the age of the Son and would conclude with the end of history.

Within these respective ages, Joachim posited different orders of grace, different modes of religious life and different chosen people, in which the former gave way to the latter according to a supersessionist logic. For instance, the Jewish people gave way to the Greek church, which in turn had given way to

---

[16]Joachim of Fiore, "The Book of Concordance, Book 2, Part 1, Chapters 2-12," in *Apocalyptic Spirituality—Treatises and Letters of Lactantius, Adso of Montier-En-Der, Joachim of Fiore, The Spiritual Francsicans, Savonarola*, trans. Bernard McGinn (Mahwah, NJ: Paulist Press, 1979), p. 123.

[17]See Whalen, *Dominion of God*, 104. See also Henri de Lubac, *Medieval Exegesis: The Four Senses of Scripture*, trans. E. M. Macierowski (Grand Rapids: Eerdmans, 2009), 3:341-59.

[18]See Whalen, *Dominion of God*, pp. 103-8.

the Roman church as the elect whom God had chosen as the principal human agents in the drama of salvation.[19] In addition, the time in which one period overlapped with another was a period of transition and was marked by tribulation, and none was more troubled than the transition between the age of the Son and the age of the Spirit.

It was here, in the time of transition, that a whole series of figures, events and images coalesced in Joachim's scheme, giving it the feel of a Hollywood movie but also providing an opening for contemporary human involvement in the unfolding of the divine plan. For Joachim prophesied the appearance during this period of a kind of monastic elite made up of "spiritual men," whose principal task was the reform and preparation of Western Christendom for the dawning of the new age.[20] Together their task was the reform and preparation of Western Christendom for the dawning of the final age. In fact, reform of church and society was so central to Joachim's vision that scholars have come to describe it as a "reformist apocalyptic."[21] Among the tasks of reform was the conversion (or suppression) of Jews, pagans, heretics and infidels, and the recovery of the Holy Land.[22] These reforms would equip the church for the spiritual struggle against the forces of Antichrist, after which history would fully enter the third status, or Sabbath Age. The Sabbath Age, also deemed the age of the Spirit, would be marked by the palpable presence of the Spirit on earth, which would embody itself in the pacification of the world through the extension of the borders of Christendom to include the whole earth, the reunification of the Greek and Latin churches (under the supervision of the West) and the final conversion or suppression of the "religious other" (i.e., Jews, pagans, heretics and Muslims).

---

[19]Ibid., pp. 108-18.

[20]See Marjorie Reeves, *Joachim of Fiore and the Prophetic Future: A Medieval Study in Historical Thinking* (Gloucestershire: Sutton, 1999), p. 29.

[21]See Bernard McGinn, "Apocalypticism and Church Reform: 1100–1500," in McGinn, Collins and Stein, *Continuum History of Apocalypticism*, pp. 273-98.

[22]It should be noted that Joachim was not a supporter of the military Crusade as the appropriate method for recovery of the Holy Land. See E. R. Daniel, "Apocalyptic Conversion: The Joachite Alternative to the Crusades," *Traditio* 25 (1969): 127-54. Whalen argues that though Joachim was ambivalent about the Crusades, his apocalyptic scheme was nonetheless easily assimilated with earlier forms of crusader ideology (Whalen, *Dominion of God*, 133-76); while Jay Rubenstein raises the possibility that this assimilation may have been possible because crusader ideology was always already apocalyptic. See his *Armies of Heaven: The First Crusade and the Quest for Apocalypse* (New York: Basic Books, 2011).

Three things need to be noted here. First, Joachim saw the final age, the age of the Spirit, as an age that was fully within history. In other words, Joachim's apocalyptic was millennialist, in that he believed that the Sabbath Age was not in eternity but was a distinct period within history.

Second, we need to highlight the performative character, to use Catherine Keller's apt description, of Joachim's apocalyptic eschatology.[23] Simply put, in Joachim's thought human beings had a significant role to play in realizing the millennial kingdom of the Spirit, which was to be the final apotheosis of history. The apocalyptic drama would unfold with the help of key actors on the world stage. Though Joachim had associated these historical actors with religious orders, numerous followers, both powerful rulers and revolutionary outsiders, would come to claim the mantle of those who would—and, because divinely commissioned, should—move history into its final age.[24]

And third, we need to note the problematic status of the complex category of "religious others." Through its emphasis on the spiritual purity of the body politic of the chosen, Joachimite apocalyptic theologically reinforced an "insider/outsider" ordering within its theological anthropology. Though the average Christian—not to mention the lax, especially among the leadership—needed to be reformed and purified, Catholic Christians were nonetheless insiders who belonged within Christendom. The same could not be said for the "stranger among us," who was representatively styled as the Jew, the heretic (significantly including Greek Christians) and the pagan (especially witches). These would have to be converted, and if they proved recalcitrant—that is, if they were servants of Antichrist—they would have to be suppressed, which meant eradicated. This logic was easily exported so that, as the boundaries of Christendom expanded—theoretically to cover the face of the earth—and more "others" were confronted (i.e., Muslims), these too would have to be converted or suppressed. In either case, whether internal or external, the stranger (i.e., the non-Western, non-Catholic) was rendered theologically problematic and "other" to the Western Christian.

---

[23]Catherine Keller, *Apocalypse Now and Then: A Feminist Guide to the End of the World* (Boston: Beacon, 1996), p. 152.

[24]For a discussion of the pervasive influence of Joachimite ideas that marked almost every level of society in the later medieval and early modern periods, see Reeves, *Joachim of Fiore and the Prophetic Future.*

New World Apocalypse

The story of the dissemination, development and alteration of Joachim's ideas, which subsequently came to be called the "Joachimite tradition," is even more labyrinthine than the apocalyptic scenarios themselves. What is undeniable is that Joachimite, pseudo-Joachimite and related forms of apocalyptic eschatology were central components in religious, political, social and intellectual projects throughout Europe in the late medieval and early modern era, in some cases stretching up into the eighteenth and twentieth centuries.[25]

Nowhere was the influence of Joachimite apocalyptic more consequential than in the statecraft practiced by the nascent late medieval/early modern nation-states of Europe, especially in their respective colonial endeavors. By the time we come to the late fifteenth century, Joachimite apocalyptic schemes had melded with crusade ideology and papal and national foreign policy, such that much of the early period of "discovery" can only properly be understood as motivated by concerns to move history into its final stage. This potent mix would not only frame the "discovery"—a locution freighted with eschatological and apocalyptic meaning—and conquest of the New World but also continue to exert a profound influence on the histories of both North and South America. One of the best exemplars of colonialism as apocalyptic mission is found in Christopher Columbus (1451–1506).

The last thirty years have seen the appearance of numerous publications that highlight the theological, and especially apocalyptic, motivations of the "Enterprise to the Indies."[26] They render a picture of Columbus—as well as the

---

[25]For a discussion of the apocalyptic motivations of Maritime expeditions in the early fifteenth century, see Peter Russell, *Prince Henry "the Navigator": A Life* (New Haven, CT: Yale University Press, 2001). For a discussion of the role of apocalyptic in royal ideology in England, see Richard Bauckham, *Tudor Apocalypse: Sixteenth Century Apocalypticism, Millenarianism and the English Reformation: From John Bale to John Foxe and Thomas Brightman* (Oxford: Sutton Courtney Press, 1978). For a broader discussion of the early modern period see Richard H. Popkin et al., eds., *Millenarianism and Messianism in Early Modern Europe*, 4 vols. (Boston: Kluwer, 2001). For a discussion of the influence of apocalyptic thought on modern European philosophy, see Jacob Taubes, *Occidental Eschatology* (Stanford: Stanford University Press, 2009).

[26]See, for example, Pauline Moffitt Watts, "Prophecy and Discovery: On the Spiritual Origins of Christopher Columbus's 'Enterprise to the Indies,'" *American Historical Review* 90, no. 1 (1985): 73-102; Leonard I. Sweet, "Christopher Columbus and the Millennial Vision of the New World," *The Catholic Historical Review* 72, no. 3 (1986): 369-82; Djelal Kadir, *Columbus and the Ends of the Earth: Europe's Prophetic Rhetoric as Conquering Ideology* (Berkley: University of California Press, 1992); and John Hubers, "'It Is a Strange Thing': The Millennial Blindness of Christopher Columbus," *Missiology: An International Review* 37, no. 3 (2009): 333-53.

Spanish monarchs who funded his venture—as apocalyptic crusader. Why did Columbus go west? What was the real purpose of his voyage? Though a desire for more access to the wealth of the East cannot be denied, this was not the primary motivating factor in Columbus's journey. Rather, Columbus was moved above all by the desire to retake Jerusalem, thereby ushering in the Sabbath Age. The "Expedition to the Indies" was largely animated by the Joachimite vision of history, and Columbus believed himself to be a key figure in the unfolding drama of the apocalypse.

The objective of retaking Jerusalem for the purpose of fulfilling apocalyptic prophecy dominates Columbus's writings from 1492 until his death. Exemplary is the 1498 "Deed of Entail," written before the fateful third voyage, which makes clear that Columbus's thought world was firmly within a Joachimite orbit: "[As] I undertook to set out upon that discovery of the Indias, it was with the intention of supplicating the King and Queen, our lords, that whatever moneys should be derived from the said Indias should be invested in the conquest of Jerusalem."[27] In his *Book of Prophecies*, Columbus included a letter addressed to Ferdinand and Isabella specifically referencing Joachim.

> Already I pointed out that for the execution of the journey to the Indies I was not aided by intelligence, by mathematics or by maps. It was simply the fulfillment of what Isaiah had prophesied, and this is what I desire to write in this book, so that the record may remind Your Highnesses, and so that you may rejoice in the other things that I am going to tell you about our Jerusalem upon the basis of the same authority. If you have faith, you may be certain that there will be success also in that other project. . . . The Abbot Joachim, a Calabrian, said that the restorer of the House of Mt. Zion would come out of Spain.[28]

The initial goal of the "Enterprise to the Indies" was inextricably linked to the liberation of Jerusalem, a key event in the unfolding of the last days.

After encountering the new lands and new peoples of the Western Hemisphere, Columbus's thought certainly shifted, but it never left the orbit of Joachimite apocalyptic. For example, after his encounter with the mouth of the Orinoco River off the coast of modern-day Venezuela, Columbus believed that he had quite possibly found the entrance to the original Garden of Eden,

---

[27]Paul Leicester Ford, ed., *The Writings of Columbus Descriptive of the Discovery and Occupation of the New World* (New York: Charles L. Webster & Co., 1892), pp. 99-100.
[28]*The* Libro de las profecias *of Christopher Columbus*, p. 111.

which would become the site of the new Jerusalem.[29] The shift from New World as way station to old Jerusalem, to New World as site of new Jerusalem, became even more significant in the generations to follow in both the North and South Atlantic.

Others have noted the influence of Joachimite apocalyptic in the Iberian Americas all the way into the twentieth century.[30] John Leddy Phelan's narrative in particular suggests that the early Franciscan missionaries in Mexico were fueled by apocalyptic expectations and visions. Gerónimo de Mendieta (1525–1604), a Franciscan missionary and historian of the period, viewed New Spain as the site of the primitive church, from which Joachim's "spiritual men" would arise. Significantly the human raw material from which the "spiritual men" would arise were the indigenous inhabitants, recently freed from idolatry by the conquistador Hernán Cortés, Mendieta's "new Moses."[31] As Phelan notes, in his correspondence with court officials and in his *Historia eclesiástica Indiana*, Mendieta sought to convince anyone who would listen "that the New World could be the geographical theater in which could unfold the climactic chapter not only in the history of the mendicant orders but also in the history of mankind."[32] Though it was in fact Cortés who finally persuaded Charles V to combine colonial and missional policy in Mexico, he nonetheless shared Mendieta's twofold paternalistic vision of Spanish presence in the New World: the colonizing and evangelizing of the indigenous inhabitants, and the building of the primitive church that would evangelize the world and usher in the final age of history.

Though Protestants in the North Atlantic sought to distance themselves and their colonial policies and practices from those of the Spanish and the Portuguese, there is substantial evidence to suggest a shared theological-apocalyptic interpretation of colonialism. Both the Virginia colony and the Puritan migration to North America were styled as auspicious events in a larger

---

[29]See *The Writings of Columbus*, pp. 140-41.
[30]See West, "Medieval Ideas"; John Leddy Phelan, *The Millennial Kingdom of the Franciscans in the New World* (Berkeley: University of California Press, 1970); Thomas M. Cohen, *The Fire of Tongues: António Vieira and the Missionary Church in Brazil and Portugal* (Stanford: Stanford University Press, 1998); and Frank Graziano, *The Millennial New World* (Oxford: Oxford University Press, 1999).
[31]See Phelan, *Millennial Kingdom*, pp. 29-38, 44-68.
[32]Ibid., p. 58.

apocalyptic economy.[33] In both the North and the South Atlantic, therefore, colonialism was fueled and, when necessary, interpreted by recourse to apocalyptic theology.

TOWARD A POSTCOLONIAL TRINITARIAN APOCALYPTIC

Against the Joachimite-inspired apocalyptic mission that fueled the colonial enterprise, we propose instead a retrieval and recovery of apocalyptic modes of thought that are centered on the life, death and resurrection of the Jew from Nazareth, and on the pouring out of the Spirit of the resurrection on all flesh. One of the central problems at work in Joachimite apocalyptic is its lack of connection to Christology. This is not to say that Jesus Christ is not a figure of some importance in Joachim. The issue, rather, is that the earthly history of Jesus plays no role in determining the content and shape of God's apocalyptic action for Joachim. By this separation, apocalyptic functions only as a time signature signifying that momentous and cataclysmic events are unfolding; meanwhile the contours of the apocalyptic action of God are in no way informed by the lowly history of the suffering Son of Man. In fact, Joachim's apocalyptic scheme makes it possible that human or communal participation in God's apocalyptic economy might look very different, even counter, to the history enacted in Jesus of Nazareth.

Whereas Christology and eschatology have been effectively severed from each other in the abbot of Fiore's account, the alternative we propose begins with a reintegration of Christology and pneumatology with eschatology.[34] The apocalyptic unveiling is thus not of a coming age of the Spirit but the revelation of the full depth and power of the messianic life, manifest in the Jewish carpenter from Nazareth, now working among those who have been filled with the Spirit of his resurrection. The Spirit-anointed Christ and his Spirit-anointed followers together embody a challenge to the status quo because the form of life raised from the dead in Jesus, and now shared by the Spirit of the resurrection, is radically different from the world "as it is."

---

[33]See Jorge Cañzinares-Esguerra, *Puritan Conquistadors: Iberianizing the Atlantic, 1550–1700* (Stanford: Stanford University Press, 2006); and Avihu Zakai, *Exile and Kingdom: History and Apocalypse in the Puritan Migration to America* (Cambridge: Cambridge University Press, 1992).

[34]See Christian T. Collins Winn, "Kingdom," in *Prophetic Evangelicals: Envisioning a Just and Peaceable Kingdom*, ed. Bruce Ellis Benson, Malinda Elizabeth Berry and Peter Goodwin Heltzel (Grand Rapids: Eerdmans, 2012), pp. 90-99.

A postcolonial trinitarian apocalypse is also performative, albeit not according to the logic of Joachim's drama. What is performed instead is living in the power of the Spirit of the life and death of Jesus the Jew. If Joachim's apocalyptic mission involved defining the new people of the spirit over against Jews, pagans, infidels and so on, a postcolonial trinitarian apocalypse is unveiled as a participation in Jesus' Jewish flesh. The church comes to see that its identity is configured in and by the humanity of a son of Israel—a humanity and identity that is not self-enclosed or self-determined by the logics of race, ethnicity or colonialism but determined by participation in the gift of covenant.[35] Thus the *place* of Jesus and the messianic Spirit—that is, Jesus' Jewish flesh, or a humanity that is radically determined in and through covenant—is a liminal or *choratic* place, one that is open to the "other" rather than being determined by the logics and boundaries of colonialism. Jesus' life was marked by covenantal obedience (see Mt 5:17), but an obedience that was not an expression of racial, cultural or religious purity; rather it was a life history performed as radical solidarity with those who were "outsiders."

The performative character of a postcolonial trinitarian apocalyptic, then, will involve living into *one* of the modalities of the story of Israel: the diasporic modality, which here refers to Jesus' solidarity with the outsider, the stranger, those on "the underside" of history and society. Rather than Joachim's logic of *either* conversion *or* eradication, the apocalyptic event of Jesus of Nazareth involves instead an embrace of any and all "others" who call on the name of the Lord (Acts 2:21) or who fear God and do what is right (Acts 10:35). The truly apocalyptic performance is thus not the performance of conquest or crusade but that of suffering love, which witnesses in our bodies to the life of the one who emptied himself for others, for it is in and through this Spirit-empowered performance that God unveils the redemption of the cosmos accomplished in the apocalypse of Jesus Christ.[36]

---

[35]For a discussion of the covenantal nature of Jewish humanity, see J. Kameron Carter, *Race: A Theological Account* (Oxford: Oxford University Press, 2008), pp. 22-30, 354-66.

[36]See Amos Yong, *The Spirit Poured Out on All Flesh: Pentecostalism and the Possibility of Global Theology* (Grand Rapids: Baker Academic, 2005); also Yong, *In the Days of Caesar: Pentecostalism and Political Theology* (Grand Rapids: Eerdmans, 2010), pp. 316-58.

8

JESUS/CHRIST THE HYBRID

Toward a Postcolonial Evangelical Christology

Joya Colon-Berezin and Peter Goodwin Heltzel

.... ☧ ....

*Because of the history of immigration,
the narratives are no longer outside but are already
inside the metropolitan centers, and the dominant white culture
does not know how to deal with the challenges of
diversity and multiculturalism.*

KWOK PUI-LAN[1]

*If Jesus Christ is to be described as God,
we may not speak of his divine being, nor of his omnipotence,
nor his omniscience; but we must speak of this weak man among sinners,
of his manger and his cross. If we are to deal with the deity of Jesus,
we must speak of his weakness. In Christology, one looks at the
whole historical man Jesus and says of him, that he is God.*

DIETRICH BONHOEFFER[2]

---

[1]Kwok Pui-lan, *Postcolonial Imagination and Feminist Theology* (Louisville, KY: Westminster John Knox, 2005), pp. 173-74.
[2]Dietrich Bonhoeffer, *Christ the Center*, trans. Edwin H. Robertson (New York: HarperCollins, 1978), p. 104.

INTRODUCTION

Vital to the task of evangelical theology today is the construction of a Christology that emphasizes the subjugated flesh of Jesus of Nazareth. While the Council of Chalcedon pointed to the full humanity and full divinity of Jesus Christ conceived without confusion, change, division or separation, this theological formulation must be reimagined for today's postcolonial context. In spite of many other contemporary theological perspectives, evangelical faith has maintained its abstract emphasis on the *deity of Christ*, with an uncompromising affirmation of the virgin birth, the sinless incarnation of Jesus Christ and his bodily resurrection.

Black liberation theology is a postcolonial discourse that offers an essential corrective to white evangelical Christology. One of its axioms is the historical suffering of Jesus of Nazareth, as well as Jesus' identification with the suffering, and liberation, of humanity. When applied to the context of North America, this means connecting the historical context of Jesus of Nazareth to the historical freedom struggles of those on the underside of European colonialism and white supremacy.[3]

In this chapter we argue that evangelical Christology can be strengthened by the black liberationist critique. In so doing it must go beyond a false theological dichotomy of a historical "Jesus" and an eternal, divine "Christ." We argue that the postcolonial concept of *hybridity* invites Christology today toward a blurring of the divine/human union, simultaneously claiming the kataphatic ("is") of Jesus and the apophatic ("is not") dimensions of our apprehension of Christ. We argue that this simultaneous *historical assertion* and *divine apophasis* create the conditions for a postcolonial evangelical Christology.

THE CHRISTOLOGICAL PROBLEM
IN AMERICAN EVANGELICAL THEOLOGY

Within American evangelical systematic theology there has been and continues to be an overwhelming emphasis on the *deity* of Christ. We can see this emphasis clearly in the theology of American Reformed evangelical theologian Carl F. H. Henry.[4] Born to German immigrant parents in 1919, Henry became

---

[3]James H. Cone, *God of the Oppressed* (New York: Seabury, 1975).
[4]We would like to note that Henry represents only one branch of evangelicalism, albeit a very significant and dominant one.

arguably the greatest theologian in the Reformed evangelical movement that
emerged in the 1940s. As Billy Graham was evangelicalism's global evangelist,
Carl F. H. Henry was one of evangelicalism's theological architects.[5] He served
as the first editor in chief of the magazine *Christianity Today*, established to
serve as a voice for evangelical Christianity and a challenge to the more liberal-
leaning *Christian Century*.

Theologically Henry was a tough-minded conservative who faithfully
sought to defend a Christology rooted in the *five fundamentals*. These fundamentals emerged in the late nineteenth century to reaffirm certain theological tenets and defend them against the challenges of liberal theology and
scholarly criticism.[6] The term *fundamentalist* was popularized by publication
of *The Fundamentals*, a collection of twelve books on five subjects written in
1910 by Milton and Lyman Stewart. The first formulation of the five fundamentals can be traced to the Niagara Bible Conference and the General Assembly of the Presbyterian Church, which distilled the twelve books into five
fundamental Christian theological assertions: "The divine authority and inerrant inspiration of Scripture, the virgin birth and sinless incarnation of
Christ, His substitutionary atonement, bodily resurrection, and final personal return to glory."[7]

Four out of five of these fundamentals focus explicitly on the deity of Christ.
These affirmations are the heart of Henry's christological vision. He wrote, "Any
current theology worthy to be called Christian vindicates the propriety and
indispensability of the deity, virgin birth, substitutionary death, bodily resurrection, and second coming of Christ."[8] In the spirit of early church apologists,
Henry passionately defended the inerrancy of Scripture and a propositional
notion of doctrinal truth. He saw Scripture as revelation in the form of "rational communication conveyed in intelligible ideas and meaningful words,

[5]For an introduction to Henry's theological vision, including his writings on the problem of race, see
Peter Goodwin Heltzel, "Carl F. H. Henry's Uneasy Conscience," *Jesus and Justice: Evangelicals, Race
and American Politics* (New Haven, CT: Yale University Press, 2009), pp. 71-88. For a collection of
Henry's evangelical christological thoughts in the late 1960s, see Carl F. H. Henry, ed., *Jesus of
Nazareth: Savior and Lord* (Grand Rapids: Eerdmans, 1966).
[6]Mark A. Noll, *A History of Christianity in the United States and Canada* (Grand Rapids: Eerdmans,
1992), pp. 376-86.
[7]Carl F. H. Henry, "A Troubled Conscience Fifty Years Later" (unpublished manuscript, 1997, Carl
F. H. Henry Archives, Trinity Evangelical Divinity School, Deerfield, Illinois), p. 8.
[8]Carl F. H. Henry, *Evangelical Responsibility in Contemporary Theology* (Grand Rapids: Eerdmans,
1957), p. 66.

that is, in conceptual verbal form."[9] Henry's thoughtful defenses of biblical inerrancy and propositional doctrine are important because they are the central planks of neoevangelical Reformed theology.[10]

Henry's Christology focuses on Jesus Christ's divinity because it points to God's sovereign power. God's sovereign power in Christ becomes the basis of the inerrant Bible and the absolute truth of the doctrinal fundamentals of the faith. For Henry, Jesus is a redemptive king. He wrote, "The extent to which man centers his life and energy in the redemptive King *now* determines the extent of the divine kingdom in the present age."[11] Henry emphasized that Jesus Christ is an abstract, transcendent king. Christian individuals are called to obey him and to relinquish their agency to him.

Henry's high Christology has been the theological foundation of Reformed evangelical apologetics and evangelical ethics. In 1947 Henry sounded a clarion call within evangelicalism for social action with his manifesto *The Uneasy Conscience of Modern Fundamentalism*. For Henry, the gospel remains primarily about the salvation of individual souls, while the struggle for justice is merely awkwardly inserted into evangelical dogmatics in an ad hoc fashion. The individualist vision of Henry's evangelical dogmatics faced a moral crisis in the civil rights movement when it found itself ill-equipped to offer a constructive response to white supremacy, America's original sin.[12] Henry's failure to diagnose the problem of white supremacy is rooted in his inability to see the racism embedded in Christian triumphalism, the theological backbone of European colonialism in North America.

In the sections that follow, we take J. Kameron Carter's lead in asking, "What would it mean to receive the Jewish Savior, to enter into the body politic of the

---

[9]Carl F. H. Henry, *God, Revelation, and Authority*, vol. 2, *God Who Speaks and Shows, 15 Theses, Part 1* (Waco, TX: Word, 1976–1983), p. 21.

[10]Carl F. H. Henry's understandings of inspiration, inerrancy and infallibility are articulated in *God, Revelation, and Authority*, vol. 4, *God Who Speaks and Shows, 15 Theses, Part 3* (Waco, TX: Word, 1976–1983), pp. 103-219.

[11]Carl F. H. Henry, *The Uneasy Conscience of Modern Fundamentalism*, 3rd ed. (Grand Rapids: Eerdmans, 1982), p. 54.

[12]For a theological exploration of the problem of racism in Christian theology, see J. Kameron Carter's *Race: A Theological Account* (Oxford: Oxford University Press, 2008). For helpful overviews of evangelical participation in the civil rights movement, see Curtis J. Evans, "Evangelicals and the Civil Rights Movement" (master's thesis, Gordon-Conwell Theological Seminary, 1999); Michael D. Hammond, "Conscience in Crisis: Neo-Evangelicals and Race in the 1950s" (master's thesis, Wheaton College, 2002); and Heltzel, "Carl F. H. Henry's Uneasy Conscience," pp. 82-88.

wounded, not triumphalist, flesh disclosed there, and so be saved?"[13] After providing a brief genealogy of the origins of the social and theological problem of white supremacy, we will engage James Cone's black liberation theology and his emphasis on the Jewishness of Jesus, followed by our own postcolonial evangelical Christology as a response.[14]

GENEALOGY OF RACISM: A SOCIAL *AND* THEOLOGICAL PROBLEM

If we are going to articulate a theology that is truly postcolonial, we as North Americans are going to have to acknowledge and take seriously the history of racism embedded in European colonialism in North America. White supremacy took on systemic form in every institution of life in the United States, including government, financial, educational, recreational and religious ones.[15] Racialized violence was integral to the process of colonial conquest. White colonial Christians embraced the promise of the New World at the expense, labor and death of black and brown bodies. Enslaved Africans and Native Americans became instruments of colonial production in the emerging New

---

[13]J. Kameron Carter, "Race and the Experience of Death: Theologically Reappraising American Evangelicalism," in *The Cambridge Companion to Evangelical Theology*, ed. Timothy Larsen and Daniel J. Treier (Cambridge: Cambridge University Press, 2007), p. 194. J. Kameron Carter calls on American evangelical Christians to deconstruct this legacy of theological triumphalism; however, he argues this can *only* be done by "displacing American evangelical belief into the liminally tight and eerily dark space of the death-bound-subject." For Carter this "death-bound-subject" refers to the African Americans of the transatlantic slave trade. Carter argues that we need to recover a "theologically profound counter-tradition . . . which in fact retrieves crucial aspects of the broader catholic Christian traditions that were in some sense lost to modernity" (ibid., p. 189).

[14]Mabiala Kenzo and John Franke call for a postcolonial evangelicalism in their essay, "The Future of Evangelical Theology in an Age of Empire: Postfoundational and Postcolonial," in *Evangelicals and Empire*, ed. Bruce Ellis Benson and Peter Goodwin Heltzel (Grand Rapids: Brazos, 2008), pp. 267-77.

[15]Works on race and religion that have shaped our thinking include Cornel West, *Prophesy Deliverance! An Afro-American Revolutionary Christianity* (Louisville, KY: Westminster John Knox, 1982); Anthony B. Pinn, *Terror and Triumph: The Nature of Black Religion* (Minneapolis: Fortress, 2003); Dwight Callahan, *The Talking Book: African Americans and the Bible* (New Haven, CT: Yale University Press, 2006); George M. Fredrickson, *Racism: A Short History* (Princeton, NJ: Princeton University Press, 2002); Eddie S. Glaude Jr., *Exodus! Religion, Race, and Nation in Early Nineteenth-Century Black America* (Chicago: University of Chicago Press, 2000); Colin Kidd, *The Forging of the Races: Race and Scripture in the Protestant Atlantic World, 1600–2000* (Cambridge: Cambridge University Press, 2006); Michael Omi and Howard Winant, *Racial Formation in the United States: From the 1960s to the 1990s* (New York: Routledge, 1994); Emile Townes, *Womanist Ethics and the Cultural Production of Evil* (New York: Palgrave, 2006); Gayraud S. Wilmore, *Black Religion and Black Radicalism: An Interpretation of the Religious History of Afro-American People* (Maryknoll, NY: Orbis, 1994).

World economy. American colonies offered the illusion to Europeans of being able to leave the ancient regime of the Old World behind and begin life anew, not recognizing that others would pay the price. Richard Slotkin writes, "The first colonists saw in America an opportunity to regenerate their fortunes, their spirits, and the power of their church and nation; but the means to that regeneration ultimately became the means of violence, and the myth of regeneration through violence became the structuring metaphor of the American experience."[16] Native American bodies and cultures were victimized by this theo-logic of violence.[17]

Colonialism was driven by a theology of conquest that provided a religious rationale for racialized violence in North America.[18] Christianity provided a social imagination that internalized these acts of racialized violence in the drama of "American" redemption. Racially designating brown and black bodies as inferior became a theological strategy for justifying and legitimating white power and privilege. The racial rendering of the black and brown Other was essential to the Christian theological basis and social formation of white identity in the "New World." The roots of rendering the Other lay buried even deeper in the Christian imagination.[19]

George Frederickson argues that the genealogy of "race" can be traced back to the fourteenth- and early fifteenth-century Iberian Peninsula.[20] His theory on the origin and historical development of race points to a significant relationship between racism and religion, particularly the *Christian* tradition. By tracing the historical, social and political circumstances under which race/racism was invented Frederickson arrives at the bold conclusion

---

[16]Richard Slotkin, *Regeneration Through Violence: The Mythology of the American Frontier, 1600–1860* (Middletown, CT: Wesleyan University Press, 1973), p. 5.

[17]Russell Bourne, *Gods of War, Gods of Peace: How the Meeting of Native and Colonial Religion Shaped Early America* (New York: Harcourt, 2002); Yasuhide Kawashima, *Igniting King Philip's War: The John Sassamon Murder Trial* (Lawrence: University Press of Kansas, 2001); Jill Lepore, *The Name of War: King Philip's War and the Origins of American Identity* (New York: Vintage, 1999); Neal Salisbury, *Manitou and Providence: Indians, Europeans, and the Making of New England, 1500–1643* (New York: Oxford University Press, 1982); Alden T. Vaughan, *New England Frontier: Puritans and Indians, 1620–1675* (Oklahoma City: University of Oklahoma Press, 1995).

[18]Luis N. Rivera, *A Violent Evangelism: The Political and Religious Conquest of North America* (Louisville, KY: Westminster John Knox, 1990); George Tinker, *Missionary Conquest: The Gospel and Native American Cultural Genocide* (Minneapolis: Fortress, 1993).

[19]See Willie James Jennings, *The Christian Imagination: Theology and the Origins of Race* (New Haven, CT: Yale University Press, 2010).

[20]George M. Fredrickson, *Racism: A Short History*, p. 28.

that religion—particularly *Christianity*—is responsible for the emergence of racism.

According to Fredrickson, the period of the Black Death that swept across Europe in the mid-fourteenth century marks an early shift to "race"-based discrimination, particularly among nations on the Iberian Peninsula. Frederickson remarks that in order to identify scapegoats, myths began to develop that Jews had "poisoned the wells in a diabolical plot to exterminate the followers of Christ."[21] As a result Portugal and Spain created the doctrine of *limpieza de sangre*.[22] This doctrine, which became law in 1547, made it such that certificates of "pure blood" were administered to distinguish those of "pure Christian descent" from others.

Frederickson argues that *limpieza de sangre* constitutes a pivotal turn toward racism in Europe. He remarks that the doctrine of *limpieza de sangre* was "undoubtedly racist" because it was supported by an "ideology or worldview" that "justified such practices."[23] This racial ideology became manifest in a law that ensured that people of both Moorish and Jewish ancestry were excluded from the hegemonic power structure in Spain.

Racist ideology in North America was also "religious racism," providing a "supernatural" and theological basis for the claim that the domination of the indigenous groups by white colonists of European descent was divinely ordained.[24] Racist christological formulations are one result of this historical reality. For example, under the enormous influence of German New Testament scholarship in the nineteenth and early twentieth century, Jesus, shorn of his Jewishness, becomes "white" in much twentieth-century German theology, allowing Christianity to sever its historic connection to Judaism.

THE JEWISHNESS OF JESUS: BLACK THEOLOGY AND THE INTERROGATION OF WHITE SUPREMACY

In *Jesus and the Disinherited* Howard Thurman writes, "How different might have been the story of the last two thousand years on this planet grown old from suffering if the link between Jesus and Israel had never been severed. . . .

---

[21]Ibid., p. 26.
[22]Ibid., p. 33.
[23]Omi and Winant, *Racial Formation in the United States*, p. 33.
[24]Ibid., pp. 45-46.

[For] the Christian Church has tended to overlook its Judaic origins, . . . the fact that Jesus of Nazareth was a Jew of Palestine."[25] Why did Western Christianity sever the link between Jesus and the religion of Israel that he grew up in? Since Christianity began as a sect within Judaism, how can Christians dispense of their Jewish heritage? Christianity is unintelligible without Judaism.

Jesus' *Jewishness* remains a theological problem and a racial problem. It is this problem that is courageously confronted by black liberation theology. Inasmuch as European continental Christendom was forged through the racial otherness of the Jews, this colonial logic of racial otherness was deployed in the racialization of "blacks" in North America. Black liberation theology connects the Jewishness of Jesus with black existence in America, developing a critique of racism and, at the same time, a constructive theology of liberation.

How might we try to characterize black liberation theology in relation to postcolonial theology? Black liberation theology is the theological trajectory within the black radical movement. The black radical movement was a postcolonial discourse in the 1960s. Frantz Fanon, in *A Dying Colonialism* (1965) and *Black Skin, White Masks* (1967), offers a sharp critique of colonization and a global analysis of white supremacy.[26] Fanon heard the cries of poor people in the Third World, who were dominated by the whiteness of colonial regimes, and called for anticolonial liberation movements throughout the world.

In the 1960s the black radical tradition erupted in the black power movement, which offered a radical critique of the white colonial order of things and a reimagination of the conditions of life in a more radically democratic valence. The black power movement in turn gave birth to the black theology of James Cone, as seen in his first book, *Black Theology and Black Power* (1969). Cone sought to articulate a prophetic Christian theology that was relevant to black existence in a nation dominated by white supremacy. Therefore, a contemporary postcolonial engagement with the work of Cone makes sense because black liberation theology is a vector within the black radical movement, which in itself already was a postcolonial discourse.

For Cone the problem of racism demands a turn to sociohistorical contexts in order to give a deeper and more pointed analysis of who Jesus Christ *is*.

---

[25]Howard Thurman, *Jesus and the Disinherited* (Boston: Beacon, 1976), p. 16.
[26]Frantz Fanon, *A Dying Colonialism*, trans. Haakon Chevalier (New York: Grove Press, 1965); also, Fanon, *Black Skin, White Masks* (New York: Grove Press, 1967).

Frustrated with the theological abstractions of his white theological colleagues, Cone demanded that theology come to terms with its context(s). Cone's theological call to context took on two forms: a call to the original context of the biblical story as well as a call to the contemporary context of US theology shaped by white supremacy, anti-Semitism and colonization. Examining the concrete Jewish backgrounds of Jesus' context becomes the basis for a contextual theological analysis in the present. Cone writes, "The historical Jesus emphasizes the social context of Christology and thereby establishes the importance of Jesus' racial identity. *Jesus was a Jew!*"[27] By thinking about Jesus in his concrete particularity—a poor Jew in Palestine—Cone deploys a broader critique of evangelical Christology.

The connection between Jesus' Jewishness and black existence in America invites us to develop a new postcolonial genealogy of Christianity, and a new constructive Christology. Even Cone acknowledges the limitations of the "black Christ" when he writes, "I realize that 'blackness' as a Christological title may not be appropriate in the distant future or even in every human context in our present."[28] Cone understood that Jesus' blackness as a christological title is a cultural construct. As a result of the cultural contingency of this title it remains a provisional yet direct prophetic challenge to American evangelical Christology. Evangelical Christology must offer both a robust theological account of Jesus' Jewishness and an analysis of the ways in which "whiteness" continues to function in the church, academy and society today. But such a Christology, while clearly liberationist in character, can be deepened by engaging postcolonial studies. A postcolonial evangelical Christology must build on the "black theology moment" in our own North American–situated Christology, but go beyond thinking about Jesus Christ as "black" to thinking about Jesus/Christ as hybrid.

JESUS/CHRIST'S HYBRID IDENTITY: TOWARD A POSTCOLONIAL CHRISTOLOGY

In order for twenty-first-century evangelical theology to respond to its multicultural and global context, it must begin to answer questions raised by postcolonial theorists. Postcoloniality is a space in which people are committed to amplifying the voice of those who have been silenced through patterns and

[27]Cone, *God of the Oppressed*, p. 113.
[28]Ibid., p. 135.

practices of colonization. Through colonial expansion European nations spread Western civilization, which is in itself a *social imaginary* through which people of European descent view themselves as superior to those of non-Western cultures. In addition to deconstructing Western hegemony, postcolonial theory offers conceptual resources for constructing prophetic, non-Western identities. These include notions of the subaltern, solidarity and hybridity.

Gayatri Spivak's notion of the *subaltern* is based on two word elements: "sub," meaning below, which refers to the people who are on the underside of colonization; and "altern," referring to the unique "difference" of their subjectivity.[29] For Jacques Derrida, *différance* refers to the irreducible "otherness" that is constitutive of human identity.[30] Spivak seeks to understand *différance* from the subjective position of the oppressed on the underside of modernity. Spivak explores subaltern voices, including the possibility and limits of their expression. While Western progressives are eager to forge solidarity with subaltern voices, Spivak exposes how these enterprises can veil new forms of neocolonial oppression.

One version of this form of neocolonization is the way in which non-Western cultures and persons are essentialized in the Western imagination. For example, as Edward Said has pointed out in his classic *Orientalism*, "orientals" function as an imaginary "other" constructed by the West to implement discursive hegemony in the colonial enterprise in Asia and among the Asian diaspora.[31] For example, the "Chinatowns" in US cities become an example of the Western projection of "China" that lies hidden behind the diasporic communities embodied in the Chinatowns of US urban centers.[32] In these two examples, what is "Asian" is reduced to an abstract essence in the terms "oriental" and "Chinatown."[33] When we essentialize diverse racial/ethnic com-

---

[29]Gayatri Chakravorty Spivak, "Can the Subaltern Speak?," in *Colonial Discourse and Postcolonial Theory: A Reader*, ed. Patrick Williams and Laura Chrisman (New York: Harvester Wheatsheaf, 1993), pp. 66-111.

[30]Gayatri Chakravorty Spivak's postcolonial vision presupposes Jacques Derrida's French poststructural notion of *différance*. See Jacques Derrida, "Différance," in *Margins of Philosophy*, trans. Alan Bass (Chicago: University of Chicago Press, 1982), pp. 7-8.

[31]Edward W. Said, *Orientalism* (New York: Vintage, 1979).

[32]Gayatri Chakravorty Spivak, *A Critique of Postcolonial Reason: Toward a History of the Vanishing Present* (Cambridge, MA: Harvard University Press, 1999), p. 332.

[33]For a postcolonial theological critique of Asian essentialism see Namsoon Kang, "'Who/What Is Asian?' A Postcolonial Theological Reading of Orientalism and Neo-Orientalism," in *Postcolonial Theologies: Divinity and Empire*, ed. Catherine Keller, Michael Nausner and Mayra Rivera (St. Louis:

munities in such a way, we create an imaginative interpretation that is distant from the complexities of cultural difference.

Whereas Spivak warns against the victims of colonization being assimilated into the dominant culture through their acceptance of these essentialized ethnic identities, imposed by the white dominant culture, she also warns against rejecting everything Western and adopting an imagined, purely "native," non-Western identity. As a result *solidarity* becomes a mode of relationship for subaltern voices and those outside a subaltern reality. This solidarity can extend to all people who can acknowledge their difference and common humanity. Spivak argues that a genuine acknowledgment of *différance* creates the conditions for intimacy: "Solidarity comes from exchange of information and a bonding through acknowledgement of difference."[34] True solidarity provides a way for subaltern identities not to degenerate into individualism, particularism or relativism. Solidarity provides the basis for true communication and a common human future. Spivak reminds us that multicultural solidarity can come about by moving beyond generalized notions of national identity to a posture of listening and improvisational collaboration in which difference is accepted and valued.[35]

Spivak, like other postcolonial theorists, appeals to the concept of *hybridity* to frame this dialectic between solidarity and the subaltern. The postcolonial language of hybridity provides another way of speaking about the difference and sameness that lies within the construction of all human identities. Homi Bhabha writes, "Hybridity is a problematic of colonial representation and individuation that reverses the effects of the colonialist disavowal, so that other 'denied' knowledges enter upon the dominant discourse and estrange the basis of its authority—its rules of recognition."[36] Hybridity refers to a multicultural identity that is not dominated by the hegemony of one race and ethnicity.

Kwok Pui-lan points out, in light of the importance of this notion for postcolonial Christian theology and ethics, that Christ has always been the "most hybridized concept in the Christian tradition."[37] Jesus Christ represents a bor-

---

Chalice, 2004), pp. 100-117.

[34]Gayatri Chakravorty Spivak, "Bonding in Difference, Interview with Alfred Arteaga (1993–1994)," in *The Spivak Reader*, ed. Donna Landry and Gerald MacLean (New York: Routledge, 1996), p. 20.

[35]Spivak, *Critique of Postcolonial Reason*, p. 334.

[36]Homi K. Bhabha, *The Location of Culture* (London: Routledge, 1994), p. 114.

[37]Kwok Pui-lan, *Postcolonial Imagination and Feminist Theology*, p. 171.

derland in his own body, the dangerous border between the human and the divine. Kwok Pui-lan argues against any "fixed" space between the divinity and humanity of Christ but rather for a fluidity between the natures. How does a hybrid Christology relate the human and divine natures in the person of Jesus Christ?

Theology is an exciting and endless journey in seeking to deepen our understanding of and communion with a mysterious God through *epektasis*. *Epektasis* comes from the term *epekteinomai*, meaning "to reach out after."[38] Kathryn Tanner, in her reading of Gregory of Nyssa, defines *epektasis* as "the creature's constant forward motion or journey beyond itself into the boundlessness of God's fullness as the creature's capacities are stretched by what it receives."[39] In developing this concept Gregory of Nyssa was inspired by the motif in Paul's letter to the Philippians of pressing on toward God: "Beloved, I do not consider that I have made it my own; but this one thing I do: forgetting what lies behind and straining forward to what lies ahead, I press on toward the goal for the prize of the heavenly call of God in Christ Jesus" (Phil 3:13-14). The apophatic mystery of God lures the theologian to press on, in *epektasis*, toward a deeper understanding.

Hybrid Christology also seeks to privilege the apophatic emphasis on God that is present in the Eastern theological tradition. Many theologians in the Eastern tradition like Denys and the Cappadocians, in their methodological emphasis on *apophatic* theology (often called "negative theology"), claim that God's nature is ineffable, and they focus on what we are unable to fully understand about God. This emphasis on the apophatic is in contrast to the Western Augustinian tradition, which eventually birthed modern evangelical theology and which most often relies on a *kataphatic* theological method that makes positive claims about what we can know with certainty. This kataphatic theological method is illustrated in American fundamentalists' use of the five fundamentals as tests of biblical orthodoxy. In the apophatic tradition of theology,

---

[38]Andrew Louth, *The Origins of the Christian Mystical Tradition: From Plato to Denys* (Oxford: Oxford University Press, 1981), p. 89n12. Louth writes that *epektasis* means that "the soul continually longs for God, continually reaches out for knowledge of Him. But there is no ultimate satisfaction, no final union, no ecstasy in which the soul is rapt up out of the temporal sequence and achieves union. There is simply a deeper and deeper penetration into darkness" (p. 89).

[39]Kathryn Tanner, *Jesus, Humanity, and the Trinity: A Brief Systematic Theology* (Minneapolis: Fortress, 2001), pp. 42-43.

as soon as a divine name, like Jesus Christ, is said, it is also unsaid. All of our assertions of Jesus Christ's identity invite new negations, generating a synergistic dialectic between Christ's (apophatic) divinity and his fully human Jewish flesh.

Brian Bantum, in his groundbreaking book *Redeeming Mulatto*, argues persuasively for a dialectic of hybridity by suggesting a Christology that contains a simultaneous "assertion" and "negation" within the person of Christ.[40] A mystical-prophetic evangelical theologian, Bantum argues that we need both apophatic and kataphatic discourse when we talk about Jesus Christ. Bantum comments on the hybrid nature of such a Christology, focusing "more upon what or who Christ is not, rather than who Christ is. The intermingling of positive and negative assertions highlights the possibility of Christ's mulattic nature."[41] Whereas the humanity of Christ resembles an "is," there is a simultaneous "is not." These two poles serve to "disrupt . . . our notions of what is possible . . . within the divine personhood."[42]

Pressing on to deepen our understanding of the person of Jesus/Christ, this hybrid Christology takes seriously the social world in which christological claims are being made today. Along with James Cone, whose black theological vision *is* a postcolonial discourse, we privilege the racialized Jewish Jesus, a poor man from northern Galilee who lived in solidarity with the poor and marginalized of his day. And as opposed to the conservative evangelical emphasis on the "is" of Christ's divinity, a postcolonial evangelical Christology will think more deeply about the eternal *negation* embedded in the deity of Christ—the apophatic unknowability of the Triune God, which remains the great mystery of faith that we are always seeking to better understand and more fully embody in our collective ecclesial life as the "body of Christ."

Conclusion

Through the *hybrid* identity of Jesus/Christ evangelicals can move away from a Christology that is almost exclusively Western and white to one that affirms Jesus/Christ for all people. The hybrid Jesus/Christ refuses the "is" of Christ,

---

[40]Brian Bantum, *Redeeming Mulatto: A Theology of Race and Christian Hybridity* (Waco, TX: Baylor University Press, 2010), p. 93.
[41]Ibid.
[42]Ibid., p. 94.

replacing it within the apophatic limits of our comprehension, bearing witness to the mystery of the Triune God. A hybrid Christology also refuses to be shaped exclusively by a hegemonic Western social imagination; rather, it is open to non-Western theological engagement, including the theologies of the black diaspora. These theological insights make clear links between the historical Jesus and our own current social crises in the world—the concerns of the disenfranchised, marginalized and poor. The dialectic of *historical assertion* and *divine apophasis* create the conditions for a robust antiracist, postcolonial evangelical Christology for the twenty-first century. It helps connect the people of God to our own vulnerable flesh, and our interdependence on the community of creation—the community of the Triune Creator.

9

RECOVERING THE
SPIRIT OF PENTECOST

Canon and Catholicity in Postcolonial Perspective

Megan K. DeFranza and John R. Franke

.... ☙ ....

ACCORDING TO ACTS 1:1-9 JESUS' LAST WORDS to his followers include a command to wait for the gift of the Spirit, who will empower their witness "in Jerusalem . . . and to the ends of the earth" (Acts 1:8 NIV). Acts 2:1-12 records the fulfillment of this promise when a strong wind fills the house where followers of Jesus are staying. According to the narrative they are filled with the Holy Spirit and begin to speak in other languages. A large and diverse number of "God-fearing Jews from every nation under heaven" (Acts 2:5) is gathered in Jerusalem on the day of Pentecost, and this crowd hears the Galilean disciples of Jesus speaking "in other tongues as the Spirit enabled them" (Acts 2:4). In addition, we are told that in spite of the numerous cultures represented in the crowd on that day, each of those present "heard their own language being spoken" (Acts 2:6). Those who experience this linguistic phenomenon are reportedly "amazed and perplexed" and ask each other the question: "What does this mean?" (Acts 2:12).

Inquiry into the meaning of this story has continued throughout the centuries, as Christians have wrestled with the implications of Pentecostal plurality. One of the most significant features for the concerns of this essay is the depiction of the Spirit's activity as that of decentering any particular language or culture with respect to the proclamation of the "wonders of God." The message seems to be that no single language or culture is to be viewed as the prime or inseparable conduit of the Spirit's message. This principle has been significant for the development of a Christian approach to mission. Christians have sought to make the Bible available to people in different cultures by translating it into their languages rather than insisting that new followers learn the biblical languages. Christian historian and missiologist Lamin Sanneh contrasts this approach to mission with that of Islam, which "carries with it certain inalienable cultural assumptions, such as the indispensability of its Arabic heritage in Scripture, law and religion."[1] Christian witness, following the pattern at Pentecost, prefers "to make the recipient culture the true and final locus of the proclamation, so that the religion arrives without the presumption of cultural rejection."[2] This approach and the translation of the Bible into nearly 2,400 different vernacular languages would seem to suggest that the spirit of Pentecost is alive and well in the Christian church. However, despite this commitment to the idea of mission as translation, the church has also been deeply implicated in the process of cultural imperialism and colonization in its mission activity.

In reflecting on the missionary expansion of the church over the last two centuries, missiologists have demonstrated that Western mission has been very much a European, church-centered enterprise and that the Christian message had been passed on in the "image of the church of western European culture."[3] In light of these realities, much of the conversation of postcolonial discourse has focused on rectifying the mistakes of Western mission.[4] Others have noted that the impulse to colonization goes back much further, even to the very formation of the ancient church and its sacred texts. In this essay we will explore the relationship of the Bible to colonialism by recovering some of the earliest instances of Christian colonization. By this we hope to demonstrate the value of postcolonial theology for recovering the spirit of Pentecost through a rethinking of dominant notions of catholicity.[5]

---

[1]Lamin Sanneh, *Translating the Message: The Missionary Impact on Culture* (Maryknoll, NY: Orbis, 1989), p. 20.

[2]Ibid.

[3]Darrell L. Guder, "Missional Church: From Sending to Being Sent," in *Missional Church: A Vision for the Sending of the Church in North America*, ed. Darrell L. Guder (Grand Rapids: Eerdmans, 1998), p. 4.

[4]R. S. Sugirtharajah, *The Bible and the Third World: Precolonial, Colonial and Postcolonial Encounters* (Cambridge: Cambridge University Press, 2001), p. 2, begins his introduction to colonialism thus: "Along with gunboats, opium, slaves and treaties, the Christian Bible became a defining symbol of European expansion."

[5]I.e., how, in the midst of these diverse expressions of faith, should we understand Christian unity?

THE CANON AND COLONIALISM

It is common to date the beginnings of Christian complicity with empire to the rise of the emperor Constantine and the emergence of Christendom. Yet Catherine Keller rightly observes that "there is no precolonial Christianity."[6] Christianity was birthed into a context of colonialism—"nations and languages colonized by Rome, and before that by Greece, and before that by Babylon, [which] had first dispersed the Jews into imperial space."[7] In fact, there is no more glaring example of the colonial context of the early church than the New Testament canon itself—documents witnessing to the Jewish Messiah, whose first language was most likely Aramaic, which were authoritatively recorded in Greek, the lingua franca of the Empire.[8]

Many scholars have looked on the Hellenization of the Holy Land as the work of divine providence. The preservation of the words of Jesus in Koine Greek, rather than Aramaic, facilitated the speedy dissemination of the gospel across cultural boundaries.[9] While acknowledging the benefit of a shared language for the mission of the early church, postcolonial scholars also note the underside of Hellenization—the tendency to privilege not only the language of the Greeks but also the philosophical traditions and cultural mores of empire. Keller laments that the hope of Pentecost was destroyed by the adoption of Hellenism. "In the interest of translation, the language, the logos, of Hellenism provided the *theo-logos* itself. 'Theology,' a Platonic concept, effected the syncretism of a colonized Judaism with a colonizing Hellenism."[10] The book of Acts presents us with a paradox: the miracle of Pentecost (the bridging of cultural-linguistic barriers by the power of the Spirit) is preserved in the language of the empire.

It is not only the privileging of Greek language and thought forms that illustrates the connection between the canon and colonialism. The question of linguistic primacy remains a dividing factor in the church to this day, not only as to which texts are considered original but also as to which texts constitute

---

[6]Catherine Keller, "The Love of Postcolonialism: Theology in the Interstices of Empire," in *Postcolonial Theologies: Divinity and Empire*, ed. Catherine Keller, Michael Nausner and Mayra Rivera (St. Louis: Chalice, 2004), p. 223.

[7]Ibid., p. 222.

[8]Stanley E. Porter, "Did Jesus Ever Teach in Greek?," *Tyndale Bulletin* 44, no. 2 (1993): 199-235.

[9]William D. Mounce, *Basics of Biblical Greek Grammar* (Grand Rapids: Zondervan, 1993), p. 2.

[10]Keller, "The Love of Postcolonialism," p. 222.

the canon. Members of the Assyrian Church of the East claim that it is the Syriac text tradition that preserves "the original words the Messiah and his followers actually spoke and wrote down,"[11] since Syriac is a dialect of Aramaic.[12] Other Syriac scholars are more modest in their claims. The introduction to one English translation of the Syriac Bible, the Peshitta/o, paints an alternate but no less challenging perspective.

> All such facts as these indicate that a very considerable portion of our Saviour's words were probably uttered in Syrian tongue. If this be so, much which is recorded as having been spoken by our Saviour, must have been a translation into one language, of what was spoken in another. Hence, the Syrian gospels have a special value; for whether they are to be regarded as the record of the thoughts which the Saviour spoke in the very language in which He uttered them, or whether they are to be regarded as an early translation from Greek originals *back* into the speech and idiom in which they were originally expressed, . . . we must look for the real spirit of our Saviour's teaching in the venerable idiom of the Peshitto.[13]

Not all Peshitta/o scholars demand Aramaic primacy for the documents of the New Testament; nevertheless, their reminder that most of the words of Christ were probably not originally uttered in Greek opens the door to the possibility that some things may have been lost even in the midst of faithful translations.[14]

What is also significant for our purposes is that the Peshitta/o represents not only a different text tradition but also an alternative canon. The Syriac New Testament omits 2-3 John, 2 Peter, Jude and Revelation. These texts are excluded from the lectionaries of the Syrian Orthodox Church and the Church of the East even if translations have been included in more contemporary versions of the Syriac Bible.

---

[11]Andrew Gabriel Roth, *Ruach Qadim: The Path to Life* (Mosta, Malta: Tushiyah Press, 2006), pp. 81-84.

[12]Aram was a region in the land of Syria.

[13]H. L. Hastings, "A Historical Introduction to the Peshitto Syriac New Testament," in *The New Testament or The Book of the Holy Gospel of our Lord and our God, Jesus the Messiah: A Literal Translation from the Syriac Peshitto Version*, trans. James Murdock (Boston: H. L Hastings, 1893, 1896), pp. xxxi-xxxii.

[14]Porter, "Did Jesus Ever Teach in Greek?," p. 209, argues, "The clear scholarly consensus is that whether or not Jesus originally spoke in Aramaic (as most scholars believe that he did), the [Greek] Gospels themselves are not literalistic translations, even where they purport to record Jesus' words . . . the 'translation' is not literal but literary."

Evangelical engagement in ecumenism certainly requires recognition of the contested nature of the biblical canon—not only of the Old Testament but also of the New. Evangelical postcolonial theology works to hold in tension both the authority and sufficiency of the Western canon with the history of its formation. We recognize that our canon is both a product of Roman imperialism as well as evidence of resistance to imperial Christianity.[15]

In a way similar to the Protestant rejection of the Roman canon, the Syriac canon has provided a model for both a theological identity and a resource to resist imperial forms of Christianity.[16] However, it should also be noted that this same tradition reveals its own evidence of the influence of colonization as far back as the first few centuries of its development. Upon closer inspection, one finds that even this tradition reveals capitulation to colonial influence, which resulted in the loss of certain theological insights unique to this early Christian community. It is to the first few centuries of the church in Syria that we turn in our work to recover the Spirit of Pentecost.

LOST IN TRANSLATION: THE COLONIZATION OF
EARLY SYRIAC CHRISTIANITY

Eastern Syria presents a unique window into the value of postcolonial studies. Bruce Metzger explains why.

> The churches of Eastern Syria in the Kingdom of Osrhoëne seem to have been the first to develop in a country that had not been under the influence of Hellenism. The political fortunes of Edessa, capital of Osrhoëne, present a remarkable contrast to those of other centres of early Christianity. Until A.D. 216 in the reign of the Emperor Caracalla, Edessa lay outside the Roman Empire. Christianity seems to have reached the Euphrates valley about the middle of the second century, that is, while the country was still an independent state. Its people, unlike the Greek-speaking Syrians in the west with their headquarters at Antioch, used Syriac as their mother tongue. It is not surprising that the Christianity of Edessa began to develop independently, without the admixture of Greek philosophy and Roman methods of government that at an early date

---

[15]In the early church the book of Revelation was not initially included in the Western canon, given its negative assessment of imperial Rome. Later, during the Reformation, revision of the canon served to shore up Protestant resistance to Roman Christianity.

[16]Sugirtharajah recounts how it was this ancient canon that enabled rural mountain priests to resist the pressure of Western missionaries in colonial India in *The Bible and the Third World*, pp. 17-20.

modified primitive Christianity in the West and transformed it into the amalgam known as Catholicism.[17]

Susan Ashbrook Harvey illuminates the significance of this uncolonized context by comparing the Syrian tradition to the Coptic of Egypt. She argues that the linguistic difference was "pivotal," but the uncolonized space even more so. "Unlike Coptic, Syriac found space for its own development: it built a rich literary and scholarly tradition all its own. There was little serious Hellenic presence in Syriac culture or thought until the sixth century AD, although influence begins in the fifth century; until then, we have what we may call a 'semitic christianity.'"[18]

According to Sebastian Brock the Syrian tradition offers "the only early Christian literature to have been written in one of these [Semitic] languages."[19] Freedom from the influence of Hellenism allowed the Semitic flavor of Syrian Christianity to flourish, for a time.

One unique aspect of early Syriac Christianity that has been gaining attention in recent years was its theologians' reflections on the grammatical gender of the Spirit. The word for "spirit" in Syriac/Aramaic is *ruha*, a slight modification of the Hebrew *ruah*.[20] Both Brock and Harvey have documented how *ruha* is grammatically feminine in virtually all Christian literature prior to 400 C.E. What is curious about this tradition is that it was altered during the course of a single century so that by the early 500s most theological treatises and biblical translations present the Holy Spirit as grammatically masculine.[21] Nevertheless, despite thoroughgoing revisions of biblical and theological materials, remnants of this ancient tradition can occasionally be found in a few liturgical texts. During Epiphany the following lines can still be heard in some congregations of the Church of the East and the Syrian Orthodox and Maronite Churches.

---

[17]Bruce M. Metzger, *The Canon of the New Testament: Its Origin, Development and Significance* (Oxford: Clarendon, 1997), p. 113.

[18]Susan Ashbrook Harvey, "Women in Early Syrian Christianity," in *Images of Women in Antiquity*, ed. Averil Cameron and Amélie Kuhrt (Detroit: Wayne State University Press, 1983), p. 288.

[19]Sebastian P. Brock, *The Holy Spirit in the Syrian Baptismal Tradition* (Piscataway, NJ: Gorgias Press, 2008), p. 175.

[20]In Hebrew, *ruah* is sometimes identified as a common noun—one that can be used as masculine or feminine depending on the context. While *ruah* is most often feminine (e.g., Judg 3:10, "And the Spirit of the LORD [she] came on him"; 1 Sam 10:6, "The Spirit of the LORD [she] will come upon you in power" [NIV 1984]), it is at times used with a masculine verb (e.g., 1 Kings 18:12, "the Spirit of the LORD [he] will carry you").

[21]Brock, *Holy Spirit*, pp. 176-77.

The Holy Spirit was sent,
she overshadowed the baptismal font
and in the womb of the water, in the "Jordan,"
she fashioned infants who will not die,
and they became spiritual bridegrooms
in whom there dwells Christ the King.[22]

These liturgical images hearken back at least to the third century, where the *Acts of Thomas*, "one of the most important documents of early Syriac Christianity,"[23] describes baptismal and Communion rites for this ancient Christian community.

(Section 27) Come, holy name of Christ, which is above every name; come, Power of the Most High (cp Luke 1:35), and perfect mercy; come exalted Gift (i.e. the Holy Spirit); come compassionate Mother.

(Section 50) Come, hidden Mother, . . . come and make us share in this Eucharist which we perform in your name, and cause us to share in the love to which we are joined by invoking you.

(Section 133, in the course of a trinitarian invocation over the newly baptized) We name over you the name of the Mother.[24]

Harvey works to balance the picture by noting that in the ancient world, "feminine images for the divine are not absent from Greco-Latin writers—Clement of Alexandria is perhaps the best known patristic author in this regard, with his use of images of mothering and nurturing—but no common development akin to the Syriac tradition of the feminine Spirit took place."[25]

At the same time, one must be careful to examine the ways in which Syriac writers employed feminine language not only for the Spirit but even the other persons of the Trinity. Theirs was no crude anthropomorphism but some of the most sophisticated theological poetry of the ancient church. Harvey defends this use in the face of Western preferences for philosophical theology, arguing that poetry "represents a use of language particularly suited to the work of

---

[22]Sebastian P. Brock, "Come, Compassionate Mother . . . Come, Holy Spirit: A Forgotten Aspect of Early Eastern Christian Imagery," *Aram* 3, no. 2 (1989): 254-55.
[23]Ibid., p. 251.
[24]Ibid., pp. 251-52.
[25]Clement, *Paedagogus* 1.6; Susan Ashbrook Harvey, "Feminine Imagery for the Divine: The Holy Spirit, the Odes of Solomon, and Early Syriac Tradition," *St. Vladimir's Theological Quarterly* 37, no. 2 (1993): 121.

theology . . . because of metaphor's capacity to open realms of meaning."[26] Ephrem the Syrian (306–373 C.E.), the most renowned of these poet-theologians, defends this medium in verse.

> In His love He made for Himself a countenance so that His servants might
>   behold Him;
> but, lest we be harmed by imagining He was really like this,
> He moved from one likeness to another, to teach us that He has no likeness.
> Blessed is He who has appeared to our human race under so many metaphors.
>   (31.11)[27]

Ancient Syrian writers drew on feminine imagery they found in the Hebrew Scriptures and developed these within their Christian trinitarian frameworks. Harvey suggests that some of the poems found in the *Odes of Solomon* (what may be the earliest collection of nonbiblical Syrian literature from the second century) are "remarkably 'trinitarian' for Christian literature this early."[28] Here is an example.

> A cup of milk was offered to me
> And I drank it with the sweetness of the Lord's kindness.
> The Son is the cup,
> And He who was milked is the Father,
> And she who milked Him is the Holy Spirit.
> Because His breasts were full, . . .
> The Holy Spirit opened her womb,
> And mixed the milk of the two breasts of the Father.
> And She gave the mixture to the world.[29]

Janet Martin Soskice argues that the styling of all three members of the Trinity as both masculine and feminine is a more orthodox solution than locating the feminine with the Spirit alone—a move she believes threatens to divide the Trinity or subordinate the third person.[30] Soskice reminds us that

---

[26]Harvey, "Feminine Imagery," p. 114.

[27]Ephrem, *Hymns on the Faith* 31, trans. Sebastian P. Brock, *A Garland of Hymns from the Early Church* (McLean, VA: St. Athanasius' Coptic Publishing Center, 1989), pp. 63-68; cited in Harvey, "Feminine Imagery," p. 138.

[28]Harvey, "Feminine Imagery," pp. 122-23.

[29]Ode 19; Harvey, "Feminine Imagery," p. 125.

[30]Janet Martin Soskice, *The Kindness of God: Metaphor, Gender, and Religious Language* (Oxford: University Press, 2007), pp. 114-15.

such complex, layered images can be found already in Deuteronomy 32:6, where God is named as "your Father, your Creator," and Deuteronomy 32:18, "the Rock, who fathered you; . . . the God who gave you birth" (NIV).[31] In a similar way, notes Harvey, "the earliest Syriac version of John 1:18 reads, 'the only-begotten Son, which is from the womb of the Father,' a wording kept in the Peshitto version."[32]

Brock insists that "in using feminine imagery of God . . . Syriac writers are simply following the lead set in the biblical writings themselves."[33] And yet, given the biblical precedence for feminine imagery, one must ask why, in the fifth century, do we find a thoroughgoing purge of feminine language for the Spirit from the Syriac tradition? There is no extant record justifying the changes; nevertheless, Harvey cites Brock, who suggests that the change was a result of the encroaching influence of Greek forms of discourse, adding that "the shift to a masculine Spirit occurred in concert with other changes to bring the Syrian churches into closer conformity with those of the Greco-Latin west."[34] Both authors recall Jerome's commentary on Isaiah wherein he reflects on the differences between Hebrew, Greek and Latin: In the first, the Spirit is feminine; in the second, neuter; in the third, masculine. Thus, he concludes, we learn that God is without gender.[35] But Harvey notes that Jerome's comment "may well indicate that debate on this matter was taking place, and that the imagery was seen to be too dangerous: that for some people the image was seen as identification rather than as icon, to be its object rather than to point to its source. Such a view misrepresents what our texts actually say."[36] The danger may have been felt by the misuse of such metaphors in groups deemed heretical as well as misunderstanding among new converts, particularly those coming from groups in which there existed "a divine triad of Father, Mother and Son."[37]

The colonization of Syriac grammar and early theological development came about through multiple pressures. The fear of misunderstanding and the

---

[31]Quoted in ibid., p. 79.

[32]Harvey, "Feminine Imagery," p. 126.

[33]Brock, *The Holy Spirit*, pp. 187-88.

[34]Harvey, "Feminine Imagery," p. 121. See also Sebastian P. Brock, "Aspects of Translation Technique in Antiquity," *Greek, Roman, and Byzantine Studies* 20 (1979): 69-87.

[35]Jerome, *In Isa.* 11 (on 40:9-11), CCL 73.1 (1963), p. 459, cited in Harvey, "Feminine Imagery"; also Brock, *The Holy Spirit*, p. 175.

[36]Harvey, "Feminine Imagery," pp. 121-22.

[37]Brock, *The Holy Spirit*, p. 185.

desire for Christian unity supplied strong reasons for altering both language and tradition, and yet one must ask: What was lost in this translation?

RECOVERING THE SPIRIT OF PENTECOST:
CATHOLICITY ACCORDING TO THE WHOLE

The history of early Syriac Christianity illustrates the colonizing impulse to suppress other voices and bring them into conformity with the imperial outlook. The difficulty with this attempt at assimilating the other in the desire to secure sameness and uniformity in the life of the Christian community is that it appears to be at odds with the activity of the Spirit in Acts 2. Postcolonial theology, with its emphasis on ways in which empire suppresses and attempts to erase the expression of indigenous theologies, brings the incongruity of the canonization process and the traditions that drove it into stark relief when compared to the activity of the Spirit in the narrative of Pentecost.

In relation to Syriac Christianity, the process of attempting to establish standard forms of theological discourse followed an oft-repeated pattern of suppression regarding constructions that were not authorized by the imperial powers. In the case of the Syriac tradition this resulted in the loss of hybridity and plurality within early theological reflections on the Godhead. Hybridity entails the resistance to hardened difference based on binary oppositions and the determined refusal to assimilate all difference into a universal, hegemonic whole.[38] Despite the challenges that hybridity and plurality bring to the concerns of Christian unity, Walter Brueggemann reminds us that it is these very aspects of the biblical witness that protect us from error. "Israel's rhetorical strategy to keep monotheism from becoming idolatry was to articulate the thick singularity of YHWH in a rich panoply of metaphors, each of which functioned to disclose something of YHWH, but none of which was permitted to dominate or eliminate others."[39] Recovering feminine language for God in the Bible and early Christian communities provides a necessary correction to the idolatrous ways in which masculine language for God has been interpreted within many Christian communities. While it complicates liturgical mores, allowing feminine language to stand alongside masculine terms reminds us that

---

[38]Ien Ang, "Together-in-Difference: Beyond Diaspora, into Hybridity," *Asian Studies Review* 27, no. 2 (2003): 141-54.
[39]Walter Brueggemann, *Reverberations of Faith* (Louisville, KY: Westminster John Knox, 2002), p. 139.

both male and female are created in God's image and that divine being is revealed by and transcends these aspects of creation.

Hybridity can push theologians to frustration in the ways it resists systematization. The very notion of hybridity raises challenges for the traditional construal of theology as "systematic." This nomenclature suggests that theology can be conceived as a relatively stable system of truth that is communicated in the act of revelation. In evangelical contexts the Bible is regularly read in this fashion, with the result that numerous systems of theology have been discerned in its pages and proclaimed to be the one true system of doctrine taught in Scripture. Hybridity resists this notion because it does not proceed on the assumption that various genres and strands of the biblical witness can be arranged into a uniform and universal system of teaching. While this suggestion may sound unsettling to some evangelicals, we believe this model reflects a better understanding of the Trinity wherein each person lives in harmonious relationship with the Other. They are one in the very midst of their difference.[40] Hybridity provides a powerful corrective to traditional conceptions of theology that have often led to sectarianism, as different expressions of the church conclude that they have arrived at the one true system of doctrine. In contrast to the systematic approach to theology and faith, hybridity humbles us. It reminds us that we will never master the mystery of divinity.

The history of Syriac Christianity not only points to questions concerning the nature of the Godhead and contents of the canon but also unmasks the intuitions of the imperial tradition that culminated in the formation of these canons and hegemonic forms of Christianity. As Stephen Moore notes, while all of the texts that would eventually make up the various canons of Christendom were produced at the margins of empire, "the Christianization of Rome and the Romanization of Christianity" meant that the margins moved to the center and were interpreted accordingly. "Locked in the crushing embrace of the Vulgate, the first official Bible of imperial Christianity, the primary function of the biblical texts became that of legitimizing the imperial status quo, a function that, covertly when not overtly, continued into the modern period."[41]

---

[40]For the development of this idea and its implications, see John R. Franke, *Manifold Witness: The Plurality of Truth* (Nashville: Abingdon, 2009).

[41]Stephen D. Moore, "Paul After Empire," in *The Colonized Apostle: Paul Through Postcolonial Eyes*, ed. Christopher D. Stanley (Minneapolis: Fortress, 2011), p. 22.

In other words, both the process of canon formation and the interpretation of the canonical texts that followed were part and parcel of a tradition of theological and ecclesial formation, dominant in the history of the church that is at odds with the work of the Spirit at Pentecost.[42]

How might evangelicals respond to this situation? Recognition of the contested nature of the canon within global Christianity does not undo the way in which the Western canon has and continues to function for the Greco-Roman tradition even if it does suggest a more humble approach to ecumenical engagement. Still, we propose that our awareness of the complicity of the canon in colonial oppression should lead to the adoption of a postcolonial hermeneutic that intentionally highlights the pluralities found in the canonical texts in order to make use of them to promote an inherently plural conception of catholicity. This approach to catholicity is both in keeping with the spirit of Pentecost and preserves the evangelical commitment to biblical authority.

Whether one begins with the Protestant, Roman Catholic or Syriac Bible, every student of the Scriptures must begin with the plurality found within these canons. Each canon is composed of multifaceted and diverse writings, which all contribute to the sense of the whole. Indeed, the presence of four different Gospel accounts provides a significant demonstration of diversity and alerts us to the basic pluriformity of the earliest Christian tradition. Highlighting the plurality of the canon not only points to diversity within the earliest Christian communities but also suggests that we should expect to see plurality in the contemporary church. Attempts at securing uniformity based on the assumption of an overarching and universalistic theology have failed. The plurality and diversity of the Christian community has continued to develop based on the canonical texts in spite of efforts at suppression of the theological or canonical Other.

This means that true "catholic" or "universal" faith is pluralistic. In the words of Justo González,

Believers from all the four corners of the earth bring the richness of their expe-

---

[42]Sugirtharajah, *Bible and the Third World*, pp. 15-19, admits a similar pattern with the Syriac canon. Although the Peshitta was originally written in the language of the people (Peshitta means "simple"), later, when Syriac missionaries moved east, they did not translate it into new vernaculars. Thus in the eighteenth century only a few of the mountain priests in India were able to read the ancient language, and none of the commoners had Bibles in their own tongue.

rience and perception of the gospel, so that we may all come to a fuller, more "catholic"—"according to the whole"—understanding of the gospel. The church calls all the "nations" to the gospel, not only because the "nations" need the gospel, but also because the church needs the "nations" in order to be fully "catholic." If "catholic" means "according to the whole," as long as part of the whole remains outside, or is brought in without being allowed to speak from its own perspective, catholicity itself is truncated.[43]

The universality of this understanding of catholicity is not to be found in a particular uniformity that pertains to the whole church, but rather in the singularity of its vision of plurality in the church.

That plurality and diversity have flourished in the church in spite of attempts at their suppression testifies to the power of the Spirit of Pentecost, who speaks in and through the texts of Scripture to form the church into the body of Christ—a community that is called to be a provisional demonstration of God's will for *all* people and not simply those who have earthly influence and power. In seeking to recover the spirit of Pentecost in the life of the church through attending to the witness of postcolonial theology we are seeking to be faithful to the reality of the Spirit of the living God, whom we believe to be at work in the church. It is our hope that by recovering some of the lost spaces from the past we may open up new spaces for postcolonial theological reflection. In so doing we will live into a form of catholicity according to the whole that has the potential to usher in a new way of doing theology—a way that we believe to be more faithful to both the spirit of Pentecost and the Spirit of the living God made known in Jesus Christ.

[43]Justo L. González, *Out of Every Tribe and Nation: Christian Theology at the Ethnic Roundtable* (Nashville: Abingdon, 1992), pp. 28-29.

Part Four

TRANSFORMING THE EVANGELICAL LEGACY

Introduction to Part Four

Transforming the Evangelical Legacy

⚡

THE AUTHORS IN THIS SECTION address the problem of praxis. Federico A. Roth and Gilberto Lozano, in "The Problem and Promise of Praxis in Postcolonial Criticism," track the development of postcolonial criticism within the field of biblical studies and suggest a rapprochement with liberation theology as a way to move forward.

Kay Higuera Smith documents colonial models of identity formation that were taken up and became characteristic within evangelicalism. In light of this she suggests ways that church and lay groups might gather together to imagine alternate forms of identity formation that enfranchise rather than subject the Other to social and coercive violence.

In a similar vein, Nicholas Rowe and Ray Aldred, in "Healthy Leadership and Power Differences in the Postcolonial Community: Two Reflections," invite us to consider alternate ways of constructing leadership models so as to avoid social and coercive violence. Rowe suggests that cultural distinctions can be taken more seriously as both church and secular groups consider how they lead. Aldred argues for an ethic that embraces distinction and differentiation as an important criterion of true unity. He also offers indigenous North American practices, such as communal identity formation and the practice of treaty, as ways to manage interactions between group leaders by focusing on shared space and mutual accountability.

Nicholas Rowe also coauthors a chapter with Safwat Marzouk, titled "Christian Disciplines as Ways of Instilling God's Shalom for Postcolonial Communities." Rowe challenges exclusively Western expressions of the disciplines and suggests that Christians can benefit from engaging non-Western forms, such as *indaba*, which is a form of communal dispute resolution and which, he argues, can be adapted as a Christian discipline because of its focus on confession, repentance, restoration and the wholeness characterized by shalom.

Marzouk addresses the pressing issues marked by the Arab Spring, which are occurring in Egypt and throughout the region as of this writing. He offers the biblical tradition of lament as an underutilized resource, which allows oppressed communities to challenge and demand of God justice and peace as part of exercising their own agency toward liberation and shalom.

All of these authors offer helpful and practical suggestions for people seeking to reevaluate the ways they structure themselves institutionally, socially and ecclesially.

10

THE PROBLEM AND PROMISE OF PRAXIS IN POSTCOLONIAL CRITICISM

Gilberto Lozano and Federico A. Roth

.... ⚹ ....

POSTCOLONIALISM IS COMMITTED TO resisting colonial and imperial subjugation in all forms. However, it lacks constructive and sustained attention to active dimensions, namely, praxis. Postcolonial theorists make little room for social action, thus undermining the possibility of comprehensive human and societal transformation.

In the following discussion we first trace the contours of postcolonial biblical criticism. Second, we identify reasons for the omission of praxis language in postcolonial thought. Third, we sketch the field's relationship with liberation theology in order to highlight the notion that both fields, despite having important differences, must remain partners and interlocutors. Finally, we conclude the discussion by describing one such point of convergence. Here we propose a collection of praxis trajectories for postcolonialism that are rooted in the groundbreaking work of Paulo Freire's *Pedagogy of the Oppressed*.

POSTCOLONIAL ORIGINS

Postcolonialism has grown out of the complex interaction of many academic fields working in conjunction with moments of geopolitical unrest, national revolutions and ideological resistance of many stripes. The interactions between academics and social forces have led to the manifestation of postcolonial expressions in areas as varied as political science, feminist theory, cultural studies, psychology, philosophy, anthropology, art, theater, musicology, sociology, economics, environmentalism, literary studies and still others.

This enormous diversity is representative of the field's many practitioners who hail from a multitude of disciplines and sociocultural backgrounds. However, what each iteration of postcolonial thought can agree to is that totalizing systems of thought (metanarratives) are to be rejected. Suspicion of such comprehensive systems is evinced in the movement's founding work, Edward Said's *Orientalism*.[1]

As a major catalyst for the working out of critical theory, *Orientalism* is a dazzling and intrepid articulation of the intellectual history of representation between the Western and Arab worlds. It offers an analysis of how raw power is imbued with ideology, expressed and qualified by academic authority, and made to serve campaigns for nation-building. Unlike the resistance literature of mid-century anticolonial thinkers, such as Aimé Césaire,[2] Frantz Fanon[3] and Albert Memmi,[4] Said has shown how the corrosive influence of the literary studies discipline materialized in the spheres of history and politics.[5]

What Said discovers in the academic history of dealings by the West is an immense collection of clichéd, reductive and offensive depictions of Eastern life. At worst its inhabitants are crudely sensationalized, disfigured and demonized as a fanatical, bloodthirsty, sexually deviant and belligerent hoard. At best the collective Orient is a land of adventures—a mysterious, dark place inhabited by primitive and pastoral people always happy but backward, steeped in primal tradition, resistant to societal advancement and hopelessly mummified in timeless antiquity. These coarse misrepresentations serve to define the East as the incompatible corruption of the West, which is portrayed as being civil, normative, sexually circumspect, masculine, safe, inherently good and supremely logical.

Following Edward Said's examination of the Western Orientalist metanarrative, postcolonialism seeks to unearth exploitative ideologies of all kinds.

---

[1] Edward W. Said, *Orientalism* (New York: Vintage, 1978).

[2] Aimé Césaire, *Notebook of a Return to the Native Land*, ed. Clayton Eshleman and Annette Smith, trans. Clayton Eshleman (Middletown, CT: Wesleyan University Press, 2001).

[3] Frantz Fanon, *Black Skin, White Masks*, trans. Charles Lam Markmann (1952; repr., New York: Grove Press, 1967); Fanon, *The Wretched of the Earth*, trans. Richard Philcox (1961; repr., New York: Grove Press, 2004); Fanon, *A Dying Colonialism*, trans. Haakon Chevalier (1959; repr., New York: Grove Press, 1965).

[4] Albert Memmi, *The Colonizer and the Colonized* (1957; repr., Boston: Beacon, 1965); Memmi, *Dependence: A Sketch for a Portrait of the Dependent*, trans. Philip A. Facey (Boston: Beacon, 1984).

[5] Valerie Kennedy, *Edward Said: A Critical Introduction* (Cambridge: Polity, 2000), p. 15.

Be they social, political or economic, all philosophical expressions that aim to suppress underprivileged populations are identified, critiqued and rejected outright. Consideration is given to the multifaceted relationship of power, in all its forms, by way of a ubiquitous spatial metaphor that identifies the "center" and the "margins." The field examines the unequal distribution of social, cultural, political and economic power existing between the dominant metropole (center) and those communities that live, or share, the experience of the underclasses on the peripheries (margins). As an outcrop of postcolonialism, biblical/theological studies has set out to identify its own colonial collusions via a critical *confrontation* and *discursive stance against* dominant knowledge systems responsible for influencing understanding.

More an approach than a method, postcolonial biblical criticism seeks to accomplish a pair of indispensable goals. As a style of inquiry it attempts to catalog the presence of imperialistic impulses in the biblical text as well as in the academic and ecclesial appropriation *of* the biblical text. Thus postcolonial scholarship attempts to go beyond simply identifying exegetical imperialism to "decolonizing" both texts and their interpretations through a commitment to disenfranchised groups, both in the biblical world and outside of it. For Christian communities this approach has important implications for the witness of the church, which is ever more global, dispersed and multiform. In that sense postcolonialism offers updated language for reaching a vast and postmodern world.

THE PUZZLING ABSENCE OF PRAXIS LANGUAGE

One would surmise that a field so indebted to movements of national liberation, political activism and insurgency would retain its emphasis on social action. Unfortunately postcolonial biblical interpretation, as it is currently construed, lacks constructive and sustained attention to active dimensions, namely, praxis. By failing to discuss praxis the field undermines its revolutionary roots and diminishes the possibility of comprehensive human and societal transformation.

One reason for this deficiency may be found in postcolonialism's resistance to totalizing discourses.[6] Even the articulation of praxis runs the risk of materializing one group's ideological agenda over that of others. For if each

---

[6]See R. S. Sugirtharajah, introduction to *The Postcolonial Bible*, ed. R. S. Sugirtharajah (Sheffield: Sheffield Academic Press, 1998), p. 16.

social context requires intimate knowledge of cultural norms, how can the critic possibly offer guidelines without reasserting hegemonic and universalizing discourses?

Moreover, postcolonialism retains a rather ahistorical nomenclature. The existence or absence of the controversial hyphen (i.e., post-colonialism) has been hotly debated. Critics are dissatisfied with the implications symbolized by its presence.[7] Chief among objections is the insinuation that colonialism represents a bygone era.[8] The hyphenated form implies that world societies have transcended colonial ideologies and advanced past them.[9] Wherever the hyphen remains, the mind is dulled to the reality of persistent political, cultural and economic Western, ideological *neo*imperialism.[10]

The more common unhyphenated merging of *post* with *colonialism* offers no solution. The collapsing of terms hints at a move "beyond" colonialism, not merely in a chronological sense, however, but in terms of an ethical direction and as a critical idea.[11] Fernando Segovia regards it as "a reference to that *frame of mind*, individual or collective, that problematizes the imperial/colonial phenomenon as a whole and, in so doing, attains a sense of conscientization."[12] Postcolonialism exists, therefore, "as a perpetual set of critical possibilities,"[13] deployed to address the array of neocolonial power relations in issues of cultural, racial and ethnic spheres.[14] Presumably then, the term is used to define an angle of inquiry, not to outline the enactment of tangible work.

---

[7]See Ellah Shohat, "Notes on the Post-Colonial," *Social Text* 31/32 (1992): 99-113.

[8]R. S. Sugirtharajah, *The Bible and the Third World: Precolonial, Colonial and Postcolonial Encounters* (Cambridge: Cambridge University Press, 2001), p. 268.

[9]Laura E. Donaldson, "Postcolonialism and Biblical Reading: An Introduction," *Semeia* 75 (1996): 5. See further, Anne McClintock, "The Angel of Progress: Pitfalls of the Term 'Post-Colonialism,'" *Social Text* 31/32 (1992): 85-98. Against McClintock see Bill Ashcroft, Gareth Griffiths and Helen Tiffin, *The Empire Writes Back: Theory and Practice in Post-Colonial Literatures*, 2nd ed. (London: Routledge, 2002), p. 198.

[10]Thus, notes Neil Lazarus, the hyphen, which appears mostly in the field's literature of the early 1970s, "was a periodizing term, a historical and not an ideological concept." See Neil Lazarus, introduction to *The Cambridge Companion to Postcolonial Literary Studies*, ed. Neil Lazarus (Cambridge: Cambridge University Press, 2004), p. 2.

[11]No author cited, introduction to *Postcolonial Theologies: Divinity and Empire*, ed. Catherine Keller et al. (St. Louis: Chalice, 2004), pp. 6-7.

[12]Fernando F. Segovia, "Interpreting Beyond Borders: Postcolonial Studies and Diasporic Studies in Biblical Criticism," in *Interpreting Beyond Borders*, ed. Fernando F. Segovia (Sheffield: Sheffield Academic Press, 2000), p. 12 (emphasis added).

[13]R. S. Sugirtharajah, "Charting the Aftermath: A Review of Postcolonial Criticism," in *The Postcolonial Biblical Reader*, ed. R. S. Sugirtharajah (Malden, MA: Blackwell, 2006), p. 9.

[14]Ashcroft, Griffiths and Tiffin, *The Empire Writes Back*, p. 201.

On the other hand, the unhyphenated term abstracts and depoliticizes, leaving no room for the experience of contemporary resistance.[15] Thus the term (with or without its hyphen) does not naturally lend itself to praxis. Rather, it divests the field of active and material potentialities. It is largely untethered from historical forces and concrete human concerns. Ironically a discipline born of social activism on behalf of disenfranchised and occupied groups, and committed to combating the reification of injustice, has itself been mollified and defanged by its very title.

The field also suffers greatly from a resultant obsession with hyperspecialization, which in turn furthers disconnectedness from the general populace. Gayatri Spivak has been uniquely critical of postcolonialism's rarified intonations. She has commented that what she sees in American circles is an "academico-cultural 'postcolonialism'" and warns against elite postcolonialism that appears "to be as much a strategy of differentiating oneself from the racial underclass as it is to speak in its name."[16] For her, "Postcolonial/colonial discourse studies is becoming a substantial subdisciplinary ghetto."[17] Similarly Ashcroft, Griffiths and Tiffin have warned against the lack of historical unlocatedness as leading to an unfortunate "fetishization of theory."[18] Perhaps most troublesome is the tendency of postcolonialists to employ rather esoteric writing styles, which self-quarantine the field in ways that resonate only in obscure publications or exclusive professional meetings. This brand of jargon-heavy[19] hyperprofessionalization obstructs the "ordinary reader"[20] from full access.

Finally, a regular critique of the discipline rests on its tendency to romanticize oppression. A roll call of its scholarly voices would reveal many who number among the self-exiled, wealthy and socially advantaged. Some use the

---

[15]Shohat, "Notes on the Post-Colonial," p. 104.

[16]Gayatri Chakravorty Spivak, *A Critique of Postcolonial Reason: Toward a History of the Vanishing Present* (Cambridge, MA: Harvard University Press, 1999), p. 358. Similarly Elleke Boehmer distinguishes between "cosmopolitan" and "contextual" kinds of emerging postcolonialisms. *Colonial and Postcolonial Literature: Migrant Metaphors*, 2nd ed. (Oxford: Oxford University Press, 2005), pp. 242-43.

[17]Spivak, *A Critique*, p. 1.

[18]Ashcroft, Griffiths and Tiffin, *The Empire Writes Back*, p. 198.

[19]R. S. Sugirtharajah, *Postcolonial Reconfigurations: An Alternative Way of Reading the Bible and Doing Theology* (St. Louis: Chalice, 2003), p. 109.

[20]Gerald O. West, ed., *Reading Other-Wise: Socially Engaged Biblical Scholars Reading with Their Local Communities* (Atlanta: Society of Biblical Literature, 2007).

postcolonial marker to incite Western guilt and sentimentalize subalterneity.[21]

When unexamined, postcolonialism has tended to indulge in its underclass status. Roland Boer identifies the ways in which postcolonialism "valorizes voluntary diaspora, migrancy, and itinerancy," often for commercial and academic gain.[22] We might add that there exists an unfortunate tendency to romanticize misery by celebrating victimhood as an unchanging reality. To overturn oppression through action would be to challenge the vogue of professional prestige, distinctiveness and privilege that comes with being numbered among marginal groups.

For these reasons, and certainly others, postcolonialism has slipped casually into inactivity. This is not to say that inaction equates to dormancy. Neither is it meant to imply that theory has lost its usefulness. If it is true that boots-on-the-ground-style colonialism is replayed in more sinister forms through cultural (mis)representation and social forms of all kinds,[23] then it will be vital to continue working theoretically. However, the lack of praxis, as outlined above, is a significant shortcoming eliciting some key questions. How can the field resist self-indulgent subalterneity, combat its own hyperspecialization, craft accessible language and reestablish itself in real time to address actual human suffering? Additionally, can the field move beyond its ahistorical and romanticizing tendencies, which serve only to alienate it from action? Is there a way to reconnect the field with its activist roots in a manner that does not fall into the trap of reinscribing totalizing discourses? What, if any, interdisciplinary resources exist in arriving at an answer? To reply in the affirmative, we propose that postcolonialism foster connectedness with the work of liberation theology, especially with regard to the critical area of praxis.

POSTCOLONIALISM AND LIBERATION: PARTNERS IN PRAXIS

The similarities between postcolonial criticism and liberation are hard to overlook. Both share a concern for humanizing the Other. Both are sensitive to the unique contexts in which flesh-and-blood readers reside. Both confirm that theology must be informed by social context. A regard for preserving the dignity of those

---

[21]Vinoth Ramachandra, *Subverting Global Myths: Theology and the Public Issues Shaping Our World* (Downers Grove, IL: InterVarsity Press, 2008), pp. 240-42.

[22]Roland Boer, *Last Stop Before Antarctica: The Bible and Postcolonialism in Australia*, Semeia Studies 64, 2nd ed. (Atlanta: Society of Biblical Literature, 2008), p. 101.

[23]See further, Edward Said, *Culture and Imperialism* (New York: Vintage, 1993).

considered "nonpersons," be they poor through economic or social realities, over against those in positions of power is also at the center of both interpretive vocations. While postcolonialism may not promote liberation's famous "preferential option for the poor,"[24] it does prefer readings that resist centrist agendas. Another thing they hold in common is the mutual denouncement of epistemic evil imposed on societies by those who hold social, political and economic power. Violence is seen as a comprehensive and institutionalized reality. Oppressors and oppressive systems to which they belong are to be opposed by the conscientized.[25] As such, human experience is not to be kept separate from Bible reading but is considered an indispensable element *of genuine* Bible reading. Both liberation and postcolonial approaches, to various degrees, long for a world devoid of human suffering. Both approaches are attuned to the ideological tenor of interpretive schemes, along with the need to dismantle their power relationships for the sake of engendering an alternative reality.[26] These seminal associations are strong enough to suggest that the disciplines ought to ultimately remain co-workers in the struggle for the liberation of oppressed communities.[27]

For these reasons postcolonialism is bound to address such issues, and in this regard its aims are closely connected to those of liberation theology. In other words, postcolonialism has generated a repertoire of critical-hermeneutical tools that can be allied to the practical purpose of generating human liberation, which ultimately is good news (*euangelion*). However, the absence of praxis language in postcolonial thought remains its most glaring deficiency. We recall that rather than beginning with erudite conceptual abstractions at home in the academic guild, liberation opted for the experience of the downtrodden as the theological starting point. In this regard liberation could emulate the tangible work of God to emphasize the need for social action. This was the essential move *before* reflection. In combination action and reflection together form praxis. From a liberation standpoint, praxis cannot be devoid of either aspect, but rather it is the result of the collaboration and reinforcement of action and reflection.

---

[24]Gustavo Gutiérrez, *A Theology of Liberation: History, Politics and Salvation,* trans. and ed. Sister Caridad Inda and John Eagleson (Maryknoll, NY: Orbis, 1988), pp. xxv-xxvii.

[25]The meaning of conscientization is explained below.

[26]Sugirtharajah, *Bible and the Third World,* p. 259.

[27]R. S. Sugirtharajah, *Postcolonial Criticism and Biblical Interpretation* (Oxford: Oxford University Press, 2002), p. 117.

To be sure, postcolonial scholarship strains to hear the voices of voiceless, disenfranchised communities. But because there is a fundamental suspicion of totalizing discourses, that is, grand narratives supposed to be universally applicable and to embrace/explicate all the diversity of human experience, there is also a felt reticence to discuss action on behalf of the poor that might lead to their healing and redemption. This is precisely because postcolonial thought refrains from prescribing certain courses of action in order to avoid the trap of imposing formulas that are supposed to be applicable regardless of cultural difference. As a result, the field tends to exist mainly in the intellectual space of the scholarly community. Postcolonialism remains inert and unengaged.

We propose, however, mitigating this deficiency by introducing a praxis that takes postcolonial concerns seriously and, at the same time, provides tools for engaging biblical texts from this perspective. Part of the solution is for the field of academic postcolonial criticism to rethink its relationship with liberation as it seeks *both* to develop praxis language and enact praxis behaviors. Much is at stake in this endeavor.

What might a postcolonialist praxis look like? How can the Christian community affirm with postcolonialism the dangers of allying too closely with totalizing discourses while also not forfeiting the important connection of action *and* reflection? In answer to this question, we propose that Paulo Freire's liberationist approach as presented in his seminal *Pedagogy of the Oppressed* provides valid guidelines for praxis done from the underside of history.[28]

POSTCOLONIAL PRAXIS AND *PEDAGOGY OF THE OPPRESSED*

Freire was among the first to champion the idea of using a hermeneutic of suspicion. He argued that education from above was not free of bias because it represented the interests of the powerful. Letting the oppressed speak or find their own voice was the way to do a liberating education. For Freire, education had to start where the oppressed were. It had to take into account their situation, and it had to include an analysis of their reality. Now, who are the oppressed? The oppressed are the voiceless in any context. When the voiceless begin to analyze their situation and to name it, they begin to gain their voice; they become Subjects of their own history, and though this would often involve a radicalization,

---

[28]Paulo Freire, *Pedagogy of the Oppressed*, trans. Myra Bergman Ramos (New York: Herder and Herder, 1970).

it is a welcome development.[29] The ultimate goal of this process is the liberation of both oppressed and oppressor resulting from a radically different form of society. Those who have embarked on an understanding of their own reality, or those who have embraced the cause of the voiceless, and thus have become "radicalized," reject a priori judgments and what Freire called *circles of certainty*.[30] It is the task of those who have become radicalized by grasping reality to face it fully in order transform it.[31] Freire's liberative pathway can be used profitably in other contexts as well. It is to that end that we propose using Freire to set constructive trajectories for postcolonial biblical interpretation and praxis.[32]

Freire starts with a general proposition: "This, then, is the great humanistic and historical task of the oppressed: to liberate themselves and their oppressors as well."[33] The oppressed, who have attained a certain degree of *conscientização*,[34] will strive to liberate themselves, removing the structures that have been used to dehumanize them. *Conscientization* is the awareness that is gained when the oppressed are able to name the things that oppress them and to uncover the mechanisms by which they are in situations of subjugation.

What do we do, however, if we recognize that we belong to the centers of power and not to the margins, as is likely to be the case for those interpreters from the European and North American contexts and cultures? The call for the oppressed to lead the way of their own liberation does not prevent others from contributing to that project. For that to take place Freire has proposed the following steps for academics or elite persons who want to ally themselves with the oppressed.

---

[29]As Freire, ibid, pp. 21-22, said, "Radicalization criticizes and thereby liberates. Radicalization involves increased commitment to the position one has chosen, and thus ever greater engagement in the effort to transform concrete, objective reality."

[30]Though using slightly different wording, there is a basic agreement between liberation and postcolonialism, namely, the suspicion or outright rejection of totalizing structures imposed from positions of power.

[31]Freire, *Pedagogy*, pp. 23-24.

[32]To be sure, when he began his own work, Freire did not use the nomenclature of postcolonialism. Nevertheless, his theories were shaped by the awareness that in his Brazilian context he was dealing with the sequels of hundreds of years of oppression, which had started with the Portuguese colonizers and had continued in the structures that largely remained from the colonial period.

[33]Freire, *Pedagogy*, p. 28.

[34]The Portuguese term *conscientização* has now been appropriated into the English language as *conscientization*. It is yet another point of contact between postcolonial theory and liberation. Both call for conscientization, as the understanding, recognition or apprehension of the functioning of colonialism and its consequences.

First, guilt-ridden, paternalistic attitudes that keep the oppressed in a situation of dependence should be discarded. Instead, he calls on elites to show *solidarity* with the oppressed. At its inception postcolonial theory also explicitly stressed solidarity. Somehow, however, postcolonial studies have become theoretical battlegrounds, and this initial aspect has been lost. Thus it is pertinent that this is where Freire starts. In this first step toward building a postcolonial, liberating paradigm the scholar takes sides—with the oppressed, which involves affirming the varieties of human experience. This should help us to refrain from judgment—that is, to see that difference is the norm and that the Bible can be seen in terms of *their* values, and not solely those of the elites.[35] Additionally, liberating education, even when done by scholars or elite persons, requires *naming* or identifying the structures of oppression. This is possible only by becoming conscious (gaining consciousness) of the oppression, and this, in turn, is possible only by way of "reflection and action upon the world in order to transform it."[36]

A second step in Freire's model and our proposal for a postcolonial interpretation and praxis involves allies from the social, political or economic center dialoguing with the oppressed. Liberation is not brought down to the oppressed but rather is directed by them, and others take roles as solidary participants. In terms of biblical interpretation this means that interpreters must constantly be in dialogue with those not in the centers of power. Moreover, their exegetical proposals should be set forth only after much reflection and significant input from those who have previously been excluded. Freire's pedagogy is born at this junction. Dialogue with the oppressed about *their* actions generates an authentic pedagogy *of the oppressed*. For that reason Freire warns, "No pedagogy which is truly liberating can remain distant from the oppressed by treating them as unfortunates and by presenting for their emulation models from among the oppressors. The oppressed must be their own example in the struggle for their redemption."[37] It must be reiterated, however, that the ul-

---

[35]Paulo Freire and Antonio Faundez, *Learning to Question: A Pedagogy of Liberation*, trans. Tony Coates (Geneva: WCC Publications, 1989), pp. 10-19.

[36]Ibid., p. 36. Also as Gustavo Gutiérrez, *On Job: God-talk and the Suffering of the Innocent*, trans. Matthew J. O'Connell (Maryknoll, NY: Orbis, 1987), p. 211, says, "Theologizing done without the mediation of contemplation and *practice* does not meet the requirements of the God of the Bible" (emphasis added).

[37]Freire, *Pedagogy*, p. 39. This is constantly stressed in Freire's work. See also Freire and Faundez, *Learning to Question*, pp. 28-29. See also how Elsa Tamez, "The Bible and the Five Hundred Years

timate goal of this enterprise is the liberation of all human beings—both oppressed *and* oppressor.

The third step, Freire alerts us, requires that the process of liberation or postcolonial praxis be initiated and guided by the oppressed themselves. When it comes to interpretation, it is imperative that scholars and allies from the West surrender, or at least be flexible with, their models of biblical interpretation. It is essential that Western interpreters recognize that they mistook the Bible as yet another object at their disposal.[38] Because of this, even after taking the side of the oppressed, the solidary still show signs of their origin, that is, "their prejudices and their deformations, which include a lack of confidence in the people's ability to think, to want, and to know."[39] Even while trying to give up control over the oppressed, the solidary insist on being the chief architects and managers of the process, and they do so mainly out of distrust of the people. That is why *trust* in the people is an essential requirement in the process of postcolonial conscientization and praxis.[40]

Trust is also promoted when those in positions of power realize that the oppressed tend to self-depreciate as a result of internalizing the opinions that the oppressors have of them.[41] Biblical interpreters solidary with their colleagues understand this mechanism and thus reaffirm the worthiness of their colleagues' views. This is a profoundly humanistic vocation, since, as Freire points out, "the oppressed must see themselves as men engaged in the ontological and historical vocation of becoming more fully human."[42]

The fourth stage for those desiring solidarity with the oppressed in this liberating enterprise consists of discovering the oppressors' identities. Only after the oppressed have identified the oppressors and have organized themselves around the struggle for their liberation can they believe in themselves. Freire

---

of Conquest," in *Voices from the Margin: Interpreting the Bible in the Third World*, ed. R. S. Sugirtharajah, 3rd ed. (Maryknoll, NY: Orbis, 2006), p. 23, has articulated this.

[38]Freire, *Pedagogy*, p. 44.

[39]Ibid., p. 46.

[40]For Freire, ibid., p. 47, learning to trust the other and surrender one's wish to control points to nothing less than the rebirth of the oppressor to a new way of being that is not oppressive anymore.

[41]See the work of Memmi, *Colonizer and the Colonized*; and *Dependence: A Sketch for a Portrait of the Dependent*. Also of great importance is Ashis Nandy, *The Intimate Enemy: Loss and Recovery of Self Under Colonialism* (Delhi: Oxford University Press, 1983). Mulk Râj Anand's *Untouchable* (London: Penguin, 1940), is a stirring narrative account of the sense of inferiority and self-depreciation experienced by the so-called untouchable caste of India.

[42]Freire, *Pedagogy*, p. 52.

states the eminently practical nature of this aspect of liberative education in this fashion: "This discovery cannot be purely intellectual but must involve action; nor can it be limited to mere activism, but must include serious reflection: only then will it be a praxis."[43] So in Freire's view praxis is not simply action but rather is constituted both by action and by reflection on that action. Only then does it constitute authentic praxis.

The fifth element of this complex pedagogy is the awareness that knowledge is not a fixed depository from which teachers or experts draw in order to enlighten the masses. Freire calls this the "banking" model of education. He calls instead for a radical concept in which "knowledge emerges only through invention and re-invention, through the restless, impatient, continuing, hopeful inquiry men pursue in the world, with the world, and with each other."[44] In other words, the knowledge generated is seen always as preliminary and susceptible to the transformations brought by the acquisition of new knowledge, which is generated as people have new experiences in the world. This is also stressed by postcolonial theory as a way of rejecting traditional, totalizing readings of the Bible, written once and for all time.

Noticeable in Freire's proposal is a certain eschatological thrust; that is, the ultimate goal of any liberating effort is to achieve the liberation of both oppressed and oppressor and to transform society so that oppression ceases. This goal implies the transformation of both the oppressed and oppressor. We have previously used the language of metropole and periphery, or margins, in order to describe how postcolonialism views the dominant center and the fringes of society. But Freire would contest that categorization. In his view, "The oppressed are not 'marginals,' are not men living 'outside' society. They have always been 'inside'—inside the structure which made them 'beings for others.'"[45] So instead of simply proposing their integration, Freire calls for the radical transformation of society, not to include the oppressed in the structures of oppression, but to change the very structure so that the oppressed become "beings for themselves."[46]

The last step in this model consists of calling into question authority for

---

[43]Ibid.
[44]Ibid., p. 58. For Freire, education is always remaking itself (p. 72).
[45]Ibid., p. 55.
[46]Ibid., p. 61.

authority's sake. Contrary to so many vertical models of education and interpretation, a postcolonial/liberative approach posits that "arguments based on 'authority' are no longer valid; in order to function, authority must be *on the side of* freedom, not *against* it. Here, no one teaches another, nor is anyone self-taught. Men teach each other, mediated by the world, by the cognizable objects which in banking education are 'owned' by the teacher."[47] Therefore, this model is collaborative. We have stressed that this praxis of interpretation should be done in dialogue with others.[48]

The foregoing are trajectories or paths set out as suggestions for interpreters seeking to generate a focus on praxis within postcolonial criticism, and thus, to more faithfully align postcolonialism with the ethos of evangelicalism. At the same time, we would like to draw attention to the fact that there does not exist a single, comprehensive model for doing postcolonial biblical interpretation with a praxis-oriented approach. Those scholars engaged in this form of criticism have used a wide variety of tools and interpretive frameworks.

CONCLUSION

From showing how colonialists portray their subjects and thus construct the image of the colonized, to pointing toward approaches for challenging those structures, postcolonial work has been characterized by being highly theoretical in nature, to the detriment of practical approaches. The absence of praxis is particularly acute in biblical studies.

In view of this absence of praxis, we have proposed broad strategies that will drive postcolonial interpretation toward achieving the promise of its potential. We have suggested that liberation and postcolonial interpretations share similar objectives. For this reason we have proposed ways by which interpreters can engage biblical texts in solidarity and dialogue with communities who traditionally have been excluded from the process.

Thus, using Paulo Freire's *Pedagogy of the Oppressed*, we have offered some trajectories that might prove useful in the practice of postcolonial biblical criticism and praxis. Along with Freire, we believe that the ultimate goal of such

---

[47]Ibid., p. 67 (emphasis original).

[48]Freire, ibid., p. 74, was convinced that "the pursuit of full humanity . . . cannot be carried out in isolation or individualism, but only in fellowship and solidarity. . . . No one can be authentically human while he prevents others from being so. Attempting *to be more* human, individualistically, leads to *having more*, egotistically: a form of dehumanization."

an endeavor is to overcome structures of oppression. Affirming the diversity of human experience and human knowledge, we have proposed that truth is found in the joint and collaborative efforts of people across multiple boundaries of wealth, geography, class, gender and so forth. Believing that postcolonial biblical interpretation should itself overcome the logic of colonialism, we suggest that interpretation should be done collectively by allies in solidarity with the oppressed and with them as full partners.

11

EMBRACING THE OTHER

A Vision for Evangelical Identity

Kay Higuera Smith

····························· ⚸ ·····························

T HE HISTORY OF CHRISTIAN EMPIRE is marked by a long-lived but violent kind of identity formation—one that constructs binary opposites between groups as a way to assert power. In such binary models, including Christian ones, group members identify themselves by what or who they are *not*. In constructing our own identity over against the group that we are *not*, we create out of whole cloth a new identity—that of the binary "Other." This model of identity formation, in imperial operations, results in distancing, alienating, subsuming or conquering those whose very identities now are bound to ours as—falsely—constructed "Other." Central to this kind of identity formation is objectification. This occurs when we create the Other as the *object* that we, the subjective knowers, seek to define on our own terms and to our own advantage. Empires have deftly employed binary models to construct their identities because it enables them to assert and legitimize taking power for themselves.[1]

One of the challenges put before those who embrace postcoloniality is to ask how postcolonial models offer new ways to construct identities so as to avoid these binary and objectifying strategies. I suggest here that those of us who desire to engage the "Other" in a manner that rejects violence have an

---

[1]On social identity construction, see Peter Weinreich and Wendy Saunderson, eds., *Analysing Identity: Cross-Cultural, Societal and Clinical Contexts* (New York: Routledge, 2003); and Peter J. Burke and Jan E. Stets, *Identity Theory* (New York: Oxford University Press, 2009), pp. 61, 118-24. On binary identity construction, see Homi Bhabha, *The Location of Culture*, 2nd ed. (New York: Routledge, 2006).

exciting opportunity to rethink how we construct our own identities with purposefulness toward our colonial and imperial past. To think about constructing identity in a way that is ethical and that avoids the pitfalls of "othering," I suggest three approaches that can be implemented at the social, institutional and ecclesiological levels: (1) that we interrogate and change how we construct power, including how we objectify others; (2) that we collectively and consciously work to involve ourselves with others at all levels of the social spectrum; and (3) that we explore the social memories of others and seek to uncover the conscious social "forgetting" of others' stories within our own cultural narratives.

Evangelicals have a well-documented history of engaging in binary identity construction. Certainly this is not unique to evangelicals. However, members of any group that purports to take seriously the words of Christ must account for why they have chosen a model of empire that builds on this kind of violent identity construction with respect to those who are different. A central task for a community of faithful disciples will be that of interrogating power and how we wield it. John Howard Yoder has written, "To constitute a visible community, there has to be an answer to the problem of power."[2] It is this problem of power that I will address below.

In this effort, I write as a woman of mixed culture—white, Spanish and Mexican—who has benefited from the privileges of white culture but who also much more closely resonates with my Latin@ traditions. I write as a person who has occupied the margins and who also has experienced privilege—being both colonizer and colonized. Given my social location this endeavor is uniquely important to me.

COLONIAL MODELS OF IDENTITY FORMATION

Colonial discourse constructed identity using binary modes as a way to maintain power over others.[3] One way of doing this was by constructing fixed identities, both for the colonial self and for others as a way to mark off colonized people groups as Object to be controlled. Colonial elites created narra-

---

[2]John Howard Yoder, *The Jewish-Christian Schism Revisited*, ed. Michael G. Cartwright and Peter Ochs (Grand Rapids: Eerdmans, 2003), p. 128.

[3]I define *discourse* as the combination of language, symbols, codes and logical structures of a social group.

tives about the colonized that would convince their own populace to fear the colonized and hence support elites in their task of marking the colonized either for subjugation or annihilation. If members of a subjugated group have one fixed, essential "nature," which elites can portray as unchanging and innate, then the subjugated Other can be marked as foreordained for colonial control.

As an example, colonial author Ernest Renan, philosopher and church historian, writing in 1861 in the Orientalist vein so carefully documented by Edward Said, expressed the conviction that the Syrians' essential natures made it impossible for them to be "*civilised* except by slavery."[4] By asserting that the Syrians possessed "essential natures," Renan fixed their identities as if they were monolithic and all-encompassing. This allowed him to offer what appeared to be a moral and ethical argument that justified enslaving them.

Binary, fixed identity construction also benefited colonialists because it gave them a reason to discourage or deny the possibility of any kind of social "mixing." The second form of identity construction characteristic of colonialism, then, was the prevention of social mixing between colonizer and colonized. This resulted in colonialists' rarely having an opportunity to engage the Other as subjective knowers in their own right but only as distant objects. In this way, they were able to justify their own actions as well as to control and impose an ordered structure on the people whose lands and resources they desired to exploit.[5] Robert J. C. Young notes that nineteenth-century official British colonial policy in India became "focused on an effort to prevent mixing between the British and their subject people."[6] Preventing social "mixing" and fixing strong boundaries allowed colonialists to maintain order and to keep people in their "place."

In colonial systems, social mixing was controlled, monitored, and taxonomically and legislatively regulated as a way to maintain identity and a clear sense of colonial "self" over against colonized "Other." These controls ensured that the social boundaries were as nearly impermeable as possible. The breakdown of

---

[4]Ernest Renan, Letter 25, "Amschid, January 25, 1861," in *Renan's Letters from the Holy Land: The Correspondence of Ernest Renan with M. Berthelot While Gathering Material in Italy and the Orient for "The Life of Jesus,"* trans. Lorenzo O'Rourke (New York: Doubleday, Page, 1904), p. 155; cf. Edward Said, *Orientalism* (New York: Vintage, 1978).

[5]See Burke and Stets, *Identity Theory.*

[6]Robert J. C. Young, *Colonial Desire: Hybridity in Theory, Culture and Race* (New York: Routledge, 1995), p. 144.

these boundaries would mean the breakdown of the defining boundaries of the dominant group as well. If this binary construction were to collapse, the entire colonial project would lose its legitimation and colonialists would lose their basis for justifying their existence as colonial overlords. To accomplish this, binary identity construction was chronicled in science, codified in law and ratified through ideology.[7] Fears of "mixing" actually became inscribed in the scientific journals of the time; science, racial theories and taxonomies, and philosophy all supported the ideology. As an example, Josiah Nott, writing in 1843, argued with scientific certainty that "*mulattoes* are the shortest-lived of any class of the human race . . . that they are bad breeders, bad nurses, liable to abortions, and that their children generally die young."[8] Such pseudo-scientific taxonomies convinced colonialists that their fears of mixing socially with the colonized were well founded and thus sustained and legitimized the entire system.

The third primary way that colonial discourse served to construct binary identities, which equally employed power and oppression as essential tools, was in its use of collective memory. Collective memory functions in two important ways: (1) in ideological interpretations of past events, and (2) in social "forgetting." The real messiness and complexity of history rarely fits neatly into mythic memories. Therefore, groups retell their histories in ways that reinforce their own mythic norms and ideals. These ideological interpretations are inevitably accompanied by social forgetting. It is as crucial for groups to forget parts of their past that do not fit their constructed identities as it is for them to idealize and mythologize other parts that they use to buttress ideological interests and to justify otherwise questionable activities.[9]

Because of these retellings of history, constructed memories idealizing famous colonial figures, such as Columbus or the Mayflower Pilgrims, are fraught with mythological elements that validate and justify the colonial enterprise. By the same

---

[7]See also Rachel Moran, *Interracial Intimacy: The Regulation of Race and Romance* (Chicago: University of Chicago Press, 2003).

[8]Josiah C. Nott, "The Mulatto a Hybrid—Probably Extermination of the Two Races If the Whites and Blacks Are Allowed to Intermarry," *American Journal of the Medical Sciences*, n.s., 6 (1843): 252-56; cited in Young, *Colonial Desire*, pp. 26-27; on British colonial fears of mixing, see Charles Brooke, *Ten Years in Sarawak* (London: Tinsley Brothers, 1866), pp. 331-38; and W. J. Moore, *Health in the Tropics: Or Sanitary Art Applied to Europeans in India* (London: Churchill, 1862), pp. 277, 280.

[9]On the power of memory for group identity, see Yosef Hayim Yerushalmi, *Zakhor: Jewish History and Jewish Memory*, 2nd ed. (New York: Schocken, 1989); and Shannon Sullivan and Nancy Tuana, eds., *Race and Epistemologies of Ignorance* (Albany: State University of New York Press, 2007).

token, contemporary anti-immigration policy, for instance, socially "forgets" the "illegal immigrant" Anglo-Europeans from the East Coast and the Midwest who flooded the West and Southwest in the mid-nineteenth century in violation of the law and of the property and civil rights of local indigenous and *mestizo/métis* ("ethnically mixed") populations.[10] In both of the above cases, the lived experiences of the indigenous and *mestizo/métis* peoples of the Americas were excluded from the collective memory, resulting in those groups being victimized by a kind of "social violence"—a social "forgetting" and expunging of their own social memories when they hear the collective memory recited by the dominant colonial group.

Constructing power by creating the binary, objectified, essentialized Other; discouraging and pathologizing social mixing; and creating ideological collective memories that inevitably include social forgetting of indigenous and *mestizo/métis* stories are characteristic forms of identity construction that valorized and underwrote colonialism. We will see that evangelicals in history have adopted these same strategies for their own identity construction, often resulting in similar forms of social violence against others.

EVANGELICALS AND IDENTITY FORMATION

Without an awareness of history, one might think that evangelicals would most wholeheartedly embrace postcoloniality and its critique of colonial ideology. For one, evangelicals, like Catholics and mainline Protestants, come from all geographic locations, races and ethnic backgrounds and are not limited to the European West. Further, evangelicalism has a long history of being an anti-elitist and populist tradition.[11] Moreover, evangelicals have historically been driven by a strong impulse to engage and influence culture at large. Central to evangelical identity have been social action and social advocacy.[12] Finally, lively and embodied rituals that are malleable and culturally adaptable characterize evangelicals' revivalist history.[13] Given these characteristics, one might assume

---

[10]This movement was validated by the doctrine of "Manifest Destiny." See David Goldfield, *America Aflame: How the Civil War Created a Nation* (New York: Bloomsbury, 2011), p. 30.

[11]George Marsden, *Religion and American Culture*, 2nd ed. (Orlando: Harcourt College Publishers, 2001), p. 33.

[12]Michael O. Emerson and Christian Smith, *Divided by Faith: Evangelical Religion and the Problem of Race in America* (New York: Oxford, 2000), p. 3.

[13]For a history of the function of religion and emotion in the US in the nineteenth century, see John Corrigan, *Business of the Heart: Religion and Emotion in the Nineteenth Century* (Berkeley: University of California, 2002).

that evangelicals would be at the forefront of exploring the benefits of post-coloniality for reimagining cultural identity.

In the United States, however, not only is this not the case, but evangelicals are also often suspicious of postcoloniality. Alister Chapman has chronicled the failures of Western evangelicals to take seriously the concerns of evangelicals in the Global South. Chapman largely attributes these failures to Western evangelicals' lack of desire to dialogue with others and, more importantly, their epistemology, which, he claims, "did not allow for the possibility that they might be wrong."[14]

Additionally, despite evangelicalism's global scope, evangelical churches in the United States are extremely divided racially. Christian Smith and Michael Emerson, writing in the year 2000, found that in the United States, "nearly 90 percent of Americans who call themselves evangelical are white."[15] R. Khari Brown has shown that Anglo-European evangelicals in the United States are much more likely than others to discount concerns about race and to blame nonwhites for problems associated with race.[16] Thus not only has evangelicalism in the United States failed to interrogate its colonial past, but it has also replicated it, creating churches that are highly segregated and divided, both racially and culturally.

How did this division occur? How did a movement that, worldwide, includes many races, ethnicities and cultures—a populist movement that has a history of social advocacy—develop this way? It did so by unreflectively adopting colonial forms of identity construction and ideology. Before offering alternative forms of identity construction, it is helpful to briefly track that historical development.

EVANGELICAL MODELS OF IDENTITY FORMATION

Historically, US evangelicals have employed, at different times, the three primary models of identity construction characteristic of colonialism. Again, those models are (1) constructing fixed, essentialized, objectifying identities,

---

[14]Alister Chapman, "Evangelical International Relations in the Post-Colonial World: The Lausanne Movement and the Challenge of Diversity, 1974–89," *Missiology: An International Review* 37 (2009), p. 363.

[15]Ibid.

[16]R. Khari Brown, "Denominational Differences in Support for Race-Based Policies Among White, Black, Hispanic, and Asian-Americans," *Journal for the Scientific Study of Religion* 48, no. 3 (2009): 605.

which allowed colonialists to manage and shape identity; (2) preventing social "mixing" or blurring of those fixed identity boundaries in order to be able to more clearly define and hence control each social group (colonizer and colonized); and (3) practicing social "forgetting" in order to suppress and ultimately annihilate cultural collective memory that does not reinforce the colonialists' national ideology. In all cases, when evangelicals employed these strategies for identity construction, it resulted in social violence against the binary Other, who served as foil for that construction.

For example, a common practice among eighteenth- and nineteenth-century evangelical writers and preachers in the United States was to rail against Roman Catholics. In the United States the noted evangelical preacher Lyman Beecher delivered a sermon series in 1830 in which he argued that Catholics were fundamentally opposed to American ideals, writing that "always they [Catholics] have been hostile to civil and religious liberty."[17] In remarking about the US colonial period, Robert Marsden notes that "a central theme was the extended cold war between [evangelical] Protestants and Catholics. This deep rivalry," he adds, "dominated American thought on international politics in a way not unlike the way the Cold War overshadowed everything after World War II."[18] Forming, as it did, a "central theme," anti-Catholicism, then, was a way that evangelicals and other Protestants in the United States shaped and nurtured their own identities by creating binary oppositions between themselves and Catholics. It also worked to discourage the enfranchisement of Catholics into US civic life in many regions for generations.

The second form of identity formation characteristic of colonialism was the fear of miscegenation, or social "mixing." In the United States, despite strong abolitionist sentiment after the Civil War, white Northerners joined white Southern evangelicals in voicing discomfort with African Americans being enfranchised or assimilated into society after they were freed. White Northerners wanted to ensure that African Americans stayed in their "assigned order," and white Southern evangelicals went about repenting, not for the "sin" of

---

[17]Lyman Beecher, *A Plea for the West*, 2nd ed. (Cincinnati: Truman & Smith, 1835), p. 92. See also Goldfield, *America Aflame*, p. 19. It should be noted that Beecher also defended Catholics' right to practice their religion; he just portrayed that religion as inconsistent with US ideals.

[18]George M. Marsden, "Religion, Politics, and Search for an American Consensus," in *Religion and American Politics: From the Colonial Period to the Present*, ed. Mark Noll and Luke E. Harlow, 2nd ed. (New York: Oxford University Press, 2007), p. 459.

slavery but rather for the "sin" of capitulation to a social world that disrupted that "order." Both Northern and Southern evangelicals widely called for freed slaves to be deported to Africa, where "they would provide a beacon for 'that most benighted continent,' extending Christianity and ending the slave trade along the African coast."[19] In this way evangelicals, both in the North and the South, cloaked their fear of social "mixing" in pious calls for evangelizing Africa, which they objectified as "benighted" and as lacking morality.[20] Samuel Hopkins, a precursor to the Second Great Awakening, despite being a Northern abolitionist theologian, advocated for deportation to Africa.

> This will gradually draw off all the blacks in New England, and even in the Middle and Southern States, as fast as they can be set free, by which this nation will be delivered from that which, in the view of every discerning man, is a great calamity, and inconsistent with the good of society, and is now really a great injury to most of the white inhabitants, especially in the Southern States.[21]

This fear of fully integrating African Americans into Anglo-European church life and vice versa has contributed to the current reality in which segregation reigns in US evangelical churches, resulting in misunderstanding, disenfranchisement and racial tensions.

In this way white evangelicals adopted the same general fears of social mixing prevalent in US colonial ideology. In the mid-nineteenth century, nowhere was xenophobia in the United States more apparent than in evangelical rhetoric about Mexico. Anti-Mexican sentiment brought together the ideologies of colonialism, Manifest Destiny and anti-Catholicism. In the wake of the US-Mexican War (1846–1847), in which the United States overran New Mexican and Alta California, one of the greatest fears expressed by evangelicals was that of living among non-Anglo-Europeans—this despite the reality that the Anglo-Europeans were occupying those other groups' traditional territories! Thus evangelicals expressed fears that "the spread of settlers (including a likely flood of Catholics) into millions of new acres (already churched by Rome) would secure 'a departure from Social Purity,' generate 'a downward gravitation in

---

[19]See Goldfield, *America Aflame*, p. 141. See also Marsden, *Religion and American Culture*, 23; and Gregory Boyd, *The Myth of A Christian Nation* (Grand Rapids: Zondervan, 2005), p. 150.

[20]Goldfield, *America Aflame*, p. 141; Samuel Hopkins, *The Works of Samuel Hopkins: With a Memoir of His Life and Character* (Boston: Doctrinal Tract and Book Society, 1854), 2:611.

[21]Hopkins, *Works*, 2:611.

morals, in social manners, in education, in religion,' and turn the Mexican lands into a 'great pasture ground of barbarism.'"[22] Even those evangelicals who protested the war with Mexico did so by evoking xenophobic, objectifying rhetoric. Richard J. Carwardine notes that "a chorus of [evangelical] Presbyterians protested against American attacks on 'a half-civilized, . . . weak and defenceless people.'"[23] By stressing anti-Catholic nativism and xenophobia, Anglo-European evangelicals joined others in the United States in refusing to acknowledge, accommodate or embrace the cultural Other. This nativism and xenophobia would carry forward into contemporary evangelical identity formation as well.

Finally, evangelicals also adopted the third identity-forming characteristic of colonialism—the employment of social "forgetting." We see "social forgetting" demonstrated in US textbooks, history books and shared narratives, which annihilate and suppress the histories of those Americans who were not Anglo-Europeans. This social forgetting led to extreme xenophobia and nativism among US evangelicals in the nineteenth century and, as we will see, to a reemergence of xenophobia and nativism in twenty-first-century evangelicalism as well. In evangelicalism it took its most destructive form in evangelical affirmation of the dogma of Manifest Destiny.

Evangelical self-consciousness in the United States has been shaped profoundly by this dogma.[24] It asserts that God has destined the United States to conquer, dispossess and strip other cultural groups of their lands, their traditions and their unique social identities in order to assimilate them to Western Christianity. To fulfill this destiny, then, is to practice Christian virtue. George Marsden writes of "the central belief in national virtue" that has deeply shaped evangelical self-consciousness in the United States.[25] Central to this gospel image of a "city built on a hill" (Mt 5:14) was the social forgetting of the painful and devastating side of that story.

In order to construct US foreign policy in such glowing and evangelistic

---

[22]Quoted in Richard J. Carwardine, *Evangelicals and Politics in Antebellum America* (New Haven, CT: Yale University Press, 1993), p. 147.

[23]J. McClintock to R. Emory, quoted in Richard J. Carwardine, *Evangelicals and Politics in Antebellum America* (New Haven, CT: Yale University Press, 1993), p. 146.

[24]On the doctrine of Manifest Destiny, see, in this volume, chap. 1, by Richard Twiss and L. Daniel Hawk; and chap. 6, by Kurt Anders Richardson.

[25]Marsden, *Religion and American Culture*, p. 23.

terms, the tangible loss of lives, cultures, histories and collective memories that resulted from the dogma had to be overlooked, spurned and delegitimized. Tami James Moore and Barbara Clark have chronicled this strategy in the history of Nebraska textbooks since 1867. They write, "Whether the intention of those textbooks was to maintain the White, male, Protestant social power . . . or to purposefully create a negative bias toward minorities . . . the review of textbooks used across the decades in American schools reveals a complex trail of inaccuracies and false truths."[26] These efforts of history-book authors to maintain Anglo-European privilege and to present indigenous and *mestizo/métis* people in a negative light is a classic form of social forgetting, inscribing in people's historical memories a distorted perception that reinforces the dominant culture's justification and validation of its own actions. Manifest Destiny, including its necessary element of social forgetting, provided a narrative of divinely ordained action that was widely accepted and internalized by US Anglo-European evangelicals to the great detriment of non-Anglo-European people.

EVANGELICAL IDENTITY CONSTRUCTION IN THE
TWENTIETH AND TWENTY-FIRST CENTURIES

Many evangelicals are unaware of their own historical implication in these colonizing strategies. Thus, when some evangelicals today find new Others against which to construct their identities, they are unwittingly walking a well-worn path. The new Others for contemporary evangelicals include theological liberals, so-called modernists, secularists, Communists, socialists, collectivists, Muslims, autonomous women and LGBQTI individuals. The rhetoric and discourse are the same; the strategies for constructing binary identities are the same; it is just the players who have changed.

Evangelical theologian Kenneth Kantzer has acknowledged evangelicalism's history of "belligerence in fighting" those who are different.[27] Carl Henry, an exemplar of this history, wrote in 1958 of the Christian "defensive fight for sheer survival" against secularism.[28] Here he employed the same kind of violent, "us/

---

[26]Tami James Moore and Barbara Clark, "The Impact of 'Message Senders' on What Is True: Native Americans in Nebraska History Books," *Multicultural Perspectives* 6, no. 2 (2004): 18.

[27]Carl F. H. Henry and Kenneth Kantzer, "Standing on the Promises," *Christianity Today* 40, no. 10 (1996): 30.

[28]Carl F. H. Henry, "Christian Education and the World of Culture," *The Mennonite Quarterly Review* 32, no. 4 (1958): 310.

them" rhetoric that we encountered in nineteenth-century evangelical discourse, in his discursive "war" against the theological Other. In the twentieth
century, binary constructions of identity, including essentializing and objectifying the Other as a hostile entity and discouraging social interaction, still
predominated for evangelicals in engaging the Other.

The twenty-first century has been no different. Following the Twin Towers
disaster in 2001, Muslims now became the target of the binary rhetoric. A
Times of London article in 2010 noted, "The Rev Franklin Graham, son of Billy
Graham, has suggested that the true purpose of Park51 [a proposed Islamic
center in Lower Manhattan] is to claim Ground Zero as 'Islamic land.'"[29] In
making such a claim, Graham "constructed" the Islamic center as a place of
terror and threat to his hearers. Communists and socialists continue to be
marked as "Other." In 2005 Pat Robertson, a noted evangelical televangelist,
called for the assassination of Hugo Chavez.[30] For him, killing and annihilation, even in violation of international law, are viable options for evangelical
engagement of the Other. All of these strategies represent what are often uncritical adoptions of colonial ways of knowing and being.

LOOKING FORWARD

There are, however, excellent models out there, including those being practiced
by certain evangelicals, for self-conscious identity construction that is not dependent on these colonial models.[31] Here I offer three of my own. All of these

---

[29]See Giles Whittell and David Charter, "The Wound That Will Not Heal: How 9/11 Is Still Tearing
America Apart," *The Times of London*, national edition, September 10, 2010, pp. 37-38. See also Jon
Meacham and Lisa Miller, "'Muhammad Only Leads to the Grave,'" *Newsweek*, US edition, May 17,
2010, p. 7, who note that in a 2010 *Newsweek* interview, Graham acknowledged calling Islam
"wicked and evil." Franklin Graham tends to be at the forefront among evangelicals hostile to Islam.

[30]Lynne Duke, "Preaching with a Vengeance: Pat Robertson's Fierce Rhetoric May Have Diminished
His Political Clout," *Washington Post*, October 15, 2005 (Correction Appended), sec. C01.

[31]One example is Brian McLaren, who challenges his readers to consider new ways of explicitly addressing injustice and, correspondingly, evangelical identity itself. See Brian McLaren, "Post-
Colonial Theology," *God's Politics* (blog), September 15, 2010, http://sojo.net/blogs/2010/09/15/post
-colonial-theology. On evangelicals and Muslims, see Lorraine Millot, "The Auto-Da-Fe Inflaming
America," *Liberation*, September 11, 2010 (French; translator unknown), BBC Monitoring: International Reports; Laurie Goodsteen, "Summit in US Confronts 'Anti-Muslim Frenzy': Religious
Leaders Gather to Denounce Bigotry as Government Concern Rises," *International Herald Tribune*,
September 9, 2010; on socialists, see Valerie Elverton Dixon, "What Is and Isn't Socialism," *God's
Politics* (blog), February 5, 2010, www.sojo.net/blogs/2010/02/05/what-and-isnt-socialism; on
gender, see Alan F. Johnson, ed., *How I Changed My Mind About Women in Leadership: Compel-
ling Stories from Prominent Evangelicals* (Grand Rapids: Zondervan, 2010); and on sexuality, see

can be worked out in small, local church groups meeting with the express purpose of social and cultural transformation for the sake of the "good news."

First, I suggest that we form church groups for the purpose of interrogating power in all our social relations and structures. I suggest that together we begin examining the sociocultural mechanisms that lead to discursive violence. Central to colonial identity strategies is the construction of power. To interrogate power is absolutely necessary for any change to occur. Naturally, powerful cultural movements, like evangelicalism, avoid interrogating power. John Howard Yoder urged Christians, however, to actively seek *dis*empowerment, acknowledging that, while critiquing power likely means remaining disempowered socially, it nevertheless is an advantage in following Christ.[32] Until small groups of Christians begin to address the question of power and the bases on which communities ascribe hierarchical status, there cannot be a real challenge to evangelical neocolonialism.

Second, small groups of evangelicals might examine how they themselves fall into patterns of essentializing or objectifying the Other. In a colonial model, both social groups—the culturally dominant and subaltern—employ this rhetoric, but the effect on the hybrid, subaltern Other is psychically, spiritually and emotionally exhausting and debilitating. To construct new identities will require thoughtful, purposeful and long-term involvement with those who are Other. It requires that church groups commit to meeting for sustained periods and discussing ways that they have objectified Others and ways they might alternately see the Other as fully orbed, complex, rich human beings. It will require them to seek commonalities and to consciously challenge their own proclivities to stereotype or make assumptions. It will require that people in dominant social groups be willing to change their own cultures. Group facilitators will need to be skilled in assisting fellow believers in navigating the anxieties and fears that such a move will engender.

Finally, evangelicals have an opportunity to hear and read other stories and collective memories. As mentioned above, both collective memory and collective forgetting are central to identity.[33] Dominant group members "forget"

Andrew Marin, *Love Is an Orientation: Elevating the Conversation with the Gay Community* (Downers Grove, IL: InterVarsity Press, 2009).

[32] Yoder, *Jewish-Christian Schism*, p. 45.

[33] See Matthew Wilson, "A History of Forgetting, and the 'Awful Problem' of 'Race': A New Historical Note," *Southern Literary Journal* 61, no. 1 (Fall 2008): 20-31.

the contributions of the Others around them. They "forget" that those whom they have constructed as binary opposites are actually real people with rich, complex lives that often interact with their own lives—whether it is as family members, coworkers, neighbors or local merchants. They "forget" that in their efforts to create fixed identities they have employed social memory as a weapon of destruction.[34] To be sure, these collective memories will often be uncomfortable and threatening for Anglo-European or culturally dominant evangelicals to hear. They often do not harmonize with national "myths."[35] Therefore, to discuss these issues requires extensive and sustained interaction in church groups, accompanied by a skilled mediator to guide group members in a way that brings healing and reconciliation after the hurt and anger that will likely emerge among all parties to the discussion.[36]

To be sure, to affirm postcolonial ways of being does not dismiss the possibility of expressing to others one's vibrant and deeply held faith commitments. But only when evangelization becomes a *real* sharing—one in which the humanity, the voice and the contributions of *all* parties involved lead to a conversation of mutual trust, respect and enrichment—can we envision a postcolonial evangelical approach to embracing the Other.

This task of identity construction from a new place is indeed exciting and exhilarating. It rejects the myth of fixed identities and replaces it with a new identity that is comfortable exploring the "nooks and crannies" of social interaction between the collective self and the Other. It rejects fixed, binary constructions of identity as fundamentally violent. It explores the hybrid nature of identity and the myriad ways that social groups enrich, and are enriched by, each other. It rejects xenophobia and nativism by recognizing the rich deposit of God's presence in grace throughout the world and by acknowledging that groups all over the world apprehend God through the abundance of their own social locations. Finally, it rejects social "forgetting," which when practiced by dominant groups has as its goal the expunging of the Other. In its place it explores the past in order to construct new social memories that are inclusive,

---

[34]See Amy-Jill Levine, "A Jewess, More and/or Less," in *Judaism Since Gender*, ed. Miriam Peskowitz and Laura Levitt (New York: Routledge, 1997), p. 154, for a discussion about the pressure placed on those who occupy the boundaries between these social groups.

[35]Emerson and Smith, *Divided by Faith*, pp. 9, 55.

[36]For a practical example of such an effort, see Paul Sorrentino, *A Transforming Vision: Multiethnic Fellowship in College and the Church* (S. Hadley, MA: Doorlight, 2010).

creative and affirming of non-Western, indigenous, gendered and postcolonial ways of being and knowing.

Brian McLaren writes,

> It's commonplace to talk about the extinction or evaporation of Christian faith in Europe, and in the US, we see this as a sad and tragic thing. But could it be that the faith that has been rejected in Europe is not the essential and original Christian faith, but rather the colonial Christian faith—the chauvinistic, Greco-Roman, consumerist, white-man's Christian faith? And could it be that this faith should be rejected so something better can emerge in the void it leaves behind?[37]

McLaren provides a new vision for disenchanted evangelicals, both those who are seeking liberation from their own colonized selves and those seeking liberation from colonial denials of their collective selves. Could it be, indeed?

---

[37]McLaren, "Post-Colonial Theology."

12

Healthy Leadership and Power Differences in the Postcolonial Community

Two Reflections

Nicholas Rowe and Ray Aldred

.... ☥ ....

As one country does not bear all things, that there may be a commerce,
so neither has God opened, nor will open, all to one, that there may
be a traffic in knowledge between the servants of God,
for the planting both of love and humility.

George Herbert

I want to be the white man's brother, not his brother-in-law.

Martin Luther King Jr.

Introduction

In this chapter, we consider and reflect on power differences in Christian post-colonial communities and their effects on church or community leadership. When we refer to postcolonial communities, we mean for them to consist of descendants of both the colonizer and the colonized; frequently their members have both sides in their ancestry. Having said that, the struggle of how to engage in leadership when the colonizer culture is still valued over that of the colonized continues. Both authors come from colonized contexts and reflect from within this space: Nicholas Rowe is of Afro-Caribbean descent and spent his formative years in the United Kingdom and the United States. He currently lives in South Africa. Ray Aldred is status Cree of the First Nations in Canada.

NICHOLAS ROWE: ESSENTIAL ASPECTS OF LEADERSHIP DEVELOPMENT IN THE POSTCOLONIAL COMMUNITY

There is a wealth of scholarship in the field of spirituality for leadership,[1] most of it written from a Western perspective. Thus those in postcolonial contexts have to filter their understanding of leadership through Western presuppositions and integrate it into a postcolonial perspective.

We point this out to indicate the ongoing struggle in Christian postcolonial communities to model healthy leadership development. The perspective of the colonizer still predominates in practice and gets treated with deference. The value of practice from other ethnic and cultural contexts is minimized or not heard; at best, it is expected to be validated through Western cultural understanding. This is one of the many dynamics that need to be addressed in the postcolonial context: how to validate the contributions and understandings of groups who have been previously marginalized in the colonial context.

Leadership development in postcolonial contexts arises out of a healing of relationships between the colonizer and the colonized, which occurs when the context of domination and marginalization is acknowledged with a commitment to move forward in a new way—"one new humanity in place of the two," as Paul stresses in Ephesians 2:15. But prior to that step the members of the disempowered community need to rediscover who they are. They also need to rediscover both the gifts imparted to them as a culture by the God who created them and how these gifts will be brought to the healed and restored postcolonial community—a community that arises out of the healing of relationships between the descendants of colonizer and colonized.

---

[1]See Donal Dorr, *Spirituality of Leadership: Inspiration, Empowerment, Intuition and Discernment* (Dublin: Columba Press, 2006); Richard Kreigbaum, *Leadership Prayers* (Wheaton, IL: Tyndale, 1998); Nicholas Rowe, "Taking Off Saul's Armour: A Reflection on Gifts, People and Leadership," *Southern Anglican* 14 (October 2007): 50-52; D. McRae-McMahon, "Spiritual Leadership in a Secular Context," in *Daring Leadership for the 21st Century* (Sydney, Australia: ABC Books, 2002); R. J. Starratt and R. E. Guare, "The Spirituality of Leadership," *Planning and Changing* 26, nos. 3/4 (1995): 190-203.

My wife and I had the privilege of overseeing a ministry of inner healing and reconciliation for over ten years. Two things were distinctive about the ministry, neither of which would have been extraordinary by itself. The first was that it was located in Boston's inner city, in a predominantly African American church. The second was that the team members we worked with were racially and ethnically diverse. Although the overall team varied over the years, the core consisted of people of African, European and Latino descent. What was distinctive was that the people to whom we ministered came from the full spectrum of the Boston metropolitan populace: urban and suburban, wealthy and professional elites, the working class, African Americans, Asians, Latinos and whites.

Given Boston's troublesome history of racial and ethnic divisions, we were often asked how it was that we had a ministry in which persons from the historically dominant culture, the descendants of colonizers, affirmed our leadership. They did so because all of us, regardless of background, had arrived at a place where our wounds and traumas of soul had become too much to manage. For many of us some of these traumas were directly a function of the colonial realities of racism, sexism and ethnic hostility; our very identities were always in question in a context that did not value them. But we also acknowledged that for those of privileged backgrounds there were similar traumas, although from different causes. In both cases it pleased God to heal us, often through restoring the ability to relate to each other.

But we all had to take responsibility for our part in the process. This included a commitment to vulnerability and transparency about our wounds and traumas and how we were progressing in our healing journeys. This, of course, entailed great relational risk. Imagine a black person who had grown up during the infamous, racially charged busing riots in Boston sharing her heart with a white resident about the feelings and wounds that resulted. Conversely it was powerful to hear a white man confess that he did not expect much when he traveled from the white suburbs to this inner city church ministry, but that he had met God powerfully in a transformative way.

Moreover, the discipline of listening was essential, with everyone laying down masks so that each could receive and release the need to control. Cultural fluency and cultural intelligence (to borrow Soong-Chan Rah's term[2]) were in

---

[2]See Soong-Chan Rah, *Many Colors: Cultural Intelligence for a Changing Church* (Chicago: Moody Press, 2010), pp. 127-97.

evidence. Those of the dominant culture were able to receive because the historically marginalized were vulnerable (despite the difficulty for them), but also vice versa. Finally, there was no "expert" culture—we all came in broken and in need, and as people went through the process and were healed, they often came back to be part of the team.

We mention this story to illustrate what I believe are essential aspects of leadership development in the postcolonial community: an awareness of the perspectives of the marginalized (especially by descendants of the colonizers) and recognition of what the marginalized have to offer the overall community.

Daniel 1: A postcolonial reading. As part of the process of coming to health in the new community, the previously marginalized have to define what they bring to the table. In Daniel 1 we see a powerful illustration of the reclamation of self-identity by a marginalized community. The book of Daniel describes a classic imperial context: a people defeated and subjugated, then put to use for the purposes of their new rulers. It goes on to describe a process of indoctrination, whereby young Jewish men are essentially to be made Babylonians by way of three processes. First, there is a radical change in diet. Second, the exiles are renamed, a process that reveals the degree to which their cultural self-understanding is to be transformed. The four young men (Daniel, Hananiah, Mishael and Azariah) all have names referring to the God of Judah and thus are referential to their context. The Babylonian names that replace them (Belteshazzar, Shadrach, Meshach and Abednego) all refer to Babylonian deities. Thus the new names totally obscure their Jewish identities in terms of self-reference. Finally, they are rigorously taught the "the language and literature of the Babylonians" (Dan 1:4 NIV). In these ways, their history, heritage and language—the last being the basis of cultural understanding and the lens through which any human engages and makes sense of the world—are taken from them. From this point they are to understand and see things the Babylonian way. As far as their captors are concerned, Judah, their old home and basis of their identity, is dead. The young men are valuable only to the extent that they conform to the ways and culture of their captors.

The book of Daniel itself, however, is a subversive testimony to the importance of cultural identity as a theological category. Right from the beginning, Daniel and his friends, despite their subjugated postures, take steps to retain and protect their integrity as Jews. First, they ask for a simple vegetarian diet instead of the royal (and undoubtedly nonkosher) food and drink. Second, the narrator emphasizes Daniel's Jewish name throughout the text. The narrator refers to Daniel by his Babylonian name only eight times, but he refers to the Jewish name over seventy times. This persistent use of his Jewish name makes it appear as though the narrator presents Daniel as taking charge of his own identity. Conversely, the appearance of his Babylonian name also demonstrates the determination of the Babylonians to construct Daniel the Jew according to Babylonian terms, casting his own self-definition to the margin. Finally, the narrator portrays Daniel as successfully negotiating the world of Babylonian politics on his own terms, as evidenced by his consistent practice of prayer to God before an open window facing the Jewish temple in Jerusalem.

Daniel's account illustrates how people in colonial contexts—especially those who have been subjugated or are powerless—have made sense of things when their cultural identity was not seen or valued. This stance of having to be two persons at once—both a genuine and colonized self—is a form of hybridity, a necessary cultural adaptation, particularly for the disempowered, who often have little choice but to master the dominant cultural frame while still holding to their own. This is important for Christian communities where, in cross-cultural situations, the dominant discourse determines the frame through which all activities are understood. When this occurs, the contributions, perspectives and gifts of the disempowered are often ignored.

Leadership and hybridity. In general today, authority in leadership is no longer valid simply because of its emanating from some sort of institutional structure. Within a church or community in the postcolonial context—that is, one with both descendants of the colonizer and colonized—leadership will require awareness of hybrid identities. In non-Western contexts, multiple leadership models abound; the learning and practice of such models can be part of overall leadership development within postcolonial communities and churches. If leaders have not worked outside of their own racial or ethnic context, then they will not have much credibility in cross-cultural contexts—especially among members outside of their own group. Awareness of hybrid identities will be essential for healthy leadership.

Those who historically have been subordinated have had to master this practice of hybridity as a matter of survival. Those of disempowered groups— the subjects of empire—have had to operate and learn outside of their frames of reference in order to survive. This is a common theme of imperial dynamics. As W. E. B. Du Bois put it in his *Souls of Black Folk*, "One ever feels his twoness—an American, a Negro; two souls, two thoughts, two unreconciled strivings; two warring ideals in one dark body.... The history of the American Negro is the history of this strife—this longing to attain self-conscious manhood, to merge his double self into a better and truer self."[3] And while Du Bois considered it a burden, he also stressed its potential benefit—that mastering two perspectives gives one a unique ability to enrich cross-cultural communities. Du Bois wrote, "He would not Africanize America, for America has too much to teach the world and Africa. He would not bleach his Negro soul in a flood of white Americanism, for he knows that Negro blood has a message for the world."[4]

While this reality is a given for many descendants of the marginalized, it is not impossible for descendants of the colonizers to acquire this skill as well. As Soong-Chan Rah has noted, it requires a willingness to submit and be led by those who are marginalized.[5] Healthy leadership development now requires an investment from both sides of reconciling communities. In his study of community development, John Perkins bluntly responds to a culturally ignorant supposition about "welfare mentality" in a question as to whether a suburban Christian can minister to those who are hurting while not being one of them. Perkins responds,

> Why on earth do you suppose these people have a welfare mentality? It's because outside experts have come up with programs that have hampered and dehumanized them. Yes, our best efforts to reach people from the outside will patronize them. Our best attempts will psychologically and socially damage them. We must live among them. We must become one with them. Their needs must become our needs.[6]

Perkins challenges the loaded presuppositions in the question. First, the question automatically objectifies those outside the suburban context, assuming that those in struggling communities have a "welfare mentality." There is no

---

[3]W. E. B. Du Bois, *Souls of Black Folk* (New York: Penguin, 1969), p. 45.
[4]Ibid.
[5]Soong-Chan Rah, *The Next Evangelicalism: Freeing the Church from Western Cultural Captivity* (Downers Grove, IL: InterVarsity Press, 2009), p. 205.
[6]John Perkins, *With Justice for All: A Strategy for Community Development* (Ventura, CA: Regal, 2007), p. 92.

attempted relationship implied in the question. For suburbanites, the "Others" are blank slates onto which so-called needs are presumed, projected and universalized. Second, he challenges the assumption that psychological and social damage only occurs in the inner cities and not in the suburbs. Perkins implies that marginalized communities have something to impart to those who are perceived to be privileged, and when privileged folks choose not to receive from folks in the inner cities, they themselves are impoverished. It is no surprise that there is an increasing spiritual void in the West. The automatic assumptions and presumptions of leadership models that draw from Western contexts, whether by institutional means or by means of practice, are in fact the causes of their own spiritual malnourishment. By stressing the need for suburbanites to "live among" and "to become one with them [inner city folk]," Perkins affirms the role of hybridity in a healthy leadership process. Those suburbanites who do as he suggests take the first steps toward their necessary hybridization. Submitting to the authority of the marginalized would further extend the process, leading toward the healed community to which Paul referred.

Going forward, then, I encourage people to confront these challenges to leadership practice in the postcolonial context. Certainly the matters identified above do not constitute an exhaustive list, but it is most urgent that we begin to address them together.

RAY ALDRED: EPHESIANS 2:11–14: A POSTCOLONIAL READING

The type of leadership necessary to heal the wounds of colonialism requires collaboration between both dominant and marginalized groups. This collaboration is only possible through acknowledgement of the "Other." More importantly I argue that we can find the resources for this collaboration within a First Nations understanding of treaty, which can inform an indigenous reading of Ephesians. In this reading, the author, possibly a former persecutor of the Other, creates space for the "Gentiles." He is not creating a Gentile church that must become Jewish. Nor is he demanding that the Jewish believers act like Gentiles. He is extending the blessing of God in Christ to all the families[7] or peoples of the earth by bringing peace and destroying hostility between God and people and between people and people. This kind of model is consistent

---

[7]See Gen 12:3.

with the traditional treaty model among indigenous First Nations and thus provides theological support for that model as a healthy and life-affirming model for others to adopt as well.

The author of Ephesians is thus an example of a leader being healed himself and then facilitating healing in a multicultural context. A postcolonial, indigenous understanding is thus helpful in exploring a unity that does not seek to erase the particularity of group identity but rather, by affirming that particularity, brings healing to all parties involved.

From my own denominational leadership I recount here a story about healing of relationships and the beginning of postcolonial leadership development that remind me of this Pauline way of being. For some time I had wondered if the church could or would make amends for the sins of the past committed against indigenous people. In 1995–1996 First Nations leaders of the Christian and Missionary Alliance in Canada (CMAC) sought to be reconciled corporately and individually with the denomination's Euro-Canadian leaders. In these meetings the First Nations representatives expressed the shared pain of indigenous people in Canada due to our treatment by the CMAC. One CMAC representative responded, "What do you want?" His frustration carried with it all the frustration of the dominant culture confused by other perspectives. My friend Larry Wilson said, "I want your heart. I want to share my heart with you." He responded, "But we don't do that." His response was honest. On a denominational, institutional level, we do not share our hearts. We share resources, we share strategies, but we do not share hearts—at least that is what I understood. Nevertheless, we continued to talk about reconciliation.

Later the CMAC leaders met with the First Nations Alliance Church leaders—two groups representing two peoples. We listened to each other. We expressed our pain and frustration. Finally, one of the First Nations group members asked the chair of the board of directors, "Has society's attitude toward First Nations people negatively affected how you have treated us as First Nations churches?"

He replied, "Yes it has."

I then responded, saying, "My people's attitude toward the 'Whiteman' has affected how I have treated you." At that point, when we both acknowledged our own weakness, our own pain and our own need of grace, we came together. We embraced the cultural space between us, and as a result the First Peoples were no longer a problem to be solved; they became a reservoir of healing and leadership in a fractured world.

This fractured world presents a crisis of leadership for indigenous people, who are seeking new leadership models that draw from our own egalitarian traditions rather than colonialized models. *Rotinohshonni* (Mohawk) author Taiaiake Alfred points out that the solution to this crisis lies in utilizing the resources available in the traditions and cultures of indigenous people.[8] Solving this crisis of leadership in a postcolonial Christian context will begin with an acknowledgment of the Other as fundamental to the unity brought about by Christ's new covenant—a unity that affirms rather than erases the identities of the groups involved.

The first solution, then, to offering alternate models of leadership is to affirm rather than erase cultural and identity distinctives. The drive among those in the West to erase cultural distinctives necessarily results in the dominant group's eradicating or assimilating the Other. Here is how it occurs. Western theology has rightly observed that race, as defined by modernity, is an illusion; we all belong to the human race. However, the Anglo-European church, which traditionally has constructed itself as the "majority" church, has also tended to interpret indigenous identity by using the Western-constructed category of race and has consequently sought to erase actual indigenous identity. By employing those racialized categories, legitimate indigenous efforts to affirm our own identities are reduced, in Western minds, to tribalism. As a result, Westerners have labeled our indigenous efforts as incompatible with efforts for worldwide unity.[9] Of course, this is not stated openly. Instead it is implied. We frequently hear phrases such as, "We need to work hard at making 'those people' (First Nations, Inuit, métis) part of society"—a statement that reveals an assumption that "those people" are not already part of society. This mindset creates pressure for indigenous people to leap from a colonized, shattered identity to a Western ideal defined and dictated by Westerners—an ideal that erases cultural distinction and hence limits possibilities for collaboration.[10]

The second solution to this crisis of leadership is for the dominant groups

---

[8]Taiaiake Alfred, *Peace, Power, Righteousness: An Indigenous Manifesto* (Don Mills, ON: Oxford University Press, 1999), p. xiv.

[9]See Paul Ricoeur, *Political and Social Essays* (Athens: Ohio University Press, 1975), p. 141.

[10]See Sophie McCall, "'What the Map Cuts Up, the Story Cuts Across': Translating Oral Traditions and Aboriginal Land Title," *Essays on Canadian Writing* 80 (2003): 305-28.

to acknowledge and affirm collective or communal notions of identity. The West presumes an individualist conception of identity. However, prioritizing individual identity erases a significant element of indigenous identity. To assume individual, rather than collective, identity is to superimpose a Western conception on First Peoples' understandings of their own identities. First Peoples define nation by relationships; we are nations of related people. Decolonization involves a recovery of personhood, and personhood for indigenous people cannot be conceived of outside of the group. Thus decolonization and healthy leadership require that the dominant groups acknowledge indigenous people's collective notions of indigenous personhood.

Dominant-culture Christians often justify their efforts at assimilation by citing Ephesians and the references there to the "unity of the faith" (Eph 4:13).[11] No one would dispute that central to any reading of Ephesians is this unity, which flows out of the person and work of Jesus; however, there are differences in how unity is expressed from one particular culture to the next. On the one hand, many focus on extending dignity to groups of people who have been marginalized. On the other hand, some efforts at unity seem intent on eradicating any and all difference between groups. In this latter reading, unity is defined, described and enforced by the dominant group.

Such a reading of Ephesians is not conducive to healing and reconciliation. It not only fails to offer a form of leadership that inspires others to follow the dominant group's leader but also, and more importantly, will disenfranchise and discourage indigenous groups' leaders to participate with the dominant group. To recognize the validity of another group is to acknowledge its leadership, which in itself provides opportunities for growth and even healthier leadership. Thus a preferred reading of Ephesians' "one new humanity in place of the two" (Eph 2:15 NRSV) acknowledges the Other's humanity and makes the reality of cultural difference essential as fertile ground for ongoing collaboration and mutual transformation within the community and the church.

---

[11]In Canada much early mission work had little to do with giving the gospel to First Nations but focused instead on making First Nations people like Europeans. As historian Arthur Ray, *I Have Lived Here Since the World Began: An Illustrated History of Canada's Native People* (Toronto: Lester Publishing Limited & Key Porter Books, 1996), p. 235, points out, "Most missionaries not only lobbied the Parliament to pass the legislation needed to implement the assimilation policies but also helped to administer and monitor the programs. In the economic sphere, officials sought . . . to undermine the communal orientation of Native economics."

The letter to the Ephesians helps us see that unity does not displace cultural difference. For example, in Ephesians 2:11-22, we are told that both Jews and Gentiles have peace because of the work of Christ and that they are now part of one body, which is growing together in love. Neither group's identity is erased in this new body, but a unity occurs that affirms both identities.

This unity of the body, then, does not preclude cultural difference but rather assumes it. The Pauline author's focus on unity in difference illuminates the dysfunction that existed until the coming of the Spirit. The slander and division that characterized those days, marked by ethnic and cultural separation, required the power of the Spirit to form a unity within diversity that eliminated animosity. Thus the model given to the Ephesians, which affirmed both Jewish and Gentile communal concepts of identity, leads us to healthy models of leadership and identity today as well.

What is important to note is that indigenous communities have existing resources to effectuate and demonstrate how this unity-in-diversity can work. For example, James Miller points out how treaties developed over time in Canada. Eventually, as they developed, the indigenous people began to conceive of them as living covenants in perpetuity between the newly arrived European powers and the First Nations.[12] To indigenous people, treaty implied a familial relationship between the parties overseen by the Creator.[13] Thus when Europeans participated with them in the pipe ceremony, they were invoking the presence of this Creator. The presence of missionaries and church officials at treaty negotiations, along with European appeals to the Great Spirit as Creator, marked the negotiations themselves as sacred. From the indigenous perspective, the land, therefore, could be used by anyone, since the Europeans were covenanting before their Creator to live in relationship with the indigenous group to group. Sadly, however, the Canadian federal government has long resisted the idea of treaty as covenant, group to group. They favored the individualist view, which reduced treaty to legality, removing the element of familial relationship.

It is this indigenous model of treaty, which does not focus on the uniqueness

---

[12]James R. Miller, "Compact, Contract, Covenant: The Evolution of Indian Treaty-Making," in *New Histories for Old: Changing Perspectives on Canada's Native Pasts*, ed. Theodore Binnema and Susan Neylan (Vancouver: University of British Columbia Press, 2007), pp. 66-69.
[13]Ibid., p. 84.

of individuals but seeks to build a unity group to group, that informs my reading of Ephesians regarding Christian unity and leadership development. It does so in three ways. First, it draws on the dynamic and changing nature of culture and identity. For the indigenous, the signing of treaty with the Europeans did not freeze each group into a particular cultural mode for all time. The idea was that the two would seek to live in harmony in shared space. Second, the indigenous model reminds us that leadership is contextual and includes the actual physical environments of the parties involved. First Nations assumed that the land was able to hold a variety of peoples; however, they expected that the people would be in harmony with each other and the land. Thus treaty, for indigenous, is about relationship forged in shared space. Finally, the treaty is a living agreement, or covenant, lived out between the parties to the treaty before the Creator. Originally it called for yearly renewals, and these are preserved to this day in ceremonies that occur on First Nations reservations. Treaty days are symbolic and remind us that we are now related and want to see one another flourish.

In a similar way, the author of Ephesians is not seeking to erase difference but to erase animosity, so that members of both groups can flourish. For Jews and Gentiles to flourish they are not to look down upon one another; rather, they are to realize that all have access to God in Christ Jesus. Leadership in such a context is about affirming how God has created the Other, with particularity—of history and of gifting—but of the same Creator, the same Spirit, the same faith. Also, because the letter to the Ephesians is occasional, it is written to a particular place or space about a relationship occurring in shared land or space. The author is trying to help the two groups see that one alone is incomplete. This is not merely about some abstract universal principle about unity but also about real community in a particular place.

In this model the Pauline author is an example of a leader's being healed in the midst of a multicultural context. At the same time, however, he is not merely aiming at coexistence; rather, through the healing work of the Spirit, he calls the two groups who were at odds to come together and respect one another. Thus Christ through Ephesians is at one moment erasing the wall of animosity and at the same time acknowledging difference. It is this distance between each group that is significant for development of the church and for postcolonial Christian leadership. Likewise, for First Nations, covenant or treaty acknowledges the validity of the Other in order to negotiate shared space with someone different but in relationship. It thus seeks not to erase difference but to overcome the anxiety between one group and the other, while acknowledging the importance of the Other for the ongoing development of ministry in the shared space. It is in this context that I read Ephesians 2.

Tension between groups has resulted in significant wounding and must be addressed if healthy leadership is to develop. Suffering was brought about when, during the colonial period in history, Euro-Americans sought to erase the culture and identities of indigenous people while stifling their leadership. It persists when Christian leaders fail to acknowledge this neocolonial heritage. The way forward is not to seek to erase cultural difference but to embrace the distance as fertile ground for collaboration.[14] By acknowledging the validity or right of each group to exist, Ephesians 2, informed by the treaty model, provides an opportunity to move forward.

Ironically, to embrace cultural distance opens the way to hybridity, or the dynamic development of a mosaic of peoples. Different group identities must be acknowledged and legitimated. This is particularly necessary in postcolonial contexts, because many formerly colonized people do not see value in their own identities. Thus the work of acknowledging the two groups has impact not only on the other but also on one's own group perception. As such, it works to heal indigenous people's ambivalence toward their own marred identities. This whole process is negotiated by wounded leaders who, like the Pauline author, are endeavoring to see Christ formed within groups of people in relationship—nation to nation, sharing the same land and creation. This is the gospel. This is the ministry of reconciliation.

---

[14]See McCall, "What the Map Cuts Up," p. 324.

13

CHRISTIAN DISCIPLINES AS
WAYS OF INSTILLING GOD'S SHALOM FOR
POSTCOLONIAL COMMUNITIES

Two Reflections

Nicholas Rowe and Safwat Marzouk

.... ☥ ....

INTRODUCTION

This chapter concerns the contribution of Christian spiritual disciplines in empowering postcolonial communities to experience and reflect God's holistic peace. The discussion will focus on ways in which the structures of colonialism have prevented the descendants of both the colonized and the colonizer from experiencing the peace of God. In other words, we need to unpack some aspects of the brokenness that postcolonial communities inherited from the colonial era. This prepares the way for us to explore the role Christian spiritual disciplines can play in the process of empowering people in these postcolonial communities as they discern practical and tangible ways to restore God's shalom. An essential part of this process are the practices of Christian spiritual disciplines that have evolved in colonized spaces. These can enrich the process of restoring God's shalom.

The authors of this chapter come from two different contexts in terms of cultural location and disciplinary background. Rowe, of Afro-Caribbean descent, grew up in the United Kingdom and the United States and now lives in South Africa. His scholarly background is in history and reconciliation ministry. Marzouk grew up in Egypt and now teaches biblical studies in the United States. That being said, this chapter will bring diverse perspectives in terms of the geographical locations and also the richness of two academic disciplines that will converse with one another throughout the pages of this chapter.

NICHOLAS ROWE

In this section I introduce a South African cultural practice called *indaba* or *lekgotla*, which is employed to resolve disputes, especially when relationships are deeply impaired. I will show how indaba and its African analogues are Christian disciplines when exercised for the purpose of reconciliation within the community. Finally, I discuss how the practice of indaba can speak to some of the challenges of Christians living in postcolonial contexts. Colonialism and imperialism have distorted perceptions of what it is to be human and how we relate to one another. This undermines shalom both individually and within postcolonial Christian communities. These disciplines can restore the ability to relate across the sharp lines defined by the colonial and imperial orders and address the damage done to persons who inherit systems shaped under those orders. When employed in Christian postcolonial communities, indaba can be a powerful illustration of the ministry of reconciliation and a powerful way of instilling or restoring God's shalom.

The indaba. In my experience of lay ministry in South Africa, I have often had the privilege of working with persons dealing with restoration of marriage relationships. Within African contexts, marital conflict does not simply affect the nuclear family. A marriage is the bringing together not just of two individuals but also of their extended families. Thus when a marriage experiences deep strain, the relationship between the two families of origin also suffers. Attempts to restore the relationship, therefore, will necessarily involve members from both families.

In South Africa a common process to reconcile the parties involves an indaba or lekgotla. Indaba, a Zulu term commonly used by South Africans of all backgrounds, is often translated simply as a "meeting" of any sort.[1] But the idea goes deeper than this. The term implies a meeting of the minds with the intention of reconciliation or of arriving at a common understanding. In the indaba, a group of elders from both families will hear representatives of

---

[1]Zulu is the major indigenous language in South Africa, but the term *lekgotla*, synonymous with *indaba*, is common among the Sotho family of languages, refers to the same idea and is commonly used among South Africans of all backgrounds.

both spouses explain the conflict and their understanding of its causes. It almost never happens that the spouses speak for themselves before the elders. While the elders usually consist of the senior males of both families, in practice it is often the uncles of the spouses who perform this function. Because the spouses do not speak on their own behalf, both spouses have to discuss their sides of the conflict with other family members before the process can begin. Often there is a cycle of dialogue and recess, during which the elders along with the parties involved will ruminate on the matter. This continues until there is a common understanding of what has happened. If there has been inappropriate conduct of one against the other, this is confronted as part of the process of determining what is to be done between both parties to restore relationship.

Bénézét Bujo observes that variations of this practice are common throughout Africa. He calls the idea of a coming together to find a moral resolution to a conflict "palaver," subverting the Western meaning, which defines it as idle, useless chatter. For Bujo, palaver is the continued deliberation—a recess to think things through—and coming together again in cyclical dialogue, which is a critical, communal process to determine right action.[2] It prioritizes the promotion of good human relationships in a communal context.[3] In addition, indaba and its related forms throughout the continent, generically referred to by Bujo's term "palaver," are not restricted to marital and other local disputes. Palaver has become a common African resource for peace-building in major conflicts, including Rwanda and Liberia.[4]

This practice predates colonialism (and hence, in many areas, Christianity) in Africa. However, I have observed that the practice is sometimes retained within local Christian communities as a means of resolving both marital and other types of conflict. Historically, the presence of patriarchy was (and remains) predominant in how women were and are often excluded from the role of elders. Patriarchy remains powerful and thus can be subjected to post-

---

[2]Bénézét Bujo, *The Ethical Dimension of Community: The African Model and the Dialogue Between North and South* (Nairobi: Pauline Publications, 1998), p. 36.

[3]Wilson Muoha Maina, "African Communitarian Ethics in the Theological Work of Bénézét Bujo," *Pacifica* 21 (June 2008): 204.

[4]Kenneth Omeje and Tricia Redeker Hepner, eds., *Conflict and Peacebuilding in the African Great Lakes Region* (Bloomington: Indiana University Press, 2013), p. 226; Gerald Gahima, *Transitional Justice in Rwanda: Accountability for Atrocity* (New York: Routledge, 2013), p. 26.

colonial criticism.[5] Despite this, I have seen respected women in the community perform the elder role in resolving all manner of disputes. This is particularly common in urban communities, where globalization and Western influences have challenged the preeminence and methods of traditional practices.

Indaba as a Christian discipline. The disciplines are understood to be those activities and practices that emulate those of Jesus when he was on earth as he modeled his relationship with God. If one assumes that one of the highest priorities of the Christian life is to be like Christ, one does so, as Dallas Willard suggests, by "following the overall style of life he chose for himself . . . by arranging our whole lives around the activities he himself practiced in order to remain constantly at home in the fellowship of his father." We do so, Willard adds, to "live and prepare ourselves for life as he did, so that we can be the kind of people who behave 'on the spot' like Christ."[6] Richard Foster additionally emphasizes that the disciplines are not a means of transformation as an end unto themselves but that they put us in a place where God can undertake the transformation.[7]

If we maintain our definition of the term "postcolonial Christian community" as composed of persons descended from both the colonizer and colonized, and where hybridity is present, then we are immediately faced with a challenge in writing about Christian spiritual disciplines as a concept. As early as the fifteenth century, the mystic Thomas à Kempis (ca. 1380–1471 C.E.) warned his readers that the evil one attempts to suppress one's desire to do the right thing, as it will "make you void of all good exercise" in its pursuit.[8] The centuries have seen this "good exercise" systematized and reified within Western theological traditions. This systemization makes the spiritual disciplines, as articulated in most writings, a construct from a Western space. It imposes a structure and understanding on them that coincide with a Western outlook. Within a Christian postcolonial community, this is problematic. It is a subtle way of privileging Western viewpoints about Christian spirituality against others from outside the West and implies that Christian disciplines can be understood only within this framework. This position is fundamentally flawed, as there are practices in Christian communities outside the Western

---

[5]Wilson Muoha Maina, "African Communitarian Ethics in the Theological Work of Bénézet Bujo," *Pacifica* 21 (June 2008): 208.

[6]Dallas Willard, *The Spirit of the Disciplines* (San Francisco: HarperSanFrancisco, 1991), p. ix.

[7]Richard Foster, *Celebration of Discipline* (San Francisco: Harper and Row, 1978), p. 6.

[8]Thomas à Kempis, *The Imitation of Christ* 3.7, quoted in Willard, *Spirit of the Disciplines*, frontispiece.

context that one can consider disciplines, especially using our definition above—that is, practices that emulate those of Christ during his life on earth—that we can use as exercises in becoming more like Christ. However, these have not been systematized to the same extent as in Western spirituality. I suggest creating more space in Christian postcolonial communities in which both Western and non-Western approaches to the disciplines might be more fully expressed to promote God's shalom.

Indaba is one of those non-Western approaches. It affirms at least two important principles of Christian spirituality: the centrality of confession and the role of the community in reconciliation. Because of this, it can be considered a discipline as it is practiced within Christian communities. Confession is one of the basics of traditional Christian practice and, historically, has been a critical part of maintaining healthy relationships within community and between individuals and God. In confession, one acknowledges an action that has broken relationship, has inflicted harm (physically or emotionally) or has violated a communal norm (that is, has inflicted harm on a community). However, confession can also be about fears, frailties and vulnerabilities. "In [confession]," Willard notes, "we let trusted others know our deepest weaknesses and failures. This will nourish our faith in God's provision for our needs through his people, our sense of being loved, and our humility before our brothers and sisters."[9]

In many Western contexts, however, confession is often practiced as an individual and private act. The offending party takes action as an individual, and the confessional transaction takes place privately between the individual and the offended party, whether this is another person, an emissary for God or God's own self. This way of doing confession contrasts strongly with indaba, where confession for restoring relationship is usually a community function. As an example, I witnessed a process involving South Africans sharing their stories of struggle under the apartheid regime in an effort to improve relationship across the color line. Black and colored Christians shared their stories of suffering, while white Afrikaner Christians talked about how they were conditioned by their theology, how they were complicit in the system and how they repented of the broken belief system.

Indaba as an indigenous Christian spiritual discipline from Africa can also

---

[9]Willard, *Spirit of the Disciplines*, p. 187.

be a gift to Western Christian communities. Communal confession is not exclusively an African process. It has been practiced in Western communities, usually as a means of redressing the misdeeds of ancestors against colonized communities. One author, John Dawson, has outlined a process of confession, reconciliation and restoration between the white Christians of Denver and Native Americans that is indeed communal in nature. The occasion was a process by which the white participants acknowledged, confessed and asked forgiveness for their ancestors' roles in the Sand Creek massacre of 1864.[10] This exercise of communal confession is often referred to as "identificational repentance," where a descendant stands in for his or her ancestors' wrongdoings and the contemporary effects they still have on the historical victims and their descendants. Despite Dawson's good intentions, however, this type of confession still runs on individualistic underpinnings endemic to Western thinking. Often an individual (or at best a small group of individuals) stands in for the community of either colonizer or colonized. The danger is that the process is a singular event that minimizes the reality of ongoing relationship. Indaba, by contrast, assumes that the outcome of the practice is the restoration not only of individual relationships but also of those between the representative communities. It implies that they all are now joined and must function as one people going forward. If, as we have stated, Christian disciplines put us in a position in which God can make us more like Christ, then indaba is such a discipline, as its objective is the restoration of relationship, which Christ strove to achieve in his person and among those who followed him. As a Christian discipline, indaba can enrich and deepen Western Christian spirituality by confronting its overemphasis on individualism. Moreover, the community in the indaba does not stop with those who are living but extends to those who have passed on as well. The spiritual discipline of confession in a communal sense understands that the activities of ancestors are never a one-time event but can continue to have ramifications in the present, for good or for ill.

Indaba as a discipline in postcolonial contexts. For people within postcolonial contexts, deep shame over the events of the colonial past often exists. For descendants of colonizers, recognizing that they are the contemporary beneficiaries of the acts of their ancestors can result in heavy emotional shame.

---

[10]John Dawson, *Healing America's Wounds* (Ventura, CA: Regal Books, 1994), pp. 135-59.

Moreover, they can feel (or are often told) that they were on the "wrong side of history." This results in various reactions, which include distancing themselves from the source of shame or refusing to acknowledge it (often manifested in comments such as, "The past is behind us and we should move on"). Reactions sometimes include defensiveness, which also impairs relational healing. Another reaction is a distancing of oneself from one's ancestry to remove the source of shame. This can also be expressed by intentional ignorance or forgetting of the past by adopting an extremely individualistic stance. Finally, it can express itself by a fear of losing power and control, as these are integral parts of the identity of the colonizer that get uncritically passed down through generations. Insisting on being in control is a common way to avoid the shame (and fear) of having no power.

However, for Christians in postcolonial contexts, these approaches are insufficient. Many realize that running away from the past does not undo the damage to the soul that has been caused and that can continue into the present, evidenced as deep suspicion and difficulty in relating between the descendants of those in power and those subjugated to that power. A deeper intervention is called for.

The discipline of indaba, when employed in postcolonial reconciliation, suggests possibilities for restoration and healing from the guilt and shame of sinful conduct. The discipline allows both individuals and, just as importantly, communities to relieve themselves of the burden of guilt over the past and to acknowledge the actions of the past and the trauma and pain imposed on those who were subjected to the violations to personhood that were an integral part of the colonial past.

Indaba seeks not only to acknowledge the legacy of the past but also to enter into vulnerability with others. Members of the community are now free to confess the existential pain and its invalidation of them as persons. By extension, as a discipline it allows us to listen and to hear those across the divide. We often want to hear on our own terms, making sure that the hearing does not make demands of us or require the surrender of authority and power. When the listening requires acknowledgment or confession from us it becomes tempting to resist. We must choose to enter into the place of listening as a redemptive act. Indaba provides the framework for such action.

Conclusion. This discussion of the practice of indaba illustrates a response to the mistrust and divisions that result from the historical effects of colonialism and imperialism. The mutual space for the spiritual practices that have organically developed in the African context offers an alternative way to deal with the cycle of hatred and oppression. When practiced in Christian postcolonial communities, which include descendants both of the colonizers and colonized, it is actually a spiritual discipline that helps members to realize the importance of listening to one another, of acknowledging the brokenness of one another, of confessing and lamenting with one another and of celebrating the hope in real healing and transformation. These communities will not just experience the way of God's shalom but will also transform the worlds around them.

SAFWAT MARZOUK

Growing up as a Presbyterian in Egypt allowed me to be a part of a unique socioreligious context. Christians in Egypt are a minority, and Presbyterians are the minority of a minority. In this sense I have lived out a Western spirituality in the midst of an Eastern Orthodox and an Islamic context. This spiritual heritage continues to be enriched as I teach at an Anabaptist Mennonite seminary in the United States.

The Egyptian context, shalom and the discipline of lament. I write this reflection on spiritual disciplines and God's shalom with the Egyptian Christian community in mind. I will focus on the role that prayers of lament can play as a Christian discipline in empowering Christians in Egypt to receive and actualize God's shalom in their context. This community as well as many Arabic societies are experiencing a "post-postcolonial" context. The so-called Arab Spring is changing the contexts of many communities in the Middle East, including the Egyptian Christian community. These popular movements and political changes, which seek livelihood, freedom and justice, affect the way the Egyptian Christian community perceives and practices its spiritual disciplines. The revolution that began in Egypt on the 25th of January, 2011, brought about new challenges, new hopes and new opportunities for Egyptian society in general and for the Egyptian Christian community in particular. Hoping for, working toward and praying for God's shalom in Egyptian society took a new turn. Thus Christian disciplines that seek to flesh out God's shalom in a postcolonial context will respond and interact with these changes.

Biblical traditions speak of God's shalom in order to refer to the wholeness, completeness and well-being of creation. The Hebrew word *shalom* "includes everything necessary to healthful living: good health, a sense of well-being, good fortune, the cohesiveness of the community, relationship to relatives and their state of being, and anything else deemed necessary for everything to be in order" (see Gen 29:6; Is 54:13; Jer 15:5).[11] The biblical concept of peace underlies God's desire for the well-being of humans in all aspects of our lives.[12] It is a holistic peace. The Greek word *eirene* is used in the New Testament to refer to the peace of God as a gift through Jesus Christ that abolishes enmity (see Eph 2:13-18; Col 1:15-20). Divine peace encompasses the relation between God and humans, relationships within the human community and relationships with the rest of the members of creation.

Imperial and neoimperial indigenous hegemonies, such as in Egypt, continue to stifle efforts to bring about God's shalom, not only because they ensure limited resources and possibilities but also because they cause a loss of hope to change the status quo. Although Egypt gained its independence about sixty years ago, the impact of colonialism and the new forms of imperialism continued to negatively affect people's living conditions within Egyptian society. Over the past sixty years, many Egyptian governments failed to address the needs of citizens in terms of quality of life, freedom of expression and belief, and justice and equality. The revolution of January 25th called for livelihood, freedom and social justice. This popular movement, in which Egyptians—Muslims and Christians together—decided to challenge the status quo, brought with it new waves of hope to bring about God's holistic shalom. However, corruption, abuse of power and sectarianism are persistent. In Egypt as of this writing, the actualization of God's holistic shalom seems to have been put on hold.

The current dilemma, namely, the hope for transforming those conditions, invites Egyptian Christians to reconsider their perception and their practice of Christian disciplines. To be truly relevant, Christian disciplines will lift up the

---

[11]Claus Westermann, "Peace (Shalom) in the Old Testament," in *The Meaning of Peace: Biblical Studies*, ed. Perry B. Yoder and Willard M. Swartley (Elkhart, IN: Institute of Mennonite Studies, 2001), p. 49.

[12]See Perry B. Yoder, *Shalom: The Bible's Word for Salvation, Peace, Justice* (1988; repr., Nappanee, IN: Evangel, 1997); and Willard M. Swartley, *Covenant of Peace: The Missing Peace in New Testament Theology and Ethics* (Grand Rapids: Eerdmans, 2006).

voices of the oppressed and energize a new level of hope, which will empower humans to be faithful agents of change who recognize their limits when they attempt to transform reality without the power of God.

In this essay I will explore one facet of the Christian disciplines that is concerned with bringing about God's holistic shalom in the Egyptian context described above. It involves drawing from the rich, theological and spiritual resources to be found in the prayers of lament in the Hebrew Bible. My discussion about prayers of lament is not descriptive of what is already taking place in the Egyptian Christian context but rather suggestive for a new praxis. Egyptian Christians, like many communities of faith, have not fully discovered the power of the prayers of lament.

Religious and political factors have caused prayers of lament to be marginalized in Christian Egyptian spirituality. The Islamic belief in Al-Qada' wa Al-Qadar ("fate and destiny"), as well as the Christian doctrine of divine sovereignty, are often misunderstood in Egyptian religious circles to be advocating a divine monopoly of power that suppresses human free will. These perceptions act as disincentives to empowering Egyptian Muslims and Christians to become agents of change. The popular theology of the majority of Egyptians— both Muslims and Christians—indeed comforts the oppressed and the poor, but it does so by focusing on the sovereignty of God in a way that deprives these communities of the courage to protest, in words and actions, against the injustice they experience. In some quarters within this social and religious context, questioning, lamenting and grieving suffering, despite the strong presence of the genre of lament in the biblical tradition, are unfortunately deemed to be blasphemous. Colonial authorities and local oppressive regimes instilled in the oppressed a prohibition and fear of questioning those who are in authority, including even God.

Prayers of lament express a deep concern for justice and well-being. The cries of lament, as found in the book of Psalms, for instance, expose the injustice, oppression and the hurt that the community of faith in particular and the world at large experience. The petitioner in Psalm 10:12 cries out,

> Rise up, O LORD; O God, lift up your hand
>   do not forget the oppressed.

When members of the community of faith practice this discipline of lament,

EVANGELICAL POSTCOLONIAL CONVERSATIONS

they are given tools to become agents of change as they participate themselves in urging God to change the current situation. Walter Brueggemann describes prayers of lament as "a complaint which makes the shrill insistence: 1. Things are not right in the present arrangement. 2. They need not stay this way but can be changed. 3. The speaker will not accept them in this way, for it is intolerable. 4. It is God's obligation to change things."[13] These prayers emerge out of dire psychological, political and social realities, and they keep "the justice question visible and legitimate,"[14] animating people to participate actively in advocacy for change.

Many of the psalms of lament appeal to the covenantal relation with God and to the characteristic of God as the one who shows steadfast love as the basis for their complaint. Brueggemann reflects on what is lost when lament is not incorporated into our spiritual disciplines. He writes, "One loss that results from the absence of lament is the loss *of genuine covenant interaction* because the second party to the covenant (the petitioner) has become voiceless or has a voice that is permitted to speak only praise and doxology."[15] These petitioners raise up their voice and cry out to bring to God's attention their suffering; they have the courage to do so because they understand what it means to be in a genuine, interactive covenant with God.

As a Christian discipline, prayers of lament help in forming the identity of the community of faith as God's covenantal partners, who long for and work toward bringing about God's shalom to their lives and to the surrounding world. Brueggemann notes, "Where there is lament, the believer is able to take initiative with God and so develop over against God the ego strength that is necessary for responsible faith."[16] Prayers of lament bring before God the injustice and oppression that the community suffers from. Taking the initiative by bringing social and political disorder before God in lament empowers the community of faith to become active and faithful partners to the covenant with God, whose purpose is to instill God's holistic shalom in the surrounding world. Prayers of lament are not a biblical way of venting anger at the current situations. Rather, they have the power to transform reality

---

[13]Walter Brueggemann, "The Costly Loss of Lament," *Journal for the Study of the Old Testament* 36 (October 1986): 62.

[14]Ibid., p. 63.

[15]Ibid., p. 60. Emphasis original. See, for example, Ps 6:4; 74:20.

[16]Ibid., p. 61.

because they are directed to a living God who listens and pays heed to the outcries of the oppressed and they strengthen and authorize the people to participate in acts of redemption. As such, this type of prayer is dialogic in nature rather than monologic.

Habakkuk. The prophetic book of Habakkuk invites us to grieve and lament the brokenness of our world. The prophet offers two prayers of lament pleading to God to intervene against the injustice conducted by both the local Judean and the imperial Babylonian oppressive systems. Usually the prophetic word would be directed toward humans to change their ways and to act righteously and justly according to the divine instructions. For instance, in Amos 5 the prophet criticizes the people for oppressing the poor and needy. In Jeremiah and Ezekiel, they pronounce oracles of judgment against the leaders of the people who commit violence and injustice (Jer 22; Ezek 22). The prophet Habakkuk, however, addresses his complaints about the injustice not to the people but to God.

Although the dialogue between the prophet and God is put in the form of a vision oracle, the content of the oracle is a prayer of lament raised by the prophet in challenge to God. The prophet cries out,

> O LORD, how long shall I cry for help,
>   and you will not listen?
> Or cry to you "Violence!"
>   and you will not save? (Hab 1:2)

The prophet claims that the violence and injustice is so overwhelming that the righteous ones are unable to act faithfully, with the result that justice comes out only "perverted" within Judah (Hab 1:4). The Lord answers the prophet, pointing to the fierce and mighty empire of the Babylonians, which, states the narrator, will act as a divine agent to punish the disorder that is taking place in Judah (Hab 1:5-11). This empire is compared to a leopard, a wolf and an eagle in its swiftness and might to capture, kill and destroy.

The prophet responds to the divine plan by engaging in lament against the violence and injustice that is committed by the Babylonian Empire, which is depicted as temporarily acting as a divine tool. Elizabeth Achtemeier writes, "God is bringing the Babylonian empire against Judah to wipe out Judah's wicked ways. But that does not hasten the coming of God's order. It simply replaces a chaotic society with one that is totally godless—with the rule of foreign people that makes its own might its god (1:11) and that worships that might as the source of its life."[17] This is perplexing to the prophet. It is as if the world is caught between two polarities that are alike in their injustice and oppression; these polarities are the oppressive systems of both the local Judean and the imperial Babylonian power structures.

The book of Habakkuk laments injustice in either case and refuses to give up on demanding God to establish a reign that brings shalom as an alternative to oppression by both the local and the imperial powers. Thus the prophet declares,

> I will stand at my watchpost,
>> and station myself on the rampart;
> I will keep watch to see what he will say to me,
>> and what he will answer concerning my complaint. (Hab 2:1)

Ultimately the prophet receives a message that proclaims divine judgment over the Babylonians.

> Alas for you who build a town by bloodshed,
>> and found a city on iniquity! (Hab 2:12)

He also receives a word of encouragement to the righteous to hold on to their righteousness in spite of Judean injustice.

> Look at the proud!
>> Their spirit is not right in them,
>> but the righteous live by their faith. (Hab 2:4)

J. J. M. Roberts argues, "Because the righteous person trusts in the reliability of God's promise contained in the vision, he or she is free to live in the present, no matter how unjust or oppressive it may be."[18] What gives hope and assures the righteous in the midst of chaos is that God reigns.

> But the LORD is in his holy temple;
>> let all the earth keep silence before him! (Hab 2:20)

In this liturgical setting, with all eyes fixed on the temple, the microcosm of

[17]Elizabeth Achtemeier, *Nahum-Malachi*, Interpretation: A Bible Commentary for Teaching and Preaching (Atlanta: John Knox Press, 1986), p. 40.
[18]J. J. M. Roberts, *Nahum, Habakkuk, and Zephaniah: A Commentary*, Old Testament Library (Louisville, KY: Westminster John Knox, 1991), p. 112.

the divine rule, the Lord appears as a warrior who is coming to put an end to the disorder (Hab 3:1-16). Such a vision moves the prophet to rejoice in the Lord despite the shortcomings and lack of prosperity (Hab 3:17-19).

This vision of divine sovereignty and the faith that brings joy despite the current chaos and the apparent disorder would not have taken place without the human initiative of lament. Thus despite the emphasis on divine agency, the initiative of the prophet to lament and grieve the oppression both of the local Judean power and the Babylonian imperial authority, along with the assurance that the righteous will survive, underline the element of human agency and accountability in bringing about the divine rule and the shalom of God.

Conclusion. In this essay I have highlighted the tension that Egyptian society lives through. The persistent realities of injustice and oppression that threaten the actualization of the divine shalom in the lives of the Egyptians here and now invite us to reconsider the role and the importance of the prayers of lament as important facets of the Christian disciplines. Prayers of lament create a safe space for the community of faith to put forth before God the dire reality that they experience and to urge God to fulfill God's promises to bring about God's vision of shalom. Prayers of lament also hold humans accountable as partners with God, who work with God and other fellow humans to actualize God's peace for all of the creation. Prayers of lament, however, acknowledge the limited human capacity to change the reality; therefore, they highlight the desire to trust in God to act and transform injustice and oppression into freedom, justice and peace. Members of the community of faith who offer prayers of lament are assured when they hear the words of Psalm 12:5, which gives a prophetic promise.

"Because the poor are despoiled, because the needy groan,
  I will now rise up," says the LORD;
  "I will place them in the safety for which they long."

Part Five

CLOSING THE CIRCLE

··· ☩ ···

Introduction to Part Five

The Evolution of the Postcolonial Roundtable

Joseph F. Duggan

Several events led to the development of a vision to establish the Postcolonial Roundtable and to seek collaborative partners, which in turn led to InterVarsity Press's publication of *Evangelical Postcolonial Conversations*. The key events in this process are briefly recorded below.

In 2008–2009, in the first year of the Postcolonial Theology Network (PTN) Facebook group, it is estimated that one-third of our then one-thousand-plus members were young evangelicals from around the world.[1] These evangelicals expressed a desire to analyze colonial legacy questions using frameworks that incorporated insights about gender, race, class, antioppression and postcoloniality. At the time evangelicals doing postcolonial work were not widely visible and were not more broadly recognized for their pioneering work.[2] In recognition of these trends, in the summer of 2009, the PTN invited Steve Hu to address postcoloniality and evangelicalism in a blog post. Steve wrote, "I ask my fellow evangelicals to consider seriously postcolonial discourse as a starting point for theologizing. In our globalizing world, the church cannot afford not to consider the multiple contexts in which theology begins."[3] During the same

[1]The PTN is now part of the umbrella organization Postcolonial Networks, www.postcolonialnetworks.com. See also our Decolonial Framework at http://postcolonialnetworks.com/the-decolonial-framework/.

[2]Kay Higuera Smith was one. See Kathryn J. Smith, "From Evangelical Tolerance to Imperial Prejudice? Teaching Postcolonial Biblical Studies in a Westernized, Confessional Setting," *Christian Scholar's Review* 37 (2008): 447-64.

[3]Steve Hu, "The Task of the Postcolonial Theologian," *ISAAC Blog*, September 11, 2009, http://isaac

time period, at Amahoro 2009, Mabiala Kenzo gave a paper titled "Post-colonialism and Why It Matters."[4]

The most significant event that led to the Postcolonial Roundtable was the 2008 publication of *Evangelicals and Empire: Christian Alternatives to the Political Status Quo* and the discussion that ensued at the book's American Academy of Religion (AAR) meeting.[5] I was taken aback by the way the AAR panel and audience's discussion appeared quickly to lead to the placement of full blame for American imperialism on the Religious Right and to equate this identity group with all evangelicals. Scholars participating in the AAR discussion carelessly deployed terms and categories such as Religious Right, fundamentalist, evangelical, colonialism and imperialism. Less time was spent on the discussion of the book's chapters and engagement of the content than that devoted to the demonization of all evangelicals as responsible for a George W. Bush–version imperialism.

The AAR panel was not made up of pioneering evangelical theologians, who like Mabiala Kenzo, John Franke, Christian Collins Winn and Peter Heltzel had authored several of the *Evangelicals and Empire* book's chapters. To further complicate matters, it appeared to me that some evangelical scholars in the room were ill-equipped to defend themselves, possibly due to a lack of theological sophistication about the differences between the terms *colonial, decolonial, postcolonial* and *imperial*.

My experience of that book's editors, the AAR panel and the AAR audience showed me the need not only for further evangelical theologizing on colonialism but also for a decolonial, dialogical process that would inspire all traditions to do similar anticolonial reflection, so that together theologians could help foster postcolonial churches and communities. The decolonization project is too important to risk perpetuation of polarized theologians or diminishment as a "liberal project." I wanted to facilitate a meeting where theologians from a multiplicity of contexts could engage one another, without the blame and shame of the AAR discussion that avoided the deeper denominational, theological and missiological questions that have too often been comfortably ignored by all traditions.

---

blog.wordpress.com/2009/09/11/the-task-of-the-postcolonial-theologian-by-steve-hu/.
[4]Mabiala Kenzo, "Post-colonialism and Why It Matters," *Ourmedia Online Digital Library*, June 9, 2009, http://archive.org/details/KenzoMabialaPost-colonialismandwhyitmatters-KenzoMabiala.
[5]Bruce Ellis Benson and Peter Heltzel, eds., *Evangelicals and Empire: Christian Alternative to the Political Status Quo* (Grand Rapids: Brazos, 2008).

Postcolonial Networks and Gordon College Collaborate

I shared my AAR experience with my friend Judith Oleson, who is on the faculty at Gordon College. Judith immediately saw a leadership opportunity for Gordon College. She shared our conversation with Dan Russ, then the director of Gordon College's Christian Studies Center, and arranged a conversation for the three of us. For several months the three of us worked through the roundtable concept, process and final member composition. The Postcolonial Roundtable met at Gordon College October 22–24, 2010.

Postcolonial Networks' Principles for the Postcolonial Roundtable

In closing I want to highlight the principles of Postcolonial Networks that were crucial to the success of the Postcolonial Roundtable and the publication of *Great Awakenings*. Postcolonial Networks encouraged roundtable members and coeditors to seek an audience in evangelical theological circles, to involve key evangelical schools and institutions, to honor the plurality of evangelical identities and to ensure diverse representation on the roundtable itself.

We at Postcolonial Networks hope that the publication of this book will begin a new chapter in the way people from a variety of contexts and beliefs encounter each other—that it will enable invested people to grapple with shared colonial legacies without blame or shame of only one religious group or identity. We hope readers will engage the book's content with all of their minds, hearts and souls; will address the colonial legacies in their own religious tradition; and will promote global justice collaborations for all peoples to flourish.

14

HOSTING A TRUE ROUNDTABLE

Dialogue Across Theological and Postcolonial Divides

Judith Oleson

.... ⚹ ....

THE ROUNDTABLE: CREATING A CONTAINER FOR DIALOGUE

The chapters in this book are a testimony to the dialogical process that is essential for collective attempts to decolonize theology and praxis. Communication across cultural, colonial and theological divides is challenging but not impossible. Summarizing what we learned from our interactions together is as important as the content that emerged in these chapters. Self-critique must be practiced as well as preached if postcolonial theology is to be taken seriously. Creating a container for such dialogue is far more challenging than theologians independently writing and then presenting their work in typical academic style of "I teach and you listen." It is through the committed interactive process that our cultural and historical perceptions are challenged, our positions of dominance and denial are brought to light and our internalized shame as individuals or representatives of collective groups may be liberated. Hosting a "roundtable" required both careful planning and a letting go of the plan so the participants could inform and redirect the process. It required constant adaptation as the participants bonded during the first three days together and then as membership was expanded in shorter follow-up gatherings. Making the transition from dialogue to collaborative writing and editing created tensions and opportunities for the group. In this chapter I will attempt to explain what we learned from hosting a roundtable on postcolonial theology in the hope that others will benefit as they continue this important interactive dialogue.

Planning

The Postcolonial Theological Roundtable was both the inspiration for and process that enabled this publication. Joe Duggan, founder of the Postcolonial Theology Network, initiated the roundtable. He had become aware of the growing interest in postcolonial theology among evangelical scholars. Joe approached Gordon College in the spring of 2009 to inquire if the college would host a gathering of evangelical scholars interested in "decolonizing theology." Early on there was commitment to dialogue, which would allow participants to explore issues and identify priorities among evangelical scholars, rather than the typical conference format of reading of papers with limited time for questions and answers. Round-table organizers were committed to relationship building and interactive dialogue that would be sustained across diverse cultural, national and theological perspectives, as well as historical memories of colonizer/colonized.

A list of key scholars, pastors and informed laypersons to be invited was developed, attending to diversity of culture, geography and gender. It was challenging to identify women, reflecting the overall disparity of women scholars to men in evangelical institutions. In the end, thirteen scholars attended from five different countries. Steve Hu functioned as scribe, Joe Duggan as overall moderator and myself (Judith Oleson) as dialogue facilitator. In order to expand the leadership circle, Kay Higuera Smith and Daniel Hawk were asked to assist in developing our format and work with the group in identifying priorities for dialogue. The roundtable met for three days at Gordon College in October, 2010.

The Model

The roundtable was designed not as a typical conference, but rather, in line with Bruce McCormack and Kimlyn J. Bender's model, as a "trans-disciplinary space where post-colonial scholars can suggest strategies to inspire movement from colonial isolation to interdependent postcolonial ecclesiological relationships."[1] The conceptual frame for the roundtable was grounded in

---

[1]Bruce McCormack and Kimlyn J. Bender, *Theology As Conversation: The Significance of Dialogue in Historical and Contemporary Theology: A Festschrift for Daniel L. Migliore* (Grand Rapids: Eerdmans, 2009), p. ix.

group dynamics most ideal for dialogue: a table with no space in the middle. At a round table, everyone is equally distant from the center, and there are no sharp edges. There is an assumption of equality when people meet in a circle, as there is no "head" of the table. A round table gathers members in toward each other and provides a sense of joining, even before we say a word.

The early Christians viewed the circle as a representation of eternity—with no beginning and no end. Thus the circle was considered divine. A large number of indigenous cultures utilize the circle to honor the four directions or use it to create beautiful mandalas to tell their stories. Carl Jung is widely known for his identification of the circle as an archetype of the psyche, as opposed to the square representing the body. The Chinese use the circle as the symbol of heaven, and the square as symbol of earth. In Celtic religion, the circle as a protective boundary is not to be crossed by evil.

Unfortunately the college could not provide a round table large enough for the group, so we convened a "roundtable" within a square context. This spiritual and intellectual holding of a roundtable within a square created a space for theological dialogue within our complex world of multiple edges and limited equalities. In addition to our physical space, we knew such dialogues could not be of any depth, or sustained over time, without participants developing trust among each other. The first dinner, as well as all of our meals, shared exclusively together, served as important times to learn about each other's contexts and to find common ground. The first evening was a time of sharing stories utilizing two questions: Who was inspirational in our coming to faith, and what currently brings joy to our lives? This personal discussion was necessary for establishing mutuality and affirming difference.

GROUP AGREEMENTS

On the first full day we explored the roundtable model and introduced the following guidelines for group process.

Set intention, clarify purpose. Most dialogues get off track immediately when participants are not clear about their intentions or have not clarified their purpose. This is different from determining end results. It was important that the group be committed to reaching outcomes but not attached to specific ones that were predetermined by identities and standard theological frames. The intention was dialogue, not debate. Our purpose was exploration of *both* commonality and difference, not uniformity. Nevertheless, we did have a desired outcome as well, which was greater understanding, perhaps a commitment to collaborate together in the future, but not consensus. We set intention through prayer for the Holy Spirit to guide our work to further God's grace in the world, but not to make us all alike.

Check our assumptions. It is human nature to make assumptions about others within the first two seconds of encountering them. Judgments are made from one's clothing, size, posture, dialect, accent and mannerisms. My assumptions about you go deeper when I learn the church you attend, the seminary you graduated from, the professional associations you belong to or don't, or the articles you have written and with whom. There are also judgments based on the area or region you come from, your culture or ethnic identification. In a roundtable that represents equality and mutuality, it is essential to become conscious of these assumptions and make a decision to leave them behind. These assumptions create the psychic sharp edges that we were trying to eliminate. By leaving our assumptions outside the circle, we enabled space for open-heartedness and freedom to truly engage with those different from ourselves.

Assume responsibility for engagement of all. Some of us think before we talk, and others talk as we think. To encourage engagement of all it is important for those of us who speak quickly sometimes to leave space for those who take time to gather their thoughts. It is equally important for those of us who hesitate to speak to be willing to step into the open spaces. The work in the dialogue circle is deepened when the interaction lines among members are between many and not just a few. Members can encourage this by asking others who have not spoken for a while for their thoughts or ask a probing question for those who had not had a chance to respond. Facilitators may ask for silence on occasion, not to silence vocal members, but to give the group time for prayerful reflection and to rebalance the circle of engagement.

Bring one's genuine self to the table. Trust is built on honesty, and honesty is difficult to practice without trust. This duality is a function of all groups and is key to any meaningful dialogue. Many of us come from institutions where prestige and pretense are part of the culture. Others may exist in institutions where one must hide or minimize one's views for survival. The sooner we can shed these roles and bring our genuine selves to the table, our dialogue will be enhanced and our trust deepened. As we know, using a critical spirit or sarcasm, dismissing one another by our body language or interrupting each other all destroy trust and thus the capacity for authenticity. By nature, dialogue about postcolonial theology invites self-critique but does not hold others in judgment.

Honor cultural diversity and gender differences. In the book *Theology and the Religions: A Dialogue*, Vitor Westhelle contributes a chapter titled "Multi-culturalism, Postcolonialism, and the Apocalyptic." He writes, "I surmise that the task of theology is now precisely that of gathering these fragments of plural history, multicultural reality and of a religious pluralism, and building a mosaic, knowing that we do not have to have the whole panorama encompassed within the cultural frame we have adopted—or which possesses us." He explains, "Multiculturalism in this post-colonial perspective is then the amount of departure from a particular way of seeing the world. It is a departure from the West as the gravitational Center of the world."[2] At a roundtable hosted in the West, within a primarily white institution, we attempt to be aware of our position of privilege and to explore and honor non-Western perspectives.

We also need to be conscious of dominant-culture filters that influence our capacity for cross-cultural understanding. Recent brain research affirms our intuitive knowledge that men and women often perceive and process differently. A roundtable is a place where difference is honored, not held suspect. As minorities in this group, women need space to bring forth diverse theological frames that have been historically dismissed by the church. Recognizing a range in gender identities in each of us will provide more options for creative thinking and new theological constructs.

Guard our needs for dominance or control. Many of us spend our days in charge of a classroom, or a church or perhaps an entire organization. Our work often calls us to be an effective manager, take charge when needed and be in control. For most of us these roles are so ingrained that we are not even aware of their presence in our behavior. In a roundtable dialogue we need to suspend these roles to build mutuality. In our roundtable we assume that God is at the center, and that we can trust that God creates, unfolds and sustains the mystery. Thankfully we do not have to control the outcome at this roundtable. Although we have a schedule, today does not mark the beginning nor will the last day be the end of the dialogue.

---

[2]Vitor Westhelle, "Multiculturalism, Postcolonialism, and the Apocalyptic," in *Theology and the Religions: A Dialogue*, ed. Viggo Mortensen (Grand Rapids: Eerdmans, 2003), p. 8.

Cultivate the capacity to hold creative tension. This means to accept and address our discomfort that can surface through our differences. Differentiation is the first step toward mediating common ground. Respectful disagreement affirms authenticity and creates space for expanded thinking and understanding. Creative tension is the willingness to disagree respectfully without demonizing or distancing the Other. Disagreement can evoke tension, and groups often seek to minimize tension through dismissing opinions, offering compromises or causing distractions. Members may try to avoid conflict by asking for a break, switching the subject or using humor. Humor can be an effective tool in acknowledging tension but can be destructive when used to avoid conflict or minimize another's perspective. By using tools of clarification, further probing, checking our own assumptions and active listening, we can hold the tension of disagreement. In a roundtable dialogue, there is an inherent belief that conflict can be creative—that it can lead to increased clarity, new breakthroughs and expanded perspectives.

After some clarification and discussion, each member committed to these group agreements. Participants were then challenged to "the kind of creative and synthetic thinking that breaks up any long standing impasses and moves a stalled conversation forward or that creates conditions needed for new conversations to get off the ground."[3]

PRIORITIZING

Even before the group met, organizers asked participants to reflect on personal identities and theological frames that might expand perspectives of each other and increase clarity. Roundtable members demonstrated quite early into the dialogue a commitment to camaraderie, mutual respect, good humor toward each other, genuine curiosity and a beginning capacity to hold creative tension.

General themes that rose to the surface were strata of postcolonialism, ways of talking about God that resist colonizing tendencies, grounding ourselves in the light of what's going on already and understanding hybrid and marginal identities. Other themes showed more differentiation: the role of eschatology, the theology of supersession, the problem of constructing theology out of nationalism, the connection to the theory and practice of reconciliation, and so

---

[3]McCormack and Bender, *Theology As Conversation*, p. ix.

on. After some discussion the group members chose to adopt five frameworks for discussion clusters: metanarrative, power and authority, identity, mission and reenvisioning the legacy. This was a significant point in the dialogue, where consensus was reached around priorities and use of precious time together. It was in discussion of these five frameworks that roundtable participants deeply engaged in the "difficult conversations" and manifested key components of successful dialogue.

SELF CRITIQUE: WHAT DID WE LEARN?

Patricia Romney summarizes key characteristics of dialogue articulated by leading theorists of dialogical processes. Dialogue, quite different from debate, is intended to increase understanding, expand options and inspire a change in hearts and minds.[4] It does not require agreement, nor does it insist on right responses. It is interested in process as much as content, with the outcome of building relationships, not just knowledge. William Isaacs and others at the MIT Dialogue Project define dialogue as "a unique form of conversation with potential to improve collective inquiry processes, to produce coordinated action among collectives, and to bring about genuine social change."[5] It is this emphasis on social change that motivated our roundtable organizers to attend not only to scholarship but also to action across theological and cultural divides. Isaacs identifies fragmentation as our typical mode of conversation that divides the world into parts. He proposed that fragmentation is addressed when creating and holding a healthy container for dialogue to occur. When successful, he adds, a field is created "to hold collective attention, identity images, and dynamic movement of tacit thought."[6]

Certainly "a field" was created through the roundtable that energized and expanded perspectives. At the end of the three days, participants acknowledged an overall sense of satisfaction with both content and process. It was agreed that dialogical process is by far more engaging and rewarding than the alternative, namely, reading papers and limited questions and answers; but it certainly is not easier. Participants worked hard over the three days and were

---

[4]Patricia Romney, "The Art of Dialogue: Animating Democracy," *Animating Democracy*, animating democracy.org/sites/default/files/documents/reading_room/art_of_dialogue.pdf, p. 2.
[5]W. N. Isaacs, *Dialogue and the Art of Thinking Together* (New York: Currency/Random House, 1999), p. 20.
[6]Ibid., p. 24.

successful in both prioritizing their agenda and then building a plan of action.

Creating a "field" is not limited just to thoughts but also to thoughts that stimulate action. Thus the importance of building an actual practice of interaction that has dynamic movement within the framework of theological reflection is essential. Can the group members practice what they preach? Can they close the divide where the residue of colonialism and theology still separates? Russian philosopher Mikhail Bakhtin defines the goal of dialogue as "responsive understanding." He rejected the idea of the solitary self, affirming that consciousness always evolves in the context of others. He used the term *heteroglossia* to describe the power relationships embedded in language. He defined heteroglossia as "competing languages and discourses: the dialogically-interrelated speech practices that are operative in a given society at a given moment, wherein the idioms of different classes, races, genders, generations and locales compete for ascendancy." In Bakhtin's view, dialogue "becomes the space of confrontation of differently oriented social accents."[7]

So how did the group practice heteroglossia and demonstrate a capacity for reflective understanding? One dynamic that surfaced within the roundtable was a power differential around knowledge. Familiarity with texts and authors was prolific for some and limited for others. Assumptions were made that theological terms were mutually understood, and those uncertain were reluctant to ask for clarification. A power differential existed between participants who regularly engaged in postcolonial theology and those who had more limited exposure. Some had a greater grasp of the theological terminology than others, reflecting the power relationships embedded in language. When disagreement occurred, appropriation of different definitions to terms was cited as a source of confusion.

Another limitation to our process was the minimal time we had to explore the diverse cultural contexts of participants and to own our own social identities related to colonial history/memory. Dominant-culture members were more agile and verbal, while minority-culture members were initially more hesitant to engage. White males were dominant at the table, women of color being in the smallest minority. The group's only African American woman attempted to challenge the focus of the group and, without much success, chose

[7]Quoted in Robert Stam, "Mikhail Bakhtin and Critical Left Pedagogy," in *Postmodernism and Its Discontents*, ed. Ann Kaplan (New York: Verso, 1988), p. 122.

to leave during the second day. Although numerous attempts were made to explore her discomfort, she never fully explained her desire to exit. This left the group with questions about their capacity for "responsive understanding." Using Bakhtin's idea of heteroglossia, we might have been more attentive to the competing languages and discourses, particularly in reference to race and gender differences.

Addressing the imbalance between highly verbal and less verbal participants was difficult. Agreements about dialogical process were established at the beginning (cited previously), but as one facilitator I could not catch all deviations. White males tended to take up most of the verbal space; females of color, the least. Some members became uncomfortable when others were not verbally engaged. Attempts to draw out less verbal members drew criticism of patronizing. After one private discussion with a member who had not spoken much, it became apparent that a major part of that participant's reserve was jet lag and a cold. The fact that some participants traveled halfway around the world while others could easily access the roundtable local to their home was a practical issue of social accents. Those of us hosting the roundtable, and those attending from neighboring communities, could not underestimate our ease in participating, while others had to navigate physical and cultural challenges, not to mention constantly listening and speaking in second or third languages.

In general, emphasis on talking rather than listening seemed to validate the Western context of the roundtable. Although there was significant listening, there were minimal spaces for silence and self-reflection or nonverbal expression. The use of silence as a tool for increased awareness was introduced in the initial roundtable agreements but was rarely utilized. The roundtable did pause for prayer at the beginning of our sessions; in hindsight, additional moments of silence could have provided intentional spaces for more diverse forms of reflection/processing.

Patricia Romney draws on Danah Zohar's book *Quantum Society*, where she identifies the need for new structures "that preserve the identities of participating members while drawing them into a larger working whole,"[8] going beyond the individual/collective dichotomy. Theorists in the Dialogue Project even define violence as the effort to "correct or alter whatever we do not like,"

---

[8]Danah Zohar and Ian Marshall, *The Quantum Society: Mind, Physics, and a New Social Vision* (New York: William Morrow, 1994), p. 29.

or verbal transgressions.[9] For example, it was a challenge to address one member who demonstrated dominance through body language, lecturing rather than commenting, and talking more than listening. Although this member's contributions were extremely rich, dominance and control of dialogue were counterproductive to the postcolonial vision we were trying to construct. Our dialogue process created a mirror of praxis from which to view our theological frames. "How" we spoke with each other was not always aligned with our postcolonial theology. The experience thus was both humbling and stimulating.

The group did not have an explicit dialogue about their own historical legacies with colonialism, and the parallel intersection of their respective churches. Nor was there time to compare participants' personal experiences with the residue of colonialism in the institutions each served, whether the academy or the church. The closest we came to this was a discussion of colonial influence still present in our seminaries around the globe. Our dialogue around mission did create a lively exchange, as participants held diverse perspectives that challenged each other's theological frameworks. Participants were encouraged to hold the tension of passionate disagreement while seeking to avoid condescending comments or emphatic body language that communicated dominance. Overall the roundtable participants created a container for both individual and hybrid identities and successfully resisted the tendency to construct "the Other" to advance their own positions.

A subtle but important observation around freedom, power and postcolonial theological dialogue occurred in the public event sponsored by Gordon College in conjunction with the roundtable session. Mabiala Kenzo and Brian McLaren were invited to dialogue before a public audience.[10] For their opening statements Mabiala prepared and read a formal paper while Brian, with little preparation, told some stories. Given the first is a theologian and the second a pastor, their diverse approaches were understandable. What was interesting were the assumptions that both held—one, that a comprehensive academic paper was expected and the other that his own stories (about grandparent missionaries in the Congo) would be enough. When Brian tried to elicit some of

---

[9]Isaacs, "Dialogue Project Annual Report."
[10]Brian McLaren joined the roundtable for one evening and participated in a public dialogue with Mabiala Kenzo at Gordon College.

Kenzo's stories (similar to what he shared in our small group) he was not forthcoming. Here we encounter one of the inherent difficulties of postcolonial theological dialogue—the context of the audience. Brian, as a white male speaking to a primarily white audience, felt comfortable sharing the story of his grandparents without the white audience's assuming guilt for their colonial past. Kenzo was a black, African man speaking to a primarily white, US American audience, thus naturally hesitant to share his and his grandparents' stories about white colonizers. One had freedom or inherent liberty to tell the story, and the other didn't.

The public exchange between Kenzo and McLaren, facilitated by Joseph Duggan, expanded the postcolonial discourse and allowed for multiple meanings and identities to coexist. The threads of power, privilege and historical institutional oppression of the church were woven into their conversation. The audience witnessed a powerful example of "facing history and ourselves" while yet moving beyond constructed identities to envision a level of healing and a collaborative process of "decolonizing theologies." Joe Duggan referenced the importance of Kenzo and McLaren's friendship in moving across such a divide to create new and different memories. The Postcolonial Roundtable in general exhibited the characteristics summarized above by Romney. There is, however, an inherent tension between moving ahead toward outcome (in this instance, collaborative writing toward a publication) and taking time to examine the power, privilege and historical institutional oppression that underlies most dialogue among diverse groups. Without individual and communal self-critique—both of ourselves and our interactions—postcolonial theology remains theory and not a living process. This can inhibit the important work toward healing across cultural and historical differences and can create false assumptions of theological understanding among participants. This was evident a year later, when the roundtable convened as a presession to the American Academy of Religion conference (2012) with expanded membership.

EXPANDING THE CIRCLE

By 2012 the initial group had expanded to twenty participants. The increase was because intentional invitations had been made to additional nonwhite and female theologians. This new configuration, which now included a majority who had not attended the three-day roundtable in 2010, shifted the overall focus of the group. The new group met for one day only to share drafts of book chapters, which they had been invited to contribute to this volume. By midday, largely due to the limited time available to us, it was apparent that the agenda did not allow room for new people to enter the process effectively or create the kind of exchange that was present among the participants at the first roundtable.

When planners regrouped, the format was changed and a circle created for an exchange among participants. Indigenous persons were asked to speak first, then other persons of color, then women, then the youngest in the room and finally the older white males. This created a process for learning that was not dominated by white, experienced, majority theologians who have a vested interest and strengths in writing and publishing scholarly papers. Rather it gave voice to other forms of expression and storytelling. As a result participants experienced a deeper and more meaningful connection to the group and the process. The dialogue shift was significant, as the trust level between new members and continuing members of the group was enhanced. Instead of focusing on the book product, participants found it essential to take time for relationship building. The capacity to exchange cultural and theological contexts first, before working on the project itself, proved essential and created an environment in which trust and enthusiasm for the project could be fostered among the new and returning roundtable members.

Prospects for Future Evangelical Postcolonial Theology Roundtables

Our hope is that this particular chapter will engage other evangelical scholars, pastors and laypersons in thoughtful dialogue processes focused on postcolonial theological reflection and praxis. By reviewing our planning process, exploring our model and learning from the self-critique of our dialogue, we anticipate that future participants will build even stronger and more sustainable roundtables.

It must be noted, however, that our roundtable struggled with the identity marker of "evangelical," and participants placed themselves on a wide continuum of identity and identification with evangelicalism. Mabiala Kenzo summarized, "This label is an identity we can use to deconstruct the term; using and appropriating evangelicalism in postcolonial criticism is a strategy we can use to redeem the term."[11] The hybridity of evangelicalism itself must be a part of the dialogue, both from diverse historical contexts and evolving theologies of participants. It is essential that interactive dialogue continues in addition to scholarly writing on postcolonial theology and praxis. It is in the roundtable process that both thought and praxis can flourish.

In her article, Romney summarizes three authors: Paulo Freire, David Schoem and Ximena Zúñiga, all intergroup facilitators and teachers who have contributed pedagogies of social justice in dialogue methods. She concludes that their practice and research require the following integration of critical thought and praxis in dialogue.

1. People enter into dialogue both as individuals and as members of social identity groups. Power, privilege and historical institutional oppression (recognized or unrecognized, acknowledged or unacknowledged) are threads weaving through all dialogue among diverse groups.

2. Moving from polite or angry talk to meaningful engagement requires time and a carefully structured process that encourages questioning and reflection.

3. Dialogue facilitators need not be neutral but should act as catalysts whose questions and probes deepen the dialogue.

4. Effective dialogue involves thinking and feeling, and listening and learning, as well as talking.[12]

It is this integration of critically informed theological thought and praxis that makes the roundtable process so unique. This acknowledgment of "power, privilege and institutional oppression" must be woven into the layers of the dialogue as participants examine themselves as individuals and as members of their institutions and communities. Romney acknowledges physicist David Bohm's definition of dialogue as "a free flow of meaning among all the participants." Utilizing quantum physics and the theory of relativity, Bohm focuses on development of the whole in dialogue. He stresses that each participant brings a part of the story to the table. The interaction with other participants,

---

[11]Mabiala Justin-Robert Kenzo was a member of the roundtable. He is a professor of systematic theology at Ambrose Seminary (Ambrose University College) in Calgary, Alberta, and at the Faculté de Théologie Evangélique de Boma (FACTEB) in the Democratic Republic of Congo.
[12]Romney, "Art of Dialogue," p. 9.

with their own part of the story, leads to a fuller and more complete story. According to Bohm this requires increased attention, deep inquiry and collective intelligence, with an emphasis on curiosity and questioning.[13]

As others engage in postcolonial theology and praxis, it is our hope that this sense of deep inquiry, curiosity and questioning might abound. Developing a "true" roundtable is not for rigid thinkers, isolated theologians or dogmatic preachers. It involves "thinking and feeling, and listening and learning."[14] The roundtable process requires initial agreement to group processes and dialogical principles, skilled facilitators, commitment to ongoing individual and collective self-critique and investment in relationships. It is from these relationships across cultures and diverse historical colonial memories/contexts that a true postcolonial theology can be articulated and more holistically lived in our respective institutions and communities of faith.

---

[13]David Bohm, *Wholeness and the Implicate Order* (London: Routledge and Kegan Paul, 1980), p. xi.
[14]Referencing quote above, note 12.

Benediction

Gregory W. Carmer

From its first annunciation the gospel of Jesus has been situated at the intersection of the particular and the universal: a message situated within the cultural conditions of a particular time and place yet with global claims. This tension is evident in the angelic proclamation of the savior's birth.

> But the angel said to them, "Do not be afraid. I bring you good news that will cause great joy for all the people. Today in the town of David a Savior has been born to you; he is the Messiah, the Lord." (Lk 2:10-11 NIV)

That events received, understood, interpreted and published within a particular historical social situation could lay claim over others in vastly different times and places grates against our contemporary sensitivities and smacks of cultural arrogance. Stories claiming universal authority often become the legitimizing cover for oppression, abuse and exploitation. Yet here, in Luke's Gospel, we have news of a particular day, transpiring in a location with its own political-social situation and launching a story that will be for *all* people.

There are elements of the globally important story of Jesus' birth, however, that distinguish it from what was perhaps its chief competitor—the universalizing impulses of empire. Such elements include the centrality of the voices of people subject to military occupation, abuse and violence; the entrustment of heavenly news to those of lowly social status; the reliance on extended family and ancestral identity; and the noncentral, almost hidden nature of Jesus' entrance into the world.

Evangelicals whose lives are oriented around the good news of Jesus contend that all God's people are profoundly shaped and formed by one great story, that of our participation in God's redeeming and reigning work in and through Jesus of Nazareth. But, unlike the story of empire, it is a story that is being written through the participation of *all* of God's people, each playing a unique part. Distinctive to the story is that the gospel of Jesus, at Pentecost, is received by each hearer in his or her own language (Acts 2). Likewise, the anticipated fulfillment of the story includes a blessed community composed of people from "every tribe and language and people and nation" (Rev 5:9). The honoring of diverse languages and, we must assume, the conceptual frameworks, orienting sensitivities and authority structures embedded in those languages, is central to the global character of the gospel.

However, ignorance, prejudice, pride, group bias and culturally generated legitimating narratives cause us to privilege some voices and languages over others. When that happens the story of Jesus and the advance of God's reign on earth get conflated with stories of our own devising, which come with, sometimes insidiously camouflaged, standards of rationality, authority and authenticity at odds with the gospel. In this way the globally liberating message of the gospel becomes colonized by our own idolatries, and we all become captive to self-protective stratagems. Our hope against this tendency lies in the gift of Pentecost: the Spirit of God, given to all the people of God, speaking through the people of God to one another, providing correction, instruction, insight, understanding and encouragement.

This volume bears powerful witness to that hope. May it engender suspicion toward our prejudices, provoke greater curiosity about voices not heard and aid in the displacement of old idols. If it can do these things, it will make a significant contribution to the health of the church, a body "joined and held together by every supporting ligament, [which] grows and builds itself up in love, as each part does its work" (Eph 4:16).

Dr. Richard Twiss

A Remembrance

Randy S. Woodley

ᛉ

R ICHARD, ONE OF THE CONTRIBUTORS TO THIS VOLUME, went on to the next life suddenly on February 9, 2013. He was my closest friend, but he knew how to be a good friend to many. Greater than any one friendship, Richard's friendship was an integral part of a larger community of First Nations followers of the Jesus Way.

Besides his great success in his own ministry, Wiconi International, Richard Twiss was part of a team of very close friends/siblings that eventually became NAIITS (the North American Institute for Indigenous Theological Studies). Richard was an incredible team player, and as the NAIITS community developed and matured in our theological perspectives, so did he. Richard always promoted the movement above himself, even though to many on the outside it may have appeared that "it was all about Richard." Not so. In this regard he was generous and thoughtful, and he understood his own giftings and limitations, as well as the giftings of each of us.

Richard Twiss was the undeniable "voice" of our movement, and he was an incredible innovator. Among his unique gifts was his extroverted personality coupled with his innovative mind. As his closest friends, we understood Richard's giftings and what he was accomplishing as the Spirit moved through our Native American, culturally contextual movement. No one could do what Richard was doing better than Richard himself. His unique mind, which was like a sponge, soaked up new information; then he added his distinctive twists to it, and he communicated it as newly processed information in very easy-to-understand and humorous ways. His framing on the subjects, which we all battered around for decades, was always refreshing. His humor allowed him to get by with some of the subject matter that most of us could not. Even though as a group we had many knockdown-dragout deliberations over the years, he also kept our group laughing at ourselves, and regardless of the rift, Richard was always willing to reconcile. After a while, it just became normal for us all to fight and love without holding grudges. Much of that was because of the influence of his generous spirituality and jovial demeanor.

It may be very difficult for white Americans from this individualistic society to understand how our little community worked so well together. In our Indian way, individuals move the ideas of the group forward because they are always secure in the group's identity. To try to understand Richard Twiss apart from his Native American community would result in a misunderstanding. Maybe this is the greatest lesson Richard still has to teach to America and the church.

Richard left behind his wife, four sons and daughters-in-law, two grandsons, his mother, siblings, cousins, nieces, nephews and hundreds of other relatives, whom he freely "took in" as family. He will never be forgotten.

Contributors' Biographies

Ray Aldred is assistant professor of theology at Ambrose Seminary in Calgary, Alberta. He is status Cree and also related to the Mohawk and Métis nations. He is also ordained with the Christian and Missionary Alliance in Canada and continues to work with My People International to develop indigenous leadership. He is former director for the First Nations Alliance Churches of Canada, where he worked to encourage pastors ministering to aboriginal people. He is also a chairperson of the North American Institute of Indigenous Theological Studies.

Gregory W. Carmer serves as the dean of Christian life and theologian in residence at Gordon College, Wenham, MA. He also directs the Christian Vocation Institute, a collection of programs, including the Elijah Project, which helps students explore the theological underpinnings and practical outworkings of vocation. He formerly served as the dean of chapel and director of service-learning and missions. Greg holds an MA and PhD in philosophical theology from Boston College.

Christian T. Collins Winn (PhD, Drew University) is professor of historical and systematic theology and chair of the Biblical and Theological Studies Department at Bethel University. He is the author or editor of several volumes, including *Jesus Is Victor! The Significance of the Blumhardts in the Theology of Karl Barth* (2009). His areas of research include eschatology and political theology, the theology of Karl Barth and developments in post-Reformation theology. He is a licensed minister in the American Baptist Churches (USA).

Joya Colon-Berezin is a teaching assistant at New York Theological Seminary in the fields of theology and social ethics. She earned her BA from Oberlin College and her MDiv from New York Theological Seminary. Joya works as the ecumenical relations coordinator for the Immigration and Refugee Program of Church World Service. She is a candidate for ordination in the United Church of Christ.

Gregory Lee Cuéllar is assistant professor of Old Testament at Austin Presbyterian

Theological Seminary. He received his PhD in Biblical Interpretation/Hebrew Bible from Brite Divinity School (TCU) in 2006. Author of *Voices of Marginality* (2008), he focuses in his research on the intersections of biblical interpretation, postcolonial theory, museum studies and archival theory.

Megan K. DeFranza (PhD, Marquette University) teaches the art of theological reflection, part time, at Gordon College (Wenham, MA) as well as gender, philosophy and culture at Endicott College (Beverly, MA). She is a theologian with particular interest in theological anthropology, sex and gender difference, hermeneutics, and justice and peacemaking. DeFranza is author of *Sex Difference in Christian Theology: Male, Female, and Intersex in the Image of God* (Eerdmans, forthcoming).

Joseph F. Duggan (PhD, University of Manchester) is founder of Postcolonial Networks and the scholar who initiated the postcolonial roundtable that led to the publication of this volume. He is the founding coeditor of Palgrave's series Postcolonialism and Religions. Duggan is an Episcopal priest and Episcopal Church Foundation academic fellow.

Victor Ifeanyi Ezigbo (PhD, University of Edinburgh) is associate professor of systematic and contextual theology at Bethel University in St. Paul, Minnesota. His areas of research are Christology, African Christian theologies, African indigenous religions and world Christianity. He is the founder of Center for Research in Global Christianity (center-rgc.org). His recent books are *Introducing Christian Theologies: Voices from Global Christian Communities* (Cascade, 2013) and *Re-imagining African Christologies* (Pickwick, 2010).

John R. Franke is the executive director and professor of missional theology at Yellowstone Theological Institute in Bozeman, MT; visiting professor of religious studies and missiology at the Evangelische Theologische Faculteit in Leuven, Belgium; and general coordinator for the Gospel and Our Culture Network in North America. He holds the DPhil degree from the University of Oxford and is particularly interested in engaging postmodern thought and culture from the perspective of missional Christian faith. He is the author of numerous books, including *Beyond Foundationalism: Shaping Theology in a Postmodern Context* (Westminster John Knox) with Stanley Grenz; *The Character of Theology: An Introduction to Its Nature, Task, and Purpose* (Baker Academic); *Barth for Armchair*

Theologians (Westminster John Knox); and *Manifold Witness: The Plurality of Truth* (Abingdon). His most recent book, *Missional Theology: Reforming Christianity for the Sake of the World*, is forthcoming from Baker Academic.

Gene L. Green (PhD, University of Aberdeen) is professor of New Testament at Wheaton College and Graduate School. Previously he served as professor of New Testament as well as academic dean and rector of the Seminario ESEPA in San José, Costa Rica. He has authored commentaries in Spanish (*1 Pedro y 2 Pedro* [Caribe] and *1 y 2 Tesalonicenses* [Portavoz]) and English (*1 and 2 Thessalonians* [Eerdmans] and *2 Peter and Jude* [Baker Academic]), and coauthored *The New Testament in Antiquity* (Zondervan). Gene is coeditor of *Global Theology in Evangelical Perspective* (IVP Academic) and the Majority World Theology series (Eerdmans). His research interest is the intersection of the Christian faith and cultures, both ancient and contemporary, and the theology of Peter.

L. Daniel Hawk is professor of Old Testament and Hebrew at Ashland Theological Seminary and an ordained minister in the United Methodist Church. His recent work, which includes *Joshua in 3-D: A Commentary on Biblical Conquest and Manifest Destiny* (Cascade, 2010), compares the ways that conquest narratives shape national identity in the Old Testament and American national mythology.

Robert S. Heaney is former director of postgraduate studies and research as well as senior lecturer in the School of Theology and Religious Studies at St. John's University of Tanzania, East Africa. He is presently director of the Center for Anglican Communion Studies and Assistant Professor of Christian Mission at Virginia Theological Seminary, USA.

Peter Goodwin Heltzel is associate professor of theology and director of the Micah Institute at New York Theological Seminary. Alexia Salvatierra and he are coauthors of *Faith-Rooted Organizing* (InterVarsity Press), a revolutionary manual for the growing multifaith justice movement. He is also the author of *Resurrection City: A Theology of Improvisation* (Eerdmans) and *Jesus and Justice: Evangelicals, Race and American Politics* (Yale University Press). His edited volumes include *The Chalice Introduction to Theology* (Chalice), *Evangelicals and Empire* (Brazos Press) with Bruce Ellis Benson, and *Theology in Global Context* (T & T Clark) with Amos Yong. An ordained minister in the Christian Church (Disciples of Christ), he serves as assistant pastor of evangelism at Park Avenue Christian

Church. He is currently writing a systematic theology that demonstrates the relevance of prophetic Christianity for the growing global movement for justice.

Steve Hu is a PhD student in the Department of Religious Studies at the University of California, Santa Barbara. His research focuses on Chinese popular religions, Christianity in China and the globalization of Christianity.

Jayachitra Lalitha is associate professor of New Testament and Greek, dean of women's studies and coordinator of the Church Women Centre at the Tamilnadu Theological Seminary, Madurai, Tamilnadu, India. Her research interests include post-Pauline literature, postcolonial biblical hermeneutics and feminism. She co-chairs the World Christianity group of the American Academy of Religion.

Gilberto Lozano currently teaches at the Anderson University School of Theology in Indiana. He has a BTh from the Boa Terra Theological Institute in Curitiba, Brazil; a BA in religion from Warner Pacific College; an MDiv from the Iliff School of Theology; and a PhD in biblical interpretation from the Iliff School of Theology and the University of Denver. He comes from Colombia, South America, and became a naturalized Brazilian citizen in 2011. He is interested in the intersection between life and faith, and faith and culture.

Safwat Marzouk is assistant professor of the Old Testament/Hebrew Bible at the Anabaptist Mennonite Biblical Seminary. An ordained Presbyterian minister with the Synod of the Nile, Egypt, Marzouk is passionate about empowering the voice of Middle Eastern Christians in ecclesial and academic circles. He believes that interpreting the biblical texts from a Middle Eastern perspective encounters many challenges that emerge from this geopolitical milieu, but at the same time such a hermeneutical process energizes new hope to bring about peace and justice in that region.

Brian D. McLaren is an author, speaker, activist, networker and blogger (brianmclaren.net). He served as a church planter and pastor for over twenty years and began his career as a college English teacher. His books include *A New Kind of Christian*, *A Generous Orthodoxy*, and *Why Did Jesus, Moses, the Buddha, and Mohammed Cross the Road?*

Teri Merrick is professor of philosophy and chair of the Department of Theology and Philosophy at Azusa Pacific University in Azusa, CA. Her PhD is in logic and philosophy of science from the University of California, Irvine. Her research interests include Kant and post-Kantian German philosophy, history and philosophy of science and analytic feminism.

Judith Oleson (DMin, MPA, MSW) is an associate professor in the Sociology/ Social Work Department at Gordon College. She coordinates the peace and conflict studies minor and the senior field practicum program. She also serves as a facilitator and mediator for churches, nonprofits, government agencies and collaborative networks.

Kurt Anders Richardson is an evangelical theologian whose academic focus is in constructive theology, religious philosophy and comparative monotheism, particularly among the Abrahamic faiths. He received his doctorate in theology at the University of Basel, Switzerland; has taught extensively in several evangelical seminaries; and is a member of the faculties of theology of McMaster University and of the Trinity College, University of Toronto. He is a cofounder of three research groups: Society for Scriptural Reasoning and Comparative Theology in the American Academy of Religion, and Method in Systematic Theology in the Evangelical Theological Society.

Federico A. Roth (PhD) is an assistant professor of Hebrew Bible at Azusa Pacific University in Azusa, CA. Federico's areas of expertise and teaching interests include postcolonial biblical criticism, third space theory, contextual/global approaches to biblical interpretation, pedagogy of exegetical methodology and literary/rhetorical-critical exegesis.

Nicholas Rowe holds the Benjamin Ryan Chair of Religious and Values Education and is associate professor of history at St. Augustine College of South Africa. He has also been involved in reconciliation ministry for over twenty years in both the United States and the African continent.

Kay Higuera Smith (PhD) is professor of religious studies and chair of the Department of Biblical Studies at Azusa Pacific University in Azusa, CA. Her PhD is in early Judaism and New Testament from Claremont Graduate University. Her research interests are in postcoloniality and its intersection with biblical studies.

Richard L. Twiss (1954–2013), Tayoate Ob Najin ("He Stands With His People"), was cofounder, with his wife, Katherine, of WICONI International, a group committed to empowering Native American families, and founding member of NAIITS (the North American Institute for Indigenous Theological Studies). His books include *One Church Many Tribes* (coauthored with John Dawson), *Rescuing Theology from the Cowboys* and *Dancing Our Prayers*. Richard is survived by his wife, four sons and daughters-in-law, and two grandsons. To Richard we join with his family in saying, in the Lakota language, *Toksa ake* ("We'll see you again").[1]

Reggie L. Williams is assistant professor of Christian ethics at McCormick Theological Seminary in Chicago, Ilinois. He received his PhD in Christian ethics at Fuller Theological Seminary, supervised by Glen Stassen. His research focuses on the intersection of christological hermeneutics and Christian moral formation. His current book project examines the influence of the Harlem Renaissance on the theological ethics of Dietrich Bonhoeffer (Baylor University Press, forthcoming).

Rev. Dr. Randy Woodley serves as distinguished professor of faith and culture and director of intercultural and indigenous studies at George Fox Seminary in Portland, OR. Randy is a legal descendent of the United Keetoowah Band of Cherokee Indians in Oklahoma. He is active in ongoing discussions concerning new church movements, racial and ethnic diversity, peace, social and ecojustice, interreligious dialogue and mission. He and his wife Edith, cofounders of Eagle's Wings Ministry, are considered early innovators in the "Native American Contextual Movement." He is a founding board member of NAIITS, the North American Institute for Indigenous Theological Studies. His most recent book is *Shalom and the Community of Creation: An Indigenous Vision*, 2012 (Eerdmans).

Amos Yong is J. Rodman Williams Professor of Theology and dean at the School of Divinity of Regent University in Virginia Beach, Virginia. His graduate education includes degrees in theology, history and religious studies from Western Evangelical Seminary (now George Fox Seminary); Portland State University, Portland, OR; and Boston University, Boston, MA. He has authored or edited two dozen volumes.

---

[1] From "Richard Leo Twiss 1954-2013," accessed September 2, 2013, www.wiconi.com/?cid=1276.

Name and Subject Index

SCRIPTURE INDEX

Finding the Textbook You Need

The IVP Academic Textbook Selector
is an online tool for instantly finding the IVP books
suitable for over 250 courses across 24 disciplines.

---

www.ivpress.com/academic/textbookselector